EMIGRANT WORLDS AND TRANSATLANTIC
COMMUNITIES

MCGILL-QUEEN'S STUDIES IN ETHNIC HISTORY
SERIES ONE: DONALD HARMAN AKENSON, EDITOR

1 Irish Migrants in the Canadas
A New Approach
Bruce S. Elliott
(Second edition, 2004)

2 Critical Years in Immigration
Canada and Australia
Compared
Freda Hawkins
(Second edition, 1991)

3 Italians in Toronto
Development of a National
Identity, 1875–1935
John E. Zucchi

4 Linguistics and Poetics of Latvian
Folk Songs
Essays in Honour of the
Sesquicentennial of the Birth of
Kr. Barons
Vaira Vikis-Freibergs

5 Johan Schroder's Travels in
Canada, 1863
Orm Overland

6 Class, Ethnicity, and Social
Inequality
Christopher McAll

7 The Victorian Interpretation of
Racial Conflict
The Maori, the British, and the
New Zealand Wars
James Belich

8 White Canada Forever
Popular Attitudes and Public
Policy toward Orientals in British
Columbia
W. Peter Ward
(Third edition, 2002)

9 The People of Glengarry
Highlanders in Transition,
1745–1820
Marianne McLean

10 Vancouver's Chinatown Racial
Discourse in Canada,
1875–1980
Kay J. Anderson

11 Best Left as Indians
Native-White Relations
in the Yukon Territory,
1840–1973
Ken Coates

12 Such Hardworking People
Italian Immigrants in Postwar
Toronto
Franca Iacovetta

13 The Little Slaves of the Harp
Italian Child Street Musicians
in Nineteenth-Century Paris,
London, and New York
John E. Zucchi

14 The Light of Nature and the Law
of God
Antislavery in Ontario,
1833–1877
Allen P. Stouffer

15 Drum Songs
Glimpses of Dene History
Kerry Abel

16 Louis Rosenberg
Canada's Jews
(Reprint of 1939
original)
*Edited by Morton
Weinfeld*

17 A New Lease on Life
   Landlords, Tenants, and Immigrants in Ireland and Canada
   Catharine Anne Wilson

18 In Search of Paradise
   The Odyssey of an Italian Family
   Susan Gabori

19 Ethnicity in the Mainstream
   Three Studies of English Canadian Culture in Ontario
   Pauline Greenhill

20 Patriots and Proletarians
   The Politicization of Hungarian Immigrants in Canada, 1923–1939
   Carmela Patrias

21 The Four Quarters of the Night
   The Life-Journey of an Emigrant Sikh
   Tara Singh Bains and Hugh Johnston

22 Cultural Power, Resistance, and Pluralism
   Colonial Guyana, 1838–1900
   Brian L. Moore

23 Search Out the Land
   The Jews and the Growth of Equality in British Colonial America, 1740–1867
   Sheldon J. Godfrey and Judith C. Godfrey

24 The Development of Elites in Acadian New Brunswick, 1861–1881
   Sheila M. Andrew

25 Journey to Vaja
   Reconstructing the World of a Hungarian-Jewish Family
   Elaine Kalman Naves

MCGILL-QUEEN'S STUDIES IN ETHNIC HISTORY
SERIES TWO: JOHN ZUCCHI, EDITOR

1 Inside Ethnic Families
  Three Generations of Portuguese-Canadians
  Edite Noivo

2 A House of Words
  Jewish Writing, Identity, and Memory
  Norman Ravvin

3 Oatmeal and the Catechism
  Scottish Gaelic Settlers in Quebec
  Margaret Bennett

4 With Scarcely a Ripple
  Anglo-Canadian Migration into the United States and Western Canada, 1880–1920
  Randy William Widdis

5 Creating Societies
  Immigrant Lives in Canada
  Dirk Hoerder

6 Social Discredit
  Anti-Semitism, Social Credit, and the Jewish Response
  Janine Stingel

7 Coalescence of Styles
  The Ethnic Heritage of St John River Valley Regional Furniture, 1763–1851
  Jane L. Cook

8 Brigh an Orain / A Story in Every Song
  The Songs and Tales of Lauchie MacLellan
  Translated and edited by John Shaw

9 Demography, State and Society
   Irish Migration to Britain,
   1921–1971
   Enda Delaney

10 The West Indians of Costa Rica
   Race, Class, and the Integration of
   an Ethnic Minority
   Ronald N. Harpelle

11 Canada and the Ukrainian Question, 1939–1945
   Bohdan S. Kordan

12 Tortillas and Tomatoes
   Transmigrant Mexican Harvesters
   in Canada
   Tanya Basok

13 Old and New World Highland
   Bagpiping
   John G. Gibson

14 Nationalism from the Margins
   The Negotiation of Nationalism
   and Ethnic Identities among Italian Immigrants in Alberta and
   British Columbia
   Patricia Wood

15 Colonization and Community
   The Vancouver Island Coalfield
   and the Making of the British
   Columbia Working Class
   John Douglas Belshaw

16 Enemy Aliens, Prisoners of War
   Internment in Canada during the
   Great War
   Bohdan S. Kordan

17 Like Our Mountains
   A History of Armenians in Canada
   Isabel Kaprielian-Churchill

18 Exiles and Islanders
   The Irish Settlers of Prince
   Edward Island
   Brendan O'Grady

19 Ethnic Relations in Canada
   Institutional Dynamics
   Raymond Breton
   Edited by Jeffrey G. Reitz

20 A Kingdom of the Mind
   The Scots' Impact on the Development of Canada
   Edited by Peter Rider and Heather McNabb

21 Vikings to U-Boats
   The German Experience in Newfoundland and Labrador
   Gerhard P. Bassler

22 Being Arab
   Ethnic and Religious Identity
   Building among Second Generation Youth in Montreal
   Paul Eid

23 From Peasants to Labourers
   Ukrainian and Belarusan Immigration from the Russian Empire
   to Canada
   Vadim Kukushkin

24 Emigrant Worlds and Translantic
   Communities
   Migration to Upper Canada in the
   First Half of the Nineteenth
   Century
   Elizabeth Jane Errington

Emigrant Worlds and Transatlantic Communities

Migration to Upper Canada in the First Half of the Nineteenth Century

ELIZABETH JANE ERRINGTON

McGill-Queen's University Press
Montreal & Kingston • London • Ithaca

© McGill-Queen's University Press 2007

ISBN 978-0-7735-3265-6 (cloth)
ISBN 978-0-7735-3266-3 (paper)

Legal deposit fourth quarter 2007
Bibliothèque nationale du Québec

Printed in Canada on acid-free paper that is 100% ancient forest free (100% post-consumer recycled), processed chlorine free

This book has been published with the help of a grant from the Canadian Federation for the Humanities and Social Sciences, through the Aid to Scholarly Publications Programme, using funds provided by the Social Sciences and Humanities Research Council of Canada.

McGill-Queen's University Press acknowledges the support of the Canada Council for the Arts for our publishing program. We also acknowledge the financial support of the Government of Canada through the Book Publishing Industry Development Program (BPIDP) for our publishing activities.

Library and Archives Canada Cataloguing in Publication

Errington, Elizabeth Jane, 1951–
Emigrant worlds and transatlantic communities : migration to Upper Canada in the first half of the nineteenth century / Elizabeth Jane Errington.

(McGill-Queen's studies in ethnic history ; 24)
Includes bibliographical references and index.
ISBN 978-0-7735-3265-6 (bound). – ISBN 978-0-7735-3266-3 (pbk.)

1. British – Kinship – Ontario – History – 19th century. 2. Immigrants – Family relationships – Ontario – History – 19th century. 3. Family – Ontario – History – 19th century. 4. Ontario – Emigration and immigration – History – 19th century. 5. Great Britain – Emigration and immigration – History – 19th century. I. Title. II. Series.

FC3100.B7E77 2007   306.85086'9120941   C2007-904901-X

Typeset by Jay Tee Graphics Ltd. in Adobe Garamond 11/13

Contents

Illustrations ix

Acknowledgments xi

Introduction 3

1 To Go or Not to Go 12

2 The Bustle of Preparation 49

3 A Nether World on the Atlantic 74

4 Into the "Strange Land" 111

5 Transatlantic Webs of Kin and Community 136

Conclusion 159

A Note on Sources: Reading and Writing about the Emigrants' World 167

Notes 177

Index 235

Illustrations

Map showing Upper Canada 14
Title page, *Counsel for Emigrants* 18
Title page, *Statistical Sketches of Upper Canada* 20
Title page, C. Stuart, *The Emigrant's Guide* 21
C.J. Grant, "Emigration, Detailing the Progress and Vicissitudes of an Emigrant" 22
"Wreck of the Emigrant Ship 'John'" 34
"The Parting Hour" 41
"The Last of England," frontispiece of W.S. Shepperson's *British Emigration to North America* 42
"Irish Emigrants Leaving Home" 57
"Emigrants Arriving at the Quay" 61
"At an Emigration Agent's Office" 64
"Embarkation, Waterloo Docks" 69
"Emigrants by the Ship Ganges Departing for Canada" 70
"The Departure" 71
"Embarking with Your Family for America" 75
"Quarterdeck of an Emigrant Ship" 81
"Scene Between Decks" 85
"Searching for Stowaways" 88
"Emigration Vessel – Between Decks" 94
"Dancing Between Decks" 95
"Scudding in a Gale" 96
"On the wide and boundless Sea" 100
"The Life-Boat of the 'Tagus'" 103
Quebec City, John Henry Walker 107
"The Government Inspector's Office" 109

The Port of Montreal, 1830, Robert Auchmuty Sproule   112
View of the Harbour, Montreal, 1830, Robert Auchmuty Sproule   113
The St. Lawrence, at Montreal, William Henry Bartlett   117
"Sailing up the St Laurence in an American Boiler ..."   118
The Lachine Canal, Lachine, QC, James Duncan   120
Entrance to Toronto   129

Acknowledgments

This volume would not have been possible without the encouragement and assistance of a great number of people and institutions. The research for this study was directly supported by my two universities, the Royal Military College of Canada and Queen's University, and by the Social Sciences and Humanities Research Council of Canada; and the publication of *Emigrant Worlds* was made possible by a grant from the Social Science Federation of Canada. The librarians and archivists at the National Library of Scotland, the Scottish Record Office, the British Museum, the Record Offices of Bedfordshire and Northampton, the British Library, the National Library and Archives of Canada, the McCord Museum, and Stouffer Library at Queen's willingly offered me their time and expertise; Jessica Hamilton, Sarah Gibson, and Emily Spencer combed through endless reels of microfilm; and the very talented people at McGill-Queen's University Press patiently helped me through the process.

It was primarily colleagues and friends and family who sustained me through the lengthy process of researching and writing, however. Donald Akenson was patient and encouraging in equal measure; moreover, his perceptive suggestions on how to "see" migration and how to frame this subject contributed materially to the final product. The dinner folk and their families from Queen's and from RMC listened to my stories and frustrations, and applauded my small triumphs. Paul Banfield and Mary Alice Thompson, and Emma and Lucy were and are always there to cheer me on, as are that wonderful second family of Farm Christmas. And like the people I write about here, I depended on my own familial networks to bring the project to completion – Jane and John, and the cousins and their families at my second home in England, and my more immediate family here in Canada.

EJE, 2007

EMIGRANT WORLDS AND TRANSATLANTIC
COMMUNITIES

Introduction

In June 1830 a short notice appeared in a local Upper Canadian newspaper: "Information Wanted" of Patrick Dundoon, "who had emigrated from County Limerick, Ireland about 5 years before." His mother and sisters had just arrived in the colony, it explained, and "should this meet his eye," they were "anxious to hear from him, and could be contacted by letter, addressed to Mr Makne, York. U.C."[1] The following year Benjamin Booth, an emigrant that season, was "anxious to find out his sister Elena Booth, who [had] emigrated to York about three years ago."[2] Some months later, in October 1831, Mrs McIndoe asked the public to help find her husband William. She and her children had come from Scotland that summer and made their way to Bytown, where he had been working. She had discovered, however, that he was "supposed to have left the Isthmus Rideau Canal and gone to Albany, NY." She added, "If this notice meets the eye of William McIndoe ... he is earnestly requested by his distressed wife and family ... to inform them of his place of residence." The notice concluded: "Editors of papers in NY will be doing the course of humanity a service by giving the above an insertion."[3]

Between 1815 and 1845, newspapers in Upper Canada included hundreds of notices of individuals who were looking for a family member or a friend. Colonists were a mobile lot, and most of these "cards" were placed by settlers who had lost touch with a son, daughter, husband, or companion. A significant portion of them, however, were from or directed to recently arrived emigrants, like Benjamin Booth and Mrs Dundoon. Often, "information wanted" notices were only a line or two – like that which appeared in the Kingston *Chronicle and Gazette* in March 1834: "If Patrick Brady, from Claremount County, Mayo Ireland be in Kingston, he will confer a favour by making it known to this office."[4] A year later, the *Chronicle* included a brief untitled card: "If this should meet the eyes of Mr George Smith and Ellen Standish, his wife, last of Bow Wood Park, Wiltshire England, by sending their address to Mr Frederick Wyse, Quebec, they will hear from him respecting their disconsolate father and mother."[5]

Sometimes, notices included somewhat more detail about the particular circumstances of their authors. In February 1830, for example, a young Irish woman, Jane Mayarity, announced to the readers of the *Colonial Advocate* in York that she was looking for her brother, Christopher Flinn. She explained that the family's last contact with him had been three years earlier, when he was living in Hallowell County, Prince Edward Island, but at that time he had intended to move to Upper Canada. Jane had arrived the previous fall to join him, but after more than four months of searching she was becoming impatient. Her announcement was emphatic; if Christopher had not contacted her by the spring, she intended to return home to Ireland.[6] A few who sought the public's assistance were in more difficult straits. In October 1833, Mary Anne Perry's mother was desperate. The Perry family had left Somerset, England, that summer and after landing in Quebec in July, their twenty-year-old daughter, Mary Anne, had struck out on her own. "The last account of her," the notice explained, was that she had "married a person named Wells from Scotland and was en route to York Upper Canada with the intention of opening a business." Her "distressed Parent" was now in Montreal "with a family of Five Children, completely destitute – The Father having died." Mrs Perry desperately needed help, and she asked newspapers in the upper province "as an act of charity" to print her notice so that she could find her daughter.[7]

"Information wanted" notices are tantalizing. For a brief moment, they offer us a glimpse into the lives and concerns of a few of those usually anonymous folk who arrived in Upper Canada in the first half of the nineteenth century determined to make the colony their home. The notices are also intriguing because they catch individuals at a key point of transition in their lives – the beginning of their stories of settlement and, at the same time, the end of their stories of migration. Yet even the most detailed notices are intensely frustrating. As soon as they appear, these women and men retreat back into the shadows of the historical record. We never know how each of their dilemmas was resolved or what the future held for these new arrivals and those they sought. More importantly for this study, most of the notices are largely silent about how these men, women, and children found themselves apparently alone in a strange land in the first place. What had propelled them to leave all that was familiar and to make that long and often dangerous journey to the colonies? What had they expected of this New World? Where were those kinfolk whom many obviously had expected to join? Who they would become was intimately tied to who they were before they arrived. And it is this – what it meant to be an emigrant in the first half of the nineteenth century – that is the central concern of this study.

Finding definitive answers to the many questions of who, why, and how that are raised in the "information wanted" notices is next to impossible. What is clear is that the McIndoes, Jane Mayarity, and the Perrys were taking part in what one historian has called "the great cycle of European emigration."[8] It is estimated that between 1815 and 1850, more than two and a half million English, Welsh, Scots, and Irish left home for North America.[9] The forces that encouraged and sustained this extraordinary migration are complex. The end of the Napoleonic Wars brought both relief and uncertainty. The immediate postwar depression was soon followed by the difficulties that accompanied the increasing pace of industrialization and urbanization and the ongoing agricultural "revolution." Throughout Great Britain and Ireland[10] (and indeed, the rest of Europe), local communities were transformed by shifting patterns of production and rising expectations and an unprecedented growth in population. At different times and in different regions, farmers and artisans, labourers and mechanics, gentlemen and their families, and sons and daughters were confronted with unemployment, higher rents, depressed markets, decreasing opportunities, and general economic uncertainty.[11] As national, local, and personal resources became increasingly strained, a growing portion of the population began to look for ways to cope with the changing circumstances.

Emigration was certainly not the only option. Many decided to stay where they were in anticipation that the situation would improve. Others moved within their neighbourhood or relocated to a local village or to one of the growing urban centres to find work and a future. A growing number moved from one region to another within the British Isles. But increasingly, many Irish, Scots, English, and Welsh contemplated leaving the country altogether, determined to take advantage of the opportunities that were promised in the "New World" across the Atlantic. Many already had family, friends, or a distant connection settled there, and this offered them at least an initial destination.[12] Others decided that the promise of America outweighed the possibilities at home. Most of the English, Scots, Irish, and Welsh emigrants settled in the United States – that traditional land of plenty. But a significant proportion (and between 1817 and 1837, the majority) landed and settled in British America, and most of them ended up in the newest interior colony, Upper Canada.[13] It was a few of these folk whose names appeared in the "information wanted" notices, they having discovered, to their chagrin and sometimes to their despair, that those they had hoped to join could not be found.

"Information wanted" notices do illustrate some of the contours and complexities of this world of emigration in the first half of the nineteenth century. They tell of a world inhabited by men, women, and children of all ages, ranks, and circumstances. New arrivals included an array of nuclear and extended families but into the 1830s and 1840s, a growing proportion of notices were placed by apparently "unattached" women and men who seem to have been quite young. Of the more than 350 notices that appeared in Upper Canadian newspapers, the majority were placed by Irish migrants, while about one-quarter of the advertisers stated they were from Scotland; the rest were from parts of England and Wales and a few from the United States.[14] Based on the notices alone, one might conclude, as other studies have done, that most who left home were adult men who travelled either alone or in extended family groupings. The notices do reflect a distinct class composition. Most emigrants who identified their trade were artisans or labourers.[15] Some of the "cards" told tales of desperation and destitution; but most of those looking for relatives or friends do not seem to have been impoverished, and some could even afford to stay in hotels or inns while looking for kin or compatriots.

Mapping national origins and compiling basic profiles of those who arrived in Upper Canada still does not really bring us much closer to understanding why Benjamin Booth or Mrs McIndoe or Jane Mayarity left home or what it actually meant to be an emigrant. But the notices do provide hints about the dynamics of the process and some of the factors that many considered when making the initial decision to emigrate. In addition to specifying their "national" origin – Irish, Scottish, English, or, for a very few, Welsh or American – almost all who placed "information wanted" notices carefully identified themselves and those they were seeking by their link to the local "home" community. In part, this was undoubtedly an attempt to help the public identify the individual they were looking for. But it also reflects the emigrants' own sense of continuing identification with a particular county or region; and it seems to confirm, as some scholars have eloquently argued, that *why* people left home was intimately tied to "*where* emigrants came from and *when*" they left.[16] Just as significant, the notices always indicated the author's relationship to the individual sought. There were wives looking for husbands, parents looking for children, widows looking for grown-up sons or daughters, nieces and nephews looking for more distant kin, and siblings, cousins, or friends who were travelling and, it seems, intending to settle together. The "information wanted" notices illustrate the centrality of family connections and networks to the world of emigration.

Nevertheless, the notices remain a singularly incomplete record of migration and settlement. They are like old snapshots, with their images frozen in space and time. One can never fully identify the subjects or know what they were thinking of doing at that moment when their images were captured in a few lines in a local paper. It is clear that each notice reflects a unique story, and it would seem that those who placed them arrived with widely varying expectations of what they would find in the colony. Some, like the McIndoes, knew (or thought they knew) exactly where they were going. Others seem to have had only the vaguest idea of where they might end up. The notices also suggest that many emigrants had little appreciation of just how vast the colony and the continent were. It was not unusual for individuals arriving in Kingston, for instance, to be looking for a friend or family member who was last known to have been in Nova Scotia or New York; and some, at least, hoped to be able to find a brother or sister who they had not seen or heard from in many years.

There is another window into the world of emigration that offers us some clues about that often irrevocable decision to leave home and what it must have meant to travel thousands of miles to an outpost of empire. Many who boarded ships bound for America were determined to record their experiences and to maintain contact with those they had left behind. Emigrants' letters home told of the trials and triumphs of settlement; diaries and journals recorded impressions of life aboard ship and of their authors' experiences in their new homes across the Atlantic. Extant emigrant writings also often alluded to some of the issues that had propelled the writers to leave home in the first place. For example, a few of the factors that prompted the Gemmill family of Glasgow to emigrate in 1821 and 1822 can be traced in the family correspondence that was maintained for more than a decade. John Gemmill, a stonemason, left home in the spring of 1821 to take up land in Upper Canada and to prepare the way for his wife and children. The family joined him a year later. But to John's consternation, his eldest son, Andrew, and John's brother had elected not to emigrate. Letters over the next few years chronicle the Gemmills' attempts to convince Andrew to change his mind, and they record John's growing acceptance when it became clear that neither Andrew, nor his sisters, nor John's brother, would do so. Other journals and collections of letters tell different stories – of a young Catharine Parr Traill and her husband Thomas, who in 1832 determined to emigrate to assure their status; or of Anne Langton, a single gentlewoman, who with her elderly parents and aunt, left home later that decade to join her brother John on a bush farm outside Peterborough, Upper Canada; or of a young George Forbes who left his parents' tenant farm in Scotland in 1845 to seek his fortune in the colony.

Emigrants' letters, journals and diaries provide invaluable insights into the lives and concerns of correspondents; they also allow us to follow some individuals and families as they made their way into the world of emigration and, after months and sometimes years, left it on their arrival in Upper Canada.[17] To read someone else's mail – written more than a hundred and fifty years ago – is to be something of a voyeur, however. There is a hint of eavesdropping, and like all those who engage in such activities, one is usually not privy to the beginning or end of the conversation. Sometimes, one can hear one side of the discussion and have to fill in the blanks as best one can. The difference between listening in on a private discussion and reading emigrants' letters is that the emigrants usually had no expectation of privacy; they wanted to be heard. Although their letters often included intimate details about their lives, most of them assumed – and, indeed, many directed – that their letter-journals be shared within the rest of the family and with friends and neighbours. Indeed, one reason why new arrivals and colonists wrote home was to pass on information. Some hoped to encourage others to join them. Others were emphatic that family members should stay home.

Emigrant correspondence had multiple purposes, many of which can be "lost in the translation" when read so many years later. Often, letters and journals were a way to make sense of the world. As well, the very act of writing was a declaration of the importance of continuing ties to "home" and community. And as David Gerber has recently illustrated, it was also a conscious attempt to maintain or resume relationships across time and space.[18] Emigrant letters and journals are, by definition, autobiographical, but like all autobiographies they are selective in what is included and what is not. In some cases, the silences cover topics which the writer took for granted that the reader understood or were clearly "common sense" – the identities of individuals mentioned in the letters, or perhaps the author's financial circumstances or long-term goals. In other instances, writers may have chosen to gloss over or fail to mention situations that placed them in a negative light. Yet as David Fitzpatrick and others have illustrated, emigrant letters had their own sensibilities and conventions. In the salutations and closings, in the almost ritualistic references to family and friends and to a divine power higher than both, and in the nature of the personal commentary, we begin to glimpse something of the inner thoughts, concerns, and assumptions of the writers.

For those who wrote home, like the new arrivals who placed "information wanted" notices in colonial newspapers, emigration in the first half of the nineteenth century was an ongoing family affair. The decision to go or stay was made in light of kin relationships and particular family dynamics. Many left home in the company of a family member; and many went to join kin already in the colony, whose very presence promised emotional and perhaps even financial support in the strange land. For some, emigration offered escape from a difficult family situation. Men used the opportunity to abandon their wives and children; others left home so that they would not have to look after aging parents or work the farm. The extant correspondence also periodically makes references to the opposition which prospective emigrants faced from family and friends. Yet like those who placed "information wanted" notices in colonial newspapers, without any assurance that they would receive a response, all identified themselves within the context of familial and community relationships.

What follows are stories of a few of those who made up what newspapers at the time called the "tide" that swept across the Atlantic in the years after the Napoleonic Wars. The study consciously ends in 1845, before the massive migration generated by the famines of the following years. The famine migrations are a unique story; they were also an anomaly. More Irish migrants arrived in British America in the years leading up to the famines than were unceremoniously decanted at Saint John, New Brunswick, or Quebec from the infamous coffin ships in 1847 and 1848.[19] As important, the mid-nineteenth century coincided with the beginning of a new era of migration from Europe – one in which steam travel was more readily available and North American destinations were increasingly settled and industrializing. This study of emigration – of leaving home – relies heavily on the work of scholars who have analysed and debated the dynamics of human movement and various collectivities and the broad contours of the emigrants' worlds. At the same time, it consciously steps out of many of the current debates.[20] As David Fitzpatrick has eloquently argued in his study of Irish migration to Australia, often "the individual human mover [is] invisible"[21] in accounts that ask why the Irish or the Scots or the English decided to emigrate. Like the profiles that can be compiled of those who placed "information wanted" notices in colonial newspapers, most analyses rest on "identikit figures" who conform "to some general model of motivation."[22] The stories told here are of families and individual migrants who actually made the decision to leave home, and it follows their experiences up to the time they began to find their feet in the colony. Their stories remind us of the uniqueness of emigrants' experiences. Although it is never possible to really understand why an individual left home and why other family members, friends, and neighbours did not, personal accounts "can reveal how these [often] deeply private matters" were negotiated and explained to others.[23] They also allow us to follow a few emigrants as they made their way to their new homes and to appreciate some of the emotional and physical bonds, particularly to family and the immediate community, that continued to tie them to home – bonds that were so important in forging and sustaining the emigrants' world.

The following accounts are not intended to be representative of the experiences of particular groups of migrants, whether by class, community, or ethnicity. It is nonetheless likely that thousands of others who made the often treacherous journey across the Atlantic between 1815 and 1845 would recognize something of themselves in the following pages. Whether Irish, Scottish, English, or Welsh, most would certainly, if only unconsciously, have understood what was going through Mrs McIndoe's mind as she packed up her children to leave home to join her husband. And many would have nodded to Benjamin Booth, as a fellow traveller, as he made his way up the gangplank to start his journey to America. They, too, had been convinced by reports of opportunities in the New World. And they shared with the Gemmills, the Traills, and Jane Mayarity similar experiences of leaving home.

Indeed, the very process of emigration created its own world and its own ways of thinking. As the Dundoons or the Perrys packed up their household goods and precious items, took leave of family and friends, and then negotiated the always uncomfortable and sometimes frightening Atlantic crossing, they joined hundreds and, in some years, thousands of like-minded individuals and families who, by their decisions and actions, had set themselves apart from those who stayed behind. Although the emigrant season – from April to September each year – became a fact of national life during this period, most people in Great Britain and Ireland chose not to take part in this "emigrant world."[24] Those who did take part shared certain notions of a world that offered opportunities which they believed were no longer available at home. They also shared the dangers and difficulties of life aboard ship; and they shared that anxious time of finding family or making friends in the New World and of recreating families and communities. Emigrants' experiences of this world, in both its physical manifestation of the journey itself and its emotional and psychological dimensions, varied sharply. It made some difference if one left home in the 1840s, rather than in the years immediately after the Napoleonic Wars, for government regulations were increasingly enforced, and the colonial networks of assistance were more firmly in place. More significant, however, was an emigrant's age, sex, marital status, financial resources, and, of course, personal expectations. Nonetheless, the very raison d'être of the emigrants' world – leaving home – provided a sense of shared identity, which emigrants often maintained long after they were settled in the colony. Paradoxically, at the same time that it provided a basis of community with new-found neighbours and friends, most of whom were fellow emigrants, the emigrants' world also tied them inexorably to kin and communities across the Atlantic.

CHAPTER ONE

To Go or Not to Go

"From your letter, I see you are anxious to have all the information and advice you possibly can in order to make up your minds respecting the propriety of emigration," John Scott of Berlin, Upper Canada, wrote to his uncle Andrew Redford in Selkirk, Scotland, in 1835. "This is a topic," he continued, "which as far as general observations go, is now pretty nearly exhausted ... All we can do is to detail our own views and experiences of the Country."[1] Neither John nor his father Charles, who farmed north of the village, would "urge anyone" to emigrate, he said. But at the same time he acknowledged that both he and his father thought "that if we were in your situation, we should from all we now know on the subject, come to America."

John's letter, like so many that arrived in Scottish, Irish, and English homes in the first half of the nineteenth century, included details of the family's activities clearing land and planting, and the current state of the harvest. John also talked about the opportunities that his uncle, as an "industrious, enterprising emigrant," would have if he purchased an improved farm for himself and "wild land for the boys." However, he added, "My dear uncle ... you will find much better accounts in the periodicals that are still no doubt in circulation respecting the price of land, produce, labour etc than I can give you in the short compass of a letter," and he recommended that his uncle get a copy of *Chamber's Information*, "perhaps the best account you can get." But he admitted, "No letter or writing whatever, will entirely satisfy your mind on the subject – however much you may read or hear about it a kind of uncertainty will still seem to brood over it which nothing short of an actual visit can dissipate." Moreover, he warned that it was only after "a few months residence in the country," that one began to be reconciled to "the striking contrast between the external appearance" of home and the New World.

Andrew Redford did not in the end move to Upper Canada, and it appears that despite encouragement and offers of assistance, neither did his sons. So why did one branch of the family choose to uproot itself and another decide to stay home? From the extant correspondence, it is clear that the two families had lived in the same community and been members of the same congregation, and the cousins had attended school and played together as children. They had shared common concerns and drawn on each other for financial as well as emotional support. Part of the answer may lie in John Scott's reference to his father's difficulties before he left Scotland. "I can assure you, My Dear Uncle," he concluded his letter, "that Father now deserves encouragement. He is an altered man from what he was during the last 2 or 3 years he spent in his native country – Those were indeed years of gloomy despondency and sadness, but Providence has as far as I can see, been working for wise purposes." One of John's reasons for writing was to express the family's "sincerest acknowledgments of gratitude" for his uncle's "never to be forgotten kindness" – a loan of £50 to help cover the "unavoidable" debts which the Scotts had incurred during their first year in the colony. Yet the Scotts had undoubtedly had other options when they decided to leave all that was familiar to start anew on the other side of the Atlantic in what even colonial promoters acknowledged was still a young, rude, and unformed society.

It is really impossible to unravel with any level of certainly why a particular individual or family chose to emigrate when many of their friends, neighbours, and even family members did not. Press accounts at the time spoke of the "tides of emigration" and implicitly evoked images of an inexorable force of nature that swept thousands of people away in its flow.[2] Other commentators likened the "rage for emigration" to a fever that infected the unsuspecting and encouraged them to make decisions that they were likely to regret.[3] When the Scotts left home, they were part of an unprecedented movement of people from Great Britain and Ireland. By the early 1830s, tens of thousands of emigrants were annually making their way to North America and "emigration had become a recognized fact of life"[4] in the United Kingdom. But this does not explain why particular individuals chose to join the world of emigration and why many others did not. John Scott explicitly cautioned his uncle not to be caught up in the enthusiasm. Permanently leaving home

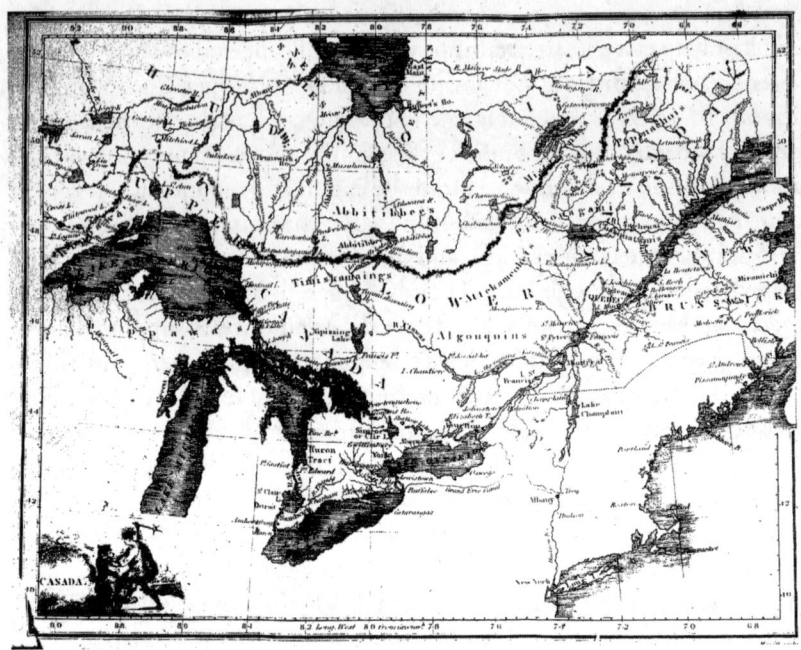

The maps printed in various guides, including this from *Counsel for Emigrants*, may have been reassuring for prospective emigrants, but did little to assist them in making a decision. Killam Library Special Collections, Dalhousie University. Photo by Cheryl DesRoches

for the colonies was a very serious decision and one not easily reversed. How one judged all the options rested on a myriad of factors. Even John Scott's often detailed letters do not really tell us why he and his family migrated or what such people experienced.[5] The transatlantic correspondence does suggest, however, some of the issues that prospective emigrants took into account when making their decisions. It also identifies and tells the stories of a few of those who were part of the migratory tide, and it offers a passing glimpse into the often sensitive negotiations in which individuals were involved as they considered whether to go or stay. When taken together with emigrants' voices, as can be faintly heard in the British and colonial press at the time, we begin to see the contours of the emigrants' world as seen by those who became part of it.

The decision to emigrate was highly personal, and the combination of factors that influenced each decision varied. Certainly, the national and local economic situation was a precipitating factor for many people.

As contemporary observers recognized, if at home there was "neither employment to yield the labourers wherewith to subsist upon nor land whereon to fix them as cultivators," then of course people considered leaving.[6] Extant government records suggest that both ethnicity and, perhaps more importantly, the economic situation in the local community shaped the decision. An individual's age, gender, marital status, place and responsibility in the family, and occupation were also essential parts of the equation. So, too, were the attitudes of one's friends and neighbours. For many, having relations, friends, friends of friends, or even more distant connections already settled in the New World made leaving home more attractive; others were attracted by the possibility that emigration afforded the chance to escape familial constraints or to avoid some other seemingly untenable situation at home.

At its most basic level, the decision to go or not to go was a family affair and was rooted in a matrix of familial relationships. Whether Scots, Irish, Welsh, or English, emigrants identified themselves and took their decisions as husbands and wives, mothers and fathers, sons and daughters, cousins and extended kin. The matter was discussed and debated in family parlours and kitchens. Family finances and personal and economic prospects in the local community were juxtaposed against the opportunities promised by the New World. People consulted various guides and settlers' accounts; they read and reread letters from those already settled in America. Having kin or friends to go to or travel with were factored in. A particular event – a marriage, the death of a parent or spouse, or eviction from one's farm – sometimes added urgency to the matter. And the general discussion was intermingled with specific questions of who might go, and where and when, and what the consequences would be for those left behind.

Residents of Great Britain and Ireland had been seeking their fortunes in America for hundreds of years, but the broad contours of the nineteenth-century world of emigration was different from that of the seventeenth and eighteenth centuries. Soon after the end of the Napoleonic Wars, commentators had been astounded at "the extraordinary emigration from all quarters of the Old World" to the New. In 1818 a Scottish newspaper editor judged that it was "a spectacle without parallel since the time of the Crusades" as all of Europe appeared "to be torn up by its roots to be precipitated upon America."[7] Many anticipated that once the economy recovered from the dislocations of the war, this unprecedented display of restlessness would abate, and in the first half of the 1820s the number of emigrants setting off from British and Irish ports did decrease. But in the early 1830s, as the members of the Scott family began to contemplate the future, an even greater number of their compatriots were leaving home for the colonies. For the thirty thousand or so men, women, and children who left home each year bound for British North American ports, emigration was not only a possibility but a viable and perhaps even desirable strategy for the future. The only hiatus in this tide of people and goods came when news of continued civil unrest in the Canadas reached the British Isles, and in 1838, 1839, and 1840 the flow temporarily ceased.

Parliament and the British public had initially been rather ambivalent about this seeming mass exodus of people. In 1815 the government briefly supported a scheme to encourage emigrants to stay within the empire and settle in Upper Canada, rather than moving to the United States, as so many were doing. These "experiments" were expensive, however, and the government was roundly criticized for actively promoting a policy that was draining the country of its most "enterprising individuals" and sapping "the nerves and sinews of national strength."[8] Apart from offering disbanded soldiers and their families land in the colonies, Parliament quickly drew back from directly supporting any subsequent programs until it had studied the matter. But the possibility of state subsidization had captured the attention of many in Great Britain and Ireland, and the Colonial Office received hundreds of petitions from individuals seeking assistance to leave home. The question of emigration continued to preoccupy policymakers in London and the colonies for the next two decades. Throughout the 1820s, various parliamentary committees considered whether state-sponsored emigration and colonization offered at least a partial solution to the pressing problems of unemployment and civil unrest at home. The emigrant enthusiast Wilmot Horton, undersecretary of state for the colonies and chair of a select committee examining emigration in the mid-1820s, convinced the authorities to support another experiment of subsidized emigration. But reports of the success of the expeditions of 1823 and 1825–26 from the south of Ireland, organized by Peter Robinson, were at best mixed. To the disappointment of many, Parliament decided in 1826 to leave emigration "to the enterprises of private or of associated speculators" and to individuals who were willing and able to cover their own expenses of relocating.[9]

This decision had little impact on the "rage" for emigration that was sweeping the nation. Most people in Great Britain and Ireland probably did not follow or understand the intricacies of the political debates that engaged parliamentarians and the national press. The controversy did, however, contribute to the wider public conversation about the benefits of emigration – for the future of the nation, of the empire, and of individuals. Increasingly, the muted concerns that had characterized reports in local newspapers and journals in the immediate postwar years – that emigration was stealing the best and brightest – had been transformed into approbation for those hardy and adventurous souls who were willing to take advantage of the opportunity offered by the New World.

This new attitude about the efficacy of emigration was fuelled by the public's growing awareness of the world on the other side of the Atlantic. After 1815, there was a veritable explosion of information and commentary about "America"[10] and British possessions around the globe. Increasingly, popular travellers' accounts introduced the British reading public to new and exciting places in far-flung parts of the world, and by the 1820s, accounts from "real" settlers told of their exploits and usually their triumphs in the colonies.[11] In addition to printing extensive reviews and excerpts of these works, newspapers and journals began to carry "reports from the colonies" or "from America"; editors commented on the relative merits of various destinations and debated the intricacies of various schemes of colonization; and newspapers often remarked on the number of emigrants leaving a particular region or community and commented on their chances of success.[12] By the mid-1820s, the British press had helped to create and sustain a world in which emigration, if not commonplace, was at least part of readers' consciousness and imagination.[13] At the same time, a plethora of pamphlets, emigrant guides, and settlers' accounts offered prospective emigrants advice on how to proceed to the New World and what they could expect when they got there. In addition to *Chamber's Information*, recommended by John Scott, prospective emigrants could consult *Counsel for Emigrants* and its *Sequel*, or Catermole's *Advantages of Emigration*, or any of a number of other collections that began to appear after 1830 and attested to the opportunities open to everyone in America.[14] The message of much of the discourse seemed clear: emigration was an option that many readers should seriously consider.

This outpouring of support for emigration was not uncontested. As the controversy over government-assisted emigration illustrates, some challenged the images of unbounded opportunity in the New World; they questioned the benefits of emigration to the nation and to the empire; and there were sharp disagreements over who should emigrate and who should stay home. "Anyone who has a prospect of making a decent livelihood in England would be a fool and a madman to remove

COUNSEL FOR EMIGRANTS,

AND

INTERESTING INFORMATION

FROM NUMEROUS SOURCES

WITH

ORIGINAL LETTERS

FROM

Canada

AND

THE UNITED STATES.

"In the multitude of Councillors there is safety."
SOLOMON.

ABERDEEN:
JOHN MATHISON, BROAD STREET.

1834.

Title page of *Counsel for Emigrants* (Aberdeen, 1834). Photo by Cheryl DesRoches

to America,"[15] a traveller commented in 1822. Others questioned whether the colonies, and particularly Upper Canada, was a fit place for any but "the Irish" or "the Scottish poor," who were "accustomed to the vicissitudes of climate and hard work" and had been "bred to the farm and handicraft work."[16] "The great error," observed a former resident, "lies in supposing that the class of persons who are overabundant at home and consequently least wanted, are exactly those most needed by the colony."[17] Many charged that "to excite and encourage such Emigration" was "as absurd as mischievous. It was cruel as well as impolitic."[18]

For the most part, however, emigration and emigrants were celebrated in the press. Moreover, whether supporting or opposing the proposition, the heated debates and extensive commentary firmly fixed the idea of emigration and images of the New World in the British and Irish imagination. The public discourse reinforced the notion that leaving home for the colonies was an option that should be considered seriously. This is not to suggest that this very public discussion alone propelled individuals and families to leave home. But farmers and artisans, daughters and sons, tenants and labourers were not immune to the conversations that swirled around them. And as more and more information about particular destinations became available (even though it was contradictory and often confusing) and as agents from the colonies began to tour the country promoting particular land schemes, emigration was undoubtedly a topic of discussion in community halls, taverns, coffee houses, churches, and homes throughout the British Isles.

Private conversations took on an immediacy when visitors or letters arrived from America or when former neighbours or friends who had already left home reappeared, disillusioned with their experiences as emigrant settlers. For most women and men, like John Scott's uncle Andrew, it was these personal recommendations – both to go or to stay – that carried the greatest weight when were trying to make up their minds about joining the world of emigration. The public discourse was nearly always mediated and filtered through an understanding gained from emigrant letters, visitors' stories, and rumours that inevitably circulated in the community. Each individual "read" the situation differently, depending on that individual's circumstances. All knew that emigration was a life-altering decision. In addition to gathering all the information they could, prospective emigrants discussed their options with neighbours and friends. And, most importantly, they discussed the situation with members of their immediate and extended family. In the end, the decision was never easy, and it was often heart rending.

In April 1833 William Hutton, a farmer who managed a sizable property in the very north of Ireland, asked to be freed from his lease. He reported to his landlord that although he was "now nearly sold out of a large and excellent crop," the result was "so distressing and so very short of what is requisite to meet our rent and expenses that we have no

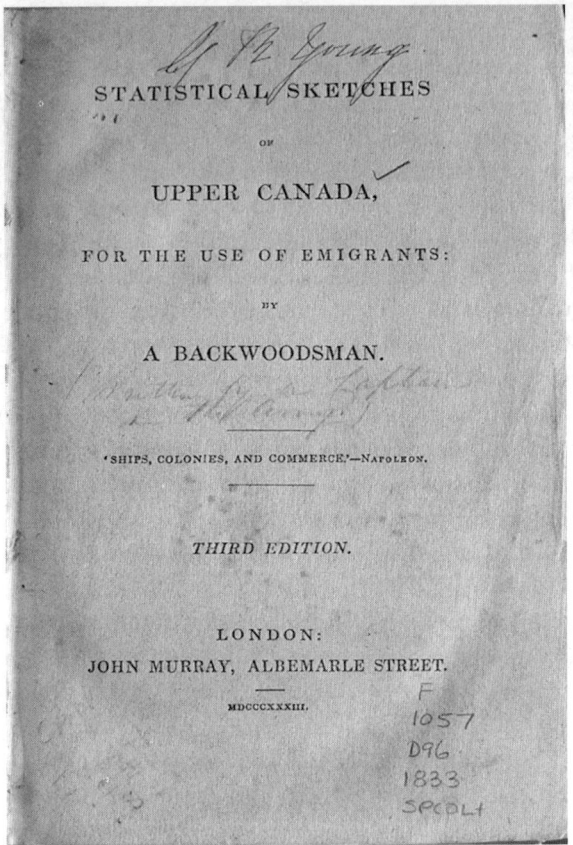

Title page of *Statistical Sketches of Upper Canada, for the Use of Emigrants* by a Backwoodsman (London, 1833). Photo by Cheryl DesRoches

recourse but to throw ourselves entirely upon your pleasure." Hutton and his wife Fanny had "been labouring nearly ten years in Grange without its ever affording us a coat to our backs, but on the contrary swallowing up every shilling of our income from other sources," he told the landlord. "With this fact before us and a family of five children, we appeal to your kindness to allow us to go elsewhere."[19] As William informed his mother in a letter written the same day, one of the options they were considering was emigrating to Canada.

The Huttons were one of thousands of farming families who considered leaving Great Britain and Ireland in the first half of the nineteenth century. The growing commercialization of agriculture, together with persistently low prices for produce, were forcing many middling and

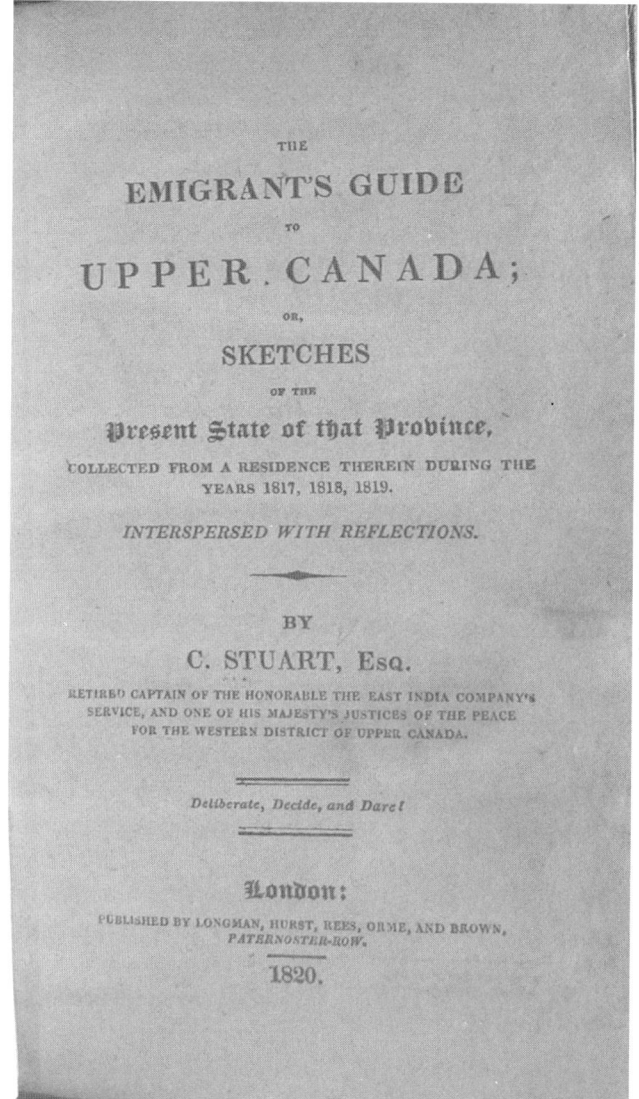

Title page, C. Stuart, *The Emigrant's Guide to Upper Canada* (London, 1820). Photo by Cheryl DesRoches

small-scale farmers, crofters, and tenants in Scotland, Ireland, and the south of England to reconsider their future.[20] It was not just farmers, however, who were under pressure. Throughout the British Isles, labourers, craftspeople, tradesmen, and individuals and families of all occupations were contemplating the apparent lack of future at home.

Although clearly intended as a satirical commentary on emigration, C.J. Grant's "Emigration, Detailing the Progress and Vicissitudes of an Emigrant," 1833 (Library and Archives Canada [LAC], e001201276, Peter Winkworth Collection [PWC], R9266-P1044) also depicts the ambivalence that at least some felt about leaving home.

Nonetheless, William Hutton does appear to fit the profile of the "typical" emigrant: male, Irish, farmer, and leaving for "America" in the 1830s.[21] Yet in many ways – and perhaps the most important way – he did not. Hutton was a "gentleman" and had considerable financial resources at his disposal. The vast majority who left Ireland and Great Britain for Upper Canada between 1815 and 1845 were certainly not destitute; they could afford the passage to America, and many – like the Irish farm families who left Tipperary during this period – were probably financially secure.[22] But few had the resources of the Huttons.

Selling up and moving, whether to the nearest village or town, to another farm or region, or across the Atlantic, was not done easily, even for someone in Hutton's position. William and Fanny Hutton had been under financial pressure for some time, and they had first begun to consider emigration as a possible solution to their predicament in the winter of 1832–33. They read emigrant guides and settlers' accounts and talked to friends and neighbours. At one point, William attended a local emigration meeting that apparently was hosted by an agent from Upper Canada, and he and his wife began to correspond with one of Fanny's cousins who had a farm near Guelph, Upper Canada.[23] Emigration was not the only option. William explored the possibility of moving to England and buying a farm in Yorkshire, but he concluded that the expenses would be too high for the expected return. In April 1833, William wrote to his mother that he and Fanny and her brother John had "been considering the propriety of [his] going out to Canada next month." Fanny's cousin was "much pleased with his prospects" in America, William noted, and had reported that the market for produce in Upper Canada was good. Moreover, many "respectable" people in the Huttons' neighbourhood were already preparing to leave. "I would much rather go now than wait here with the hope of getting a situation," William explained.[24]

William had not yet made up his mind, however. One significant problem was that Fanny was not enthusiastic: "[She] says she would rather have a situation of a £150 per annum than go to Canada; to her the idea of such a trip is odious in the extreme. No wonder, when there are five such helpless little ones about her but she thinks of two evils 'Canada or idleness' the former is the better."[25] The prospect of being able to obtain fertile, relatively inexpensive land in British America while maintaining his status as a gentleman and securing a future for his children was increasingly attractive to William. The information he had received from Fanny's cousin was enough to convince him that he should see the situation for himself, so in the spring of 1834 he left for

New York. The plan was that if the New World met his expectations, he would buy a farm and the family would move.

William Hutton was by no means the only prospective emigrant to visit the colony personally to assess its possibilities before making a final decision. John Scott had recommended this to his uncle. A number of guides unequivocally stated, "All persons intending to emigrate [should] visit the country before they move their families to it. ... It is a duty which the emigrant owes them."[26] And many did. Settlers in the colony frequently mentioned in their journals the arrival of individuals who were "prospecting the land" or on a "settling expedition."[27]

For most who were trying to decide if emigration was their best option, such a trip was well beyond their means. Over 90 percent of British and Irish emigrants paid their own way, and it was difficult enough to save or cobble together the funds to cover the cost of a single transatlantic crossing, let alone a return. Consequently, they had to rely on information that was locally available. They compared accounts in the press with presentations made by agents at local emigration or colonization society meetings. They pored over emigrant guides and settlers' accounts. Yet even the most respected journals and guides frequently contradicted each other about who should go, the best locations in which to settle, and how to get there.[28] Emigration enthusiasts and colonial promoters had their own agendas and could not always be trusted. If one could not investigate personally, the most reliable source of information about life and prospects in the New World was from someone who could be trusted and was already there and thus had first-hand experience.

In 1826 James Hendry, a farmer living near Glasgow, asked his brother-in-law John Gemmill, who had a farm in Shepherd's Mills Township, Upper Canada (probably the same John Gemmill who had emigrated in 1821), to tell him "how the farming, merchandising, manufacturing and distillery and procreative establishments are coming on at Ramsay."[29] James and John corresponded sparingly over the next six years, and in April 1832 James announced, "I am thinking of coming to America," and asked for advice on what to bring and whether he should purchase land from the Canada Company.[30] James realized there were "difficulties." He had a wife, seven children, and limited means. Thus, he would only come, he stated, if there was a good prospect of "getting over some of them." But he had obviously been encouraged by reports from his brother-in-law, who seemed "to be getting very rich."[31] A year later, James was still thinking of coming. In addition to wanting "particulars" about the possibilities for farming and the best way to travel, he tentatively asked if John would be willing to help financially.³² In March 1834 James was still trying to make up his mind. He was "pleased to hear," he wrote, that the Gemmills were "doing so well and [were] building a stone house." He had saved almost £100 for the trip, as John had advised, but he wondered if this was enough. Nonetheless, he concluded, "You might let the old [house] stand for a year or two as we might be coming."³³

We do not know if James Hendry and his family ever moved to Upper Canada. Without John Gemmill's replies, it is also impossible to know John's reaction to James's request for funds or his suggestion that the Hendrys might move into the Gemmills' old house. It appears from the tone of James Hendry's letters that his brother-in-law sent quite detailed advice, and like many other colonists, wrote home at some length about his life and work in Upper Canada. James obviously read John's letters carefully and took at least some of his advice seriously. But even with family already well established in the colony, James was not about to make a hasty decision.³⁴

Emigrant letters were of inestimable importance in encouraging family members, friends, and neighbours to consider packing up and crossing the Atlantic. Those at home often wrote to kin and friends in the colony asking for advice and information, and what they received was frequently wide ranging and detailed. New arrivals in Upper Canada told anxious relatives about their voyage and of their initial efforts getting settled. Later, they wrote about various aspects of their experiences which they thought would be of particular interest to their readers. Writing letters required time, effort, and some expense; many appear to have chosen their subjects carefully. Thus, if not responding to specific questions, new colonists included information which they thought their readers would want to know.

Tradesmen, artisans, and mechanics wrote about opportunities for work, their wages, and the price of goods, and they often requested that specific tools be sent or brought out. Farmers regularly included details about the climate, the fertility of the soil, how various crops were faring, and the state of the harvest.³⁵ Emigrant colonists were writing to kith and kin who were concerned not only for their well-being but who would appreciate the references to wages or prices for produce at the local market. Those at home undoubtedly compared what they learned about the colonies with their own situation. Unlike the tables of information that appeared in many emigrant and settlers' guides, information received from friends and family already in Upper Canada could be trusted.

By the 1830s, colonial promoters had begun to recognize the influence that personal correspondence could have in convincing prospective emigrants to take that final step into the emigrants' world. Personal testimonials could encourage readers to relocate to a particular place or community. A number of British newspapers and journals periodically published "letters home" for the edification of their readers. By 1830, emigrant guides routinely included often lengthy excerpts from the letters of new settlers to illustrate a particular piece of advice. A number of enterprising emigrant enthusiasts went one step further and published collections of letters – from the Dorking emigrants, or a party who had left from Sussex, for example – that quickly captured the public's imagination.[36] Such public endorsements from real people undoubtedly had some influence on those considering emigrating. But many viewed these collections with considerable skepticism. Readers often wondered aloud what had been omitted from the edited versions. Others charged that only those letters that supported emigration or a particular settlement were ever published.[37] If possible, it was best to rely on information from someone they knew, a family member or friend who could be trusted and who understood the particulars of their situation at home.

Those at home could not fail to realize that most who had already emigrated, like John Scott and his family, were "well pleased with [their] situation." At the same time, they were left in no doubt that, as Scott told his uncle, the New World was a foreign land in "a remote part of the World."[38] The British America of emigrant letters was not an Eden in the wilderness (as it was frequently depicted in the British press and promotional literature),[39] and there were no assurances of a better life. As John Scott explicitly reminded his uncle, "You must recollect Canada is a different country from Scotland and it requires a long apprenticeship to make a person contented with a Canadian farm."[40] Those at home were frequently warned, for example, that establishing and working a farm in British America required hard work and perseverance. John's father and brothers had to "labour long and hard with that stern Master Necessity behind them," he reported to his uncle. The only thing that helped keep "up their spirits" was "the prospect of a good remuneration from their toils."[41] Many new settlers recounted the trouble they had had with ague or fever shortly after their arrival. Periodically, they reported "sickness everywhere."[42] William Hendry, a young Scottish farm labourer, complained soon after landing in Upper Canada in 1834, "This place is pretty boring to be in sometimes. We don't see anything about us but the forest and the sky above."[43] Some emigrants obviously had difficulty settling, and they moved restlessly from place to place, looking for a situation or "the right" location.

In their letters home, most new arrivals nonetheless remained confident that they had made the right decision. And some unequivocally recommended that family members and friends join them. A year after he arrived in the colony in 1845, George Forbes, the son of a Scottish tenant farmer, emphatically told his father and brothers, "I am certain you will be better to come over here and get land of your own" instead of leasing at home.[44] Fathers and mothers often encouraged their children to join them. Brothers frequently recommended that a younger sibling or a cousin "come out"; and sons and daughters sometimes urged parents to emigrate.

Not all were willing to give such unqualified advice. "Were I to consult only my own feelings and comforts," an anonymous Aberdonian in Upper Canada wrote to his brother in 1832, "I should say without hesitation – <u>come</u> <u>come</u> <u>every</u> <u>one</u> of <u>you</u>." But perhaps concerned that he would be held responsible if things did not work out, he warned, "It cannot be concealed that there are difficulties to encounter and privations to be endured, which everyone has not resolution to face or patience to endure."[45] John Scott informed his uncle that, initially, farming in Upper Canada was expensive; but with capital he could prosper.[46] However, he was careful to point out the many hardships of life in the colony. As William Hendry explained to his mother and sisters and brothers when asked if they or their neighbours should join them, "I can well believe that they would be better here than where they are and many in addition to them, but I am not encouraging any body to come at this moment, for many are coming out who are not pleased with this place and I'm none too pleased myself with this place myself but it may be very good for all that but I know that I would be far happier if yourself and the rest of family were here."[47]

Many new settlers were clearly torn by their desire to have family join them and their concern that those reading the letters should not think that Upper Canada was a land of milk and honey. Mary McNicol, a widow who with her family ran a farm near Southwold, Upper Canada, stated in a letter to her brother in 1831, "You may tell my sister and Donald McFail her son that I do not advise them to come to this country ... It goes very hard with people at first, particularly with those who have no pieces of money with them." But McNichol's letter, like so many from North America, illustrated a profound ambivalence. "One thing I know," the letter continued, was that "when people once get themselves properly settled that they are much better off here than at home."[48] Moreover, she asked her brother to tell her sister that "if Donald McPhail has a mind to try it he better come by New York as it will be much cheaper than by Quebec." She added that if he did come, she would "let them have twenty acres of my land," which they would have to clear themselves.[49]

To people in the British Isles, the overall impression from the letters was that those who had already emigrated believed they had made the right decision. Although they were often lonely and missing family and friends and the sights of home, life appeared to be better in the New World than the Old. America, and specifically Upper Canada, offered a myriad of opportunities for those who worked hard. There was plenty of land to be cleared and cultivated, and ready employment in colonial towns and villages. William Knox, one of John Scott's cousins, wrote home in 1842 that Upper Canada was "a better Country for a poor man than the Old County."[50] Scott had assured his uncle that the colony held many opportunities for those with capital. Perhaps the most convincing testimonial was that most kin now living in Upper Canada had no intention of returning home, even if they had the means to do so. As Thomas Medd wrote his aunt in 1820, "I would not persuade anyone to come to America everyone must please themselves." At the same time he stated, "No one can persuade me to come back again."[51]

Many in Ireland, Scotland, and England were in fact persuaded to "come to America." As Marjory Harper has recently noted, "Private encouragement and practical assistance from family, friends, and community, transmitted primarily by letter and remittance but occasionally through visits home, were of inestimable and enduring importance in stimulating secondary migration and directing patterns of settlement."[52] For many of those in the Old World who were wondering whether to go or stay, having kin in the New World provided them with a specific destination and the security of a ready-made if only temporary home. Having relatives in the colony helped to temper the feeling that the New World was a completely foreign land. Bruce Elliott has concluded that for those who left Tipperary in the 1840s, it was "the location of distant kin, more than soil capability, the nearness of markets and transportation routes [that] influenced the choice of destination."[53]

As they carefully weighed their options, individuals and families had to consider other factors before they could make a final decision. The voyage was known to be long and often dangerous. In the 1820s and 1830s, British newspapers frequently included sensational accounts of ships being wrecked on the rocks off the coast of Ireland and Newfoundland or going down in a storm. There was also the matter of finances and whether one could afford to go. Often a precipitating factor – the offer of assistance, the arrival in the community of a particularly persuasive emigrant agent, or the departure of friends – prompted an individual or a family to consider the matter more seriously.[54] About 10 percent of all those who left home between 1815 and 1845 did so with financial assistance from the state, the parish, or a local benevolent organization. There were, for example, the two quite large parties of Irish Catholic emigrants (the Peter Robinson expeditions) that were funded by the Colonial Office in 1823 and 1825. In 1832 the Earl of Egremont established the Petworth Committee of Emigration, which organized parish-assisted migration from the south of England to Upper Canada until the program was stopped in 1837.[55] But even those fortunate enough to be chosen for one of these schemes still had to confront the question of what other members of the family thought of the matter. Families had to decide who should (or wanted to) go and what would happen to those left behind.

The debates in the Gemmill household in 1820 and 1821 may have been protracted. It is likely that John and Ann Gemmill of Glasgow had been considering emigration for some time before a local emigration society offered the chance of subsidized passage and land in Upper Canada. It is unclear whether financial circumstances prevented the family (which included nine children who ranged in age from two to eighteen) from traveling together or whether John and Ann had determined that it would be best for him to go ahead to begin to make a new home for the family. Whatever the case, they decided that John would go first. As they prepared for his departure, the family made tentative plans for their reunion. When John left home in late May 1821,[56] Ann and children went to live with his brother Andrew; and while they waited for news of John's safe arrival, Ann began to make preparations for their own departure.

"I am now at work on my land," John wrote home in March 1822. After providing a few particulars of the weather (which was "very healthy") and his work clearing the land, and giving news of others who had been part of the original party of emigrants, John expressed his concern that he had not heard from Ann, even though this was the third letter he had written. He nonetheless instructed his wife about what had to be done to get the family ready to leave home: "Get yourselves entered into some society and if you are not already entered get it done immediately as I wish you were all here and my brother Andrew along with you." He said that his son Andrew should register as "head of the family" because this would "entitle him to land and implements."[57] John then gave Ann detailed instructions about what she should pack, both for the voyage and for their new life in Upper Canada.

John's letter did not arrive until after Ann and the six youngest children had set out.[58] To John's great disappointment, when the family arrived in Lanark, his eldest son Andrew and two daughters, Margaret and Jean were not with them, nor was his brother. Andrew, a young man of eighteen, was apparently already settled in a job, and his sisters were in service. John was nonetheless confident that when his eldest children realized the opportunities for them in Upper Canada, they would soon change their minds.

Over the next ten years, John first instructed and then entreated his son to come to the colony and bring his sisters and uncle. There was no question, he stated again and again, that the farm could support them. "I have got Plenty of Everything that is necessary that the Earth can produce,"[59] he wrote two years after he left home; and a year later he reported that rapid improvements in the area "will render our situation more comfortable and agreeable."[60] John's letters made it clear that there were any amount of opportunities for Andrew and his sisters to find waged work if they did not want to settle on the farm. The girls could easily earn from four to six dollars a month and board as servantwomen, he and Ann wrote.[61] John declared that he needed his brother's help, since he intended to purchase another hundred acres of land;[62] and at least twice, he and Ann found son Andrew "a good birth" – once as a clerk in a tanning yard and once working for a local merchant. Indeed, John said, there were a number of other excellent opportunities which his son might have had "with very genteel salaries."[63]

It appears that for the first few years after the family left Scotland, young Andrew seriously considered emigrating. In 1824 he asked his father for "a more explicit statement" than he had so far received about conditions in Lanark. "We shall proceed to answer your numerous budget of queries just as they stand and leave you to judge in some measure for yourself,"[64] John replied. He then described his farm in detail (its size, topography, varying soil quality, rate of clearing, methods of tilling, and his crops), as well as the climate, the wildlife in the area, and the family's proximity to neighbours. But Andrew was not convinced. The issue became even more complicated when Andrew and his sisters Jean and Margaret married and set up their own households. John continued to hope that his children, their spouses, and his brother would join the rest of the family in Upper Canada, but his hopes gradually faded.

Initially, John's letters had addressed Andrew as a dependent son – someone to be instructed and directed. By 1826 his tone had begun to change: "I would be very glad were you to think of coming here yourself, but particularly your Sisters and Husbands I would honestly advise not to neglect this opportunity."[65] Two years later, implicitly recognizing that Andrew was an independent householder in his own right, John entreated, "I hope as soon as you receive this letter you will be ready to embark for this country if you can raise the means to enable you to do so." But echoing a theme in so many emigrant letters, he continued, "I hope I need not say any thing to influence you to leave Scotland."[66] At one point, Jean and her husband apparently planned to emigrate, though it is unclear from John's letters if they ever arrived. By the end of 1829, however, John wrote to Andrew, "I almost despair of your wishes of our meeting again with the rest of my family around my fireside ... [Although] that may not take place upon earth let us wish to Divine assistance and conduct ourselves in such a manner that we look forward to our meeting together in another and better world."[67]

The Gemmill story illustrates some of the issues that people confronted as they considered the question of emigration. A significant proportion of British and Irish emigrants left home as part of nuclear families. The Gemmills' decision was probably precipitated by the offer of assistance from the Glasgow Committee on Emigration during a period when John and Ann had a large family and few prospects for their future. John had the security of travelling and settling in the company of friends and neighbours, and also had the opportunity to own his own farm.[68] Although the decision was officially John's, as head of his household, it became evident a year later that Ann shared John's assessment of the situation. Certainly, she did not hesitate to assume responsibility for reuniting the family. Like many other British couples, the Gemmills had apparently decided together that emigration was to be a family undertaking. It was "a strategy of heirship"[69] that addressed not only the immediate economic dilemma but also ensured that one's sons and daughters and children into the next generation could be secure and possibly prosper.

Young Andrew Gemmill appears to have seen the matter quite differently. Apparently trained as a bookkeeper, he already had secure employment when his parents and siblings left Glasgow, and he was well integrated into a community of friends and associates. Accompanying his mother and siblings would have meant giving up what he had already worked so hard to establish, as well as sacrificing some of his personal independence. After his marriage in 1825, the dynamics changed even further. Now he had to consider the wishes of his wife and her family and friends, as well as those of his parents. Once married, his sisters had even less flexibility. As wives and soon as mothers, Jean and Margaret were, by law and custom, dependents; they had little opportunity and probably little inclination to make decisions independent of their husbands.

The negotiations that went on in the Hutton household in 1833–34 were also protracted and appear to have caused some tension between husband and wife. Even after William left for New York and Upper Canada in the early spring of 1834, Fanny continued to object to moving across the Atlantic. William believed that this was partly because Fanny was concerned about the health and welfare of her children. She was also daunted by the prospect of leaving behind family and friends and all that was familiar. Meanwhile, for almost ten weeks, William travelled and looked at prospects in both the United States and Upper Canada. As he wrote to his mother and his brother-in-law John, he was at times "bewildered" by the number of farms for sale in Upper Canada, and at one point he concluded, "I feel pretty confident that all my labours of inspection will end in my settling somewhere in the States."[70] The people he met in upstate New York were congenial, one letter related, and like many of his compatriots, William was more concerned about the quality and potential of the area than whether it was part of the British Empire. He did inspect property in the Peterborough area, on the recommendation of Lieutenant Governor Colborne of Upper Canada, but he was unimpressed and was also offended by "the depravity of the young people there."[71] A chance wind on Lake Ontario took him unexpectedly to the eastern part of the colony, and there he found what he was looking for.

William's letters home (some of which were later published in the *British Farmers' Magazine*) chronicle his concerns and careful investigation of the potential of the New World for someone in his situation. As he wrote in one letter, "I set out with the idea that I was not calculated for a life of extreme hardship and determined, if I found such to be necessary in Canada, to return."[72] In the end, the Belleville area had everything he required: local markets, easy access to larger communities, good and affordable land, a pleasing climate, and a "respectable" and prosperous society. He acknowledged that Upper Canada had many disadvantages. Wages for farm labourers were excessive, cash was scarce, and the winters were long and cold. Nonetheless, there was, he concluded, "the positive certainty that every man has of providing a comfortable maintenance for himself and his family if he have only common industry and a pair of working hands, or a small capital to supply the want of the latter."[73]

In June 1834 William announced to Fanny, without apparently any warning, that he had purchased a hundred and sixty-five acres of land within a mile and a quarter of the small village of Belleville, in the eastern part of the colony. After describing how he intended to finance the purchase (with loans from his father), William explained to his wife, "I have done my very best both in doing and in refraining from doing, and I feel very confident that if my dearest Fanny should think otherwise, she will not reproach me." William was obviously aware that Fanny was still not reconciled to emigrating. "If you feel you cannot be happy at such a distance from home, I would say certainly remain until you can train your mind to it, and send the children forward." William clearly believed that this was his decision to make. He only hoped that her love for him would prevail and that, as he told her, "You will endeavour to sooth sorrows which a separation from a beloved country and beloved friends naturally produces in a warm heart ... Enough of this, I merely wish to encourage you to hold the mastery over your spirit, to root and ground your love. I know well how grievous, how intensively grievous, your separation from all that you hold dear in Ireland must be."[74]

Fanny still had to make her decision, and it must have been agonizing. Leaving a terminally ill mother and moving permanently to a new country and new home, which William described as "bare" – and one that was difficult at best to reach – was almost impossible to conceive. Her family was adamantly opposed to the idea, and William seems to have made no attempt to consult her about where she might like to live if she agreed to go. Fanny's concerns about "the rugged path which lies before us" were further compounded when a neighbouring family returned from Upper Canada disheartened and disgruntled. "The accounts which they give of the country is miserable," Fanny wrote.[75] But she was a gentlewoman of her time. Being separated from husband and possibly children and refusing to accept the responsibilities of being a middle-class wife and mother was almost unthinkable, for someone of her rank and upbringing.[76] She began to make arrangements for the journey, and she and the children joined William in the fall of 1834.

Illustrations such as this "Wreck of the Emigrant Ship 'John,'" which appeared in the *Illustrated London News*, 19 May 1855, only served to heighten prospective emigrants' concerns about the venture (McCord Museum [MCM], M994.5.61).

Fanny's reluctance is understandable. Many men and women shared her aversion to leaving all that was familiar for the uncertainties of life in the colonies. Fanny appears to have had some choice in the matter. She had family in Ireland who were willing and financially able to support her and the children, even if this meant that, as a separated woman, her respectability might be questioned.

Wives could be in a particularly difficult situation if the husband was determined to go. Even in the most companionate marriage, they were legal dependants; and nineteenth-century sensibilities assumed that a wife would support her husband's decision. This was certainly reflected in the public discussions about emigration. The discourse of emigration was decidedly gendered.[77] "The emigrant" was by definition male, and the growing body of promotional literature was directed almost exclusively to men of the soil, gentlemen of some means, and craftsmen, tradesmen, and mechanics. Every so often, emigrant enthusiasts noted that there were opportunities for single and healthy young women. Wives, on the other hand, were assumed to be appendages of their husbands. It was the male head of the household, after all, who controlled the family finances and had the authority to direct others to follow. It was acknowledged that an emigrant might have to "persuade" his wife to leave home,[78] for women were, by nature, timid and more attached to home and hearth than men were. But in the end, it was his decision to make, and hers to follow.

Emigrants' letters did not always reflect such stark lines of authority. Although to William Hutton, "common sense" suggested that Fanny would eventually succumb to his superior knowledge and judgment, other husbands recognized that their wife's concerted opposition to leaving home was difficult if not impossible to ignore. In 1834, for example, Henry Kerr explained to his brothers, who were already in Upper Canada and apparently urging him to join them: "I do think, if my wife were not so averse to go to America that I would have come out in the Autumn – as it is I will not come at this time."[79] It was challenging enough to pack up a household and relocate thousands of miles away when both husband and wife were committed to the undertaking. If one party was actively opposed, many families probably abandoned the idea altogether.[80]

For the Gemmills, the Scotts, and many other families, both husband and wife seem to have embraced the project. Indeed, between 1815 and 1845, many Irish, English, and Scottish families emigrated, with young and not so young children. Contemporary colonial reports frequently mentioned the arrival of groups of nuclear families and of extended households who intended to settle together.[81] When Frances Stewart and her husband Thomas left Ireland in 1823, the party of two complete households included twelve children and various other assorted individuals.[82] Although the limited statistical evidence suggests that, if possible, the family emigrated together, many of the male passengers listed on ships' manifests as single or unattached were part of this pattern of familial emigration. Like William Hutton and John Gemmill, they were husbands and fathers who expected that their wives and children would soon follow.[83] For some, this strategy was a way of easing the transition. When wives such as Fanny Hutton were still unsure about leaving home, having a new home to go to in Upper Canada could make an immense difference. For many others, the two- or three-step migration of the family was the only way they could afford to go. It was not unusual for the family to be separated for a number of years, until wives and children had accumulated sufficient funds to pay for their passage. Husbands and fathers often tried to send money home to help defray the cost, but there was no assurance that these remittances ever arrived.[84] Moreover, many of these men discovered that they needed all they could earn just to survive in the New World.

The logistics of reuniting families could be complicated. Maintaining contact across the Atlantic was difficult at the best of times. Not all emigrants had the ability or could afford to write home. Moreover, as John Gemmill and many others discovered, letters could take months to cross the Atlantic, and they frequently went astray. The situation was further complicated because new emigrants moved repeatedly – to look for work or for that right piece of land. And, of course, in an untold number of instances, men took the opportunity afforded by "going ahead" to effectively dissolve their marriages and absolve themselves of any further responsibilities to their wives and children. Notices in colonial newspapers of wives looking for their husbands indicate that after months and sometimes years apart, wives were often not sure where their husbands actually lived or whether they were even still alive.

A number of families, undoubtedly anticipating the difficulties of communication, made at least tentative arrangements in advance about how and when the family would be reunited in the colonies. Although Ann Gemmill had not heard from John before she left Scotland, she seems to have made her way to New Lanark without problems, perhaps having received directions from authorities in Glasgow or Kingston. Fanny Hutton, on the other hand, waited for instructions from William before she left home; and as she made her way to board the ship that would take her to America, she was confident that her husband would be at the wharf in New York to meet her and the children. In some instances, wives were told to write when they arrived and their husbands would come and find them.[85] In 1829, for example, Mrs Spright and her children put a note in an Upper Canada newspaper to inform her husband Thomas that they had "just arrived from England."[86]

"Information wanted" notices of wives looking for their husbands that were printed in Upper Canadian newspapers tell the stories of some of those whose arrangements had gone astray. They also suggest something of the internal dynamics of family decision making and of the circumstances of women and children who were left behind. Michael Brown Kirwin's wife and child explained in the fall of 1839 that they had come from Dublin "in order to join him" and were now dismayed because they did not know where he lived. The notice asked Michael to "make known at this office [the *Christian Guardian* in York] where he is residing."[87] Irishwoman Mrs McQueen must have been delighted when, sometime in 1831, she received a letter from her husband John, "who had sailed from Glasgow, Scotland" the previous year, directing her to pack up and join him. The family had arrived in the Gananoque area of eastern Upper Canada sometime in the late summer or fall of 1831. John was not there, and for the next six months they managed as best they could while looking for him. By January 1832, Mrs McQueen and their six children were getting desperate.[88]

Not all families were willing to wait for husbands to send for them. After months of separation and often silence, which might lengthen into years, some wives packed up their children and made preparations for their own transatlantic crossing. Hannah Gadel, for example, left County Clare in 1830 to find her husband Michael Power, "for he never wrote to her."[89] Fanny Connor went "in search" of her husband in August 1833 and, she informed the public, was "disconsolate" at her lack of success. When Mrs Donevan left Ireland in 1821, she was not even sure that her husband John was still alive. He had "left Cork about three years ago" and the last word she had had of him was "at Mr Snider's near Point Fortune, about twelve months since." Anxious about the lack of news, she decided to go to Upper Canada "in search of him."[90] One wonders whether John Donevan wanted to be found. Both he and Michael Power may have used emigration as an opportunity to abscond and to reinvent themselves in the colonies.[91] Other men undoubtedly decided that their families would only be a hindrance as they moved about looking for that mythical opportunity promised in the press and the settlers' accounts.[92] Moreover, by the time their wives and children arrived at Quebec, an untold number of husbands had succumbed to the fever or had died as a result of injuries suffered while clearing their land or working in the bush or on the river.

One can only wonder how these women had coped after their husbands had emigrated. Many, like Ann Gemmill, moved in with relatives while they waited and prepared for their own journey. Others apparently depended on local charity or the parish poor rates to keep themselves and their children. Certainly, some turned to the parish for assistance for their own passage. Many had to work for years before they had the means to cover the cost of the passage. It was four years, for example, before Mrs Robert Morrisson set out to join her husband in Upper Canada.[93] She arrived in Cornwall, where he had been teaching, only to find that he had moved on. A number of women used all the funds they had just to make the trip. They landed in the colonies with little or no money or resources, confident that their financial worries would be shared with their husbands. Mary Duffy and her five children left County Kerry, Ireland, in 1829. By the time they arrived in North America, the family was "in a distressed situation" and obviously dismayed that John, "who had emigrated to Quebec" two years earlier, was not there to meet them.[94]

What is startling is the underlying optimism behind many of these notices, even those placed by wives who arrived bewildered and apparently in desperate straits. It must have been both distressing and disheartening as they began to realize how large the colony was and how difficult communications and transportation could be. This was certainly not just another part of Britain, as some at home were claiming.[95] Yet as they packed up their children and households, these mothers had decided that it would be their future home. Emigration was the only way to reunite their families and move forward.

For many, the decision about whether and when to emigrate was not so complicated. Newly married couples and single women and men (who made up a significant portion of transatlantic migrants) did not have to worry about children or packing up a household and disposing of land or a business. As historian Catharine Wilson has noted, for many young couples, emigration was "an integral part of setting up a new family."[96] Thomas and Catharine Parr Traill had only been married a few weeks when they made their way to Upper Canada in 1832. Prospects in the south of England were bleak, and Thomas's military half pay and Catharine's income from writing were not enough to support them in a lifestyle of genteel respectability. They were undoubtedly aware of the warnings in much of the public discourse of emigration about the problems that gentlemen emigrants frequently encountered.[97] But Upper Canada promised the Traills an opportunity to gain financial security. They had kin already settled in the colony; and, perhaps as important, Catharine's "dear sister Susanna" and Thomas's brother officer Dunbar Moodie were also emigrating to the colony. Catharine appears to have approached the project with a mixture of eagerness and trepidation. As she wrote to her friends James and Emma Bird on her "bridal day": "The waves will soon roll between her and all the friends of her youth." Yet she was "willing to leave all for the sake of a dear valued friend and husband to share with him all the changes and chances of settler life."[98] Three years later, Robert and Harriet Pengelly left Guernsey for Upper Canada, having been married only a few months. Harriet was not so sanguine about the prospect of her new home. Like Fanny Hutton, she feared the long voyage and at times was desperately unhappy about leaving home. But Harriet, like Catharine Parr Traill, seems to have kept most of her concerns to herself. As a young middle-class wife, she knew her place and obviously felt that it was beside her husband Robert.[99]

Many young husbands and wives were eager to leave home, however. It was an opportunity for a shared adventure. And for non-inheriting sons, emigration was their one chance to gain land and a livelihood. The transatlantic crossing affirmed the young couple's independence from their respective families. Similar factors were undoubtedly at play for young unmarried adults who left home for the colonies.

Young Abraham Bait left Scotland for Quebec sometime in 1832 or 1833 in the company of his employer/master. We know little about Abraham's circumstances other than that he had left behind his fiancée, Margaret Colquohoun, who expected to join him once he had finished his apprenticeship and set up his own household. In a poignant letter home in July 1833 he told Margaret, "I think upon you night and day[,] my mind is the same as it was when I left you." Abraham reassured Margaret that he would see her "here or in Scotland when my time is finished & I hope we shall part no more." Although he missed her and his friends, Abraham "quite liked the country." He assured her, "You would like this place if you were here."[100] The two appear to have corresponded intermittently over the next two years. In 1835 Abraham replied to Margaret's last letter: "It gave me no small joy ... that you whom I held so dear were still true[,] you said that you thought I had forgotten you in this you were far mistaken for I never forgot you one day ever since I left you." Abraham apologized for not having written sooner and again assured Margaret that there was "not another girl in the world" that he loved like her. He had managed to save some money, he reported, adding, "I think in the course of a year and a half or two years, I can have what will get a very good farm." Then the two could be together.[101]

Extant government statistics indicate that the largest single group of emigrants were unattached or unaccompanied adult men and women. An unknown portion of these were undoubtedly husbands, who like John Gemmill were going ahead to find work and begin to make a new home. It is nonetheless clear that between 1815 and 1845 the colonies, and particularly Upper Canada, were an attractive destination for many young Scottish, Irish, and English sons and daughters. Based on the "information wanted" notices and limited statistical evidence, this portion of the "stream" of migrants increased after 1840. Yet even among this group, emigration remained a family affair. Young men and women emigrated in the company of siblings or cousins; they expected (or hoped) to join kin already in the colony; and often the actual decision to leave home was made as much by the whole family as by the individual.

In the fall of 1833 Mrs Murray, a widow who lived near Edinburgh, had to decide how best to secure a future for her youngest son, William. The eldest boy, James, appears to have been well established in Aberdeen. Another son, Archibald, was in the military, and Thomas was a clerk in a Montreal merchant house. After considerable discussion within the family, Mrs Murray decided that Willy, who seems to have been in his mid-teens, would join Tom in the colonies. Over the next few months, her letters to James periodically mentioned how William was being "fitted out for Canada"; she was making him new clothes and sorting out things he would need for the voyage. She anticipated Willy's departure with a mixture of satisfaction and regret. Although she would miss him dreadfully, the colonies offered far greater opportunities than were available at home.[102] In early March 1834, Mrs Murray made the final arrangements for William's passage on board the ship that had taken Thomas to Montreal, and at the end of the month Willy was "delivered" into the care of Captain Neil. William's departure was an occasion for celebration and sadness. Mrs Murray was sorry that James had not had an opportunity to bid his brother farewell. "The Poor fellow," she wrote, was "sad at having to go." But it was for the best, and she "committed him to the care of that merciful God." The only thing left to be done was to continue to support him in his new life. As she told James, "I intend to write to him & Tom by one of the vessels that leave in April." If James had a letter ready, she said, she would put it in with hers: "It will be encouraging for him to hear from us."[103]

George Forbes, the tenant farmer's son, appears to have been rather older and more mature when he left Aberdeenshire in April 1845. In his initial letters to his parents, he recounted details of his voyage and his trip up the St Lawrence to York, where he stayed for a short time with a cousin, Alexander Forbes. Later letters reported on his situation working on a farm for John Thaines in Vaughan and then on his marriage to his employer's widow after Thaines died of typhus. About the time that George left home, his family was having trouble renegotiating the terms of a new lease. Although this was later resolved, George, as a younger son, obviously saw no future for himself in Scotland. In 1848 he replied to his parents' questions about returning: "Concerning going home, I don't know one thing I know that is if I went home that a few months would find me on my way journeying back to Canada to stay home it is useless to think of it."[104] Instead of agreeing to their wishes, George urged his parents and his brother to join him in Canada.[105]

To Go or Not to Go

A somewhat satirical depiction of parish emigrants at "The Parting Hour," in *For Emigration*, 1832 (LAC, C4987)

For these young men, and increasingly, women, emigration offered more opportunities than seemed to be available at home. Promotional literature told them and their families that "young, healthy men, if industrious and prudent could hardly fail of success"[106] and that young women would easily find positions as domestic servants, teachers, or farm girls. "And if steady, industrious and deserving," these girls might "probably soon (if they choose) become the mistress of a house of their own," one commentator confidently predicted.[107] Perhaps more importantly, as opportunities at home seemed to be diminishing, kin, friends, and former neighbours who had settled in Upper Canada were writing home that the colony was "far better than the old country."[108] As John Scott told his uncle in Scotland in 1835, there was plenty of "wild land"

"The Last of England," frontispiece of W.S. Shepperson's, *British Emigration to North America: Projects and Opinions for the Early Victorian Period* (Oxford: Basil Blackwell, 1957)

for the "boys" to develop into farms.[109] John Gemmill promised waged work for his daughters; and many emigrants who had left England for Upper Canada between 1832 and 1837 as part of the Petworth project encouraged friends, brothers, and sisters to join them. Bricklayer John Holden, for example, who had left West Sussex in 1832, told his brother, "I shall be very happy to see you come ... next summer, as I think it would be much the best for you." Like many new arrivals, he refused to "persuade" his brother or cousins, but if they came, he assured them, "You will find a home" and "plenty of work."[110]

For William Murray, George Forbes, Abraham Bait, and countless other young people, emigration was part of their rite of passage into adulthood, and for some it offered independence from the parental household. This did not mean that the rest of the family was not involved in the decision to leave home or that kin were not important in deciding where they went and when. Willy Murray's future had obviously been the topic of considerable discussion by his family before he left home. Like many other young emigrants, he was joining a brother already in the colonies.

Transatlantic correspondence and "information wanted" notices in colonial newspapers tell stories of sisters, brothers, and cousins travelling and settling together, many of them expecting to join a sibling or other family member. For example, Eliza, Isabele, and Margaret Taylor left the parish of Drowhome, County Donegal, in the spring of 1837 to join their brother John, who had left home two seasons before.[111] Catherine Armstrong left Longford, Ireland, in 1835 to join her sister and brother-in-law. Her notice suggests that she was expected and that although they were not waiting for her at the wharf in Montreal, she knew their address: "Care of Colonel Crawford, Third Township, U.C."[112]

Having relatives in the colony, even if they had not been seen or heard from for years, appears to have been a significant consideration for many young women and men when they were deciding whether to emigrate or not. A family member or members who were already settled provided a destination; they also offered the possibility of financial assistance, or at least a place to stay while one looked for work. And, of course, kin were a touchstone of familiarity in a foreign land, and by their very presence they provided a sense of security. For some, the pull of family spanned years as well as the Atlantic. Semeon D.W. Drown, for example, decided to emigrate to Upper Canada in 1817 to join his brother, whom he thought was in the Kingston area. But he was not even sure "whether he is now dead or living."[113] Margaret Young left Ireland in the spring of 1834, perhaps drawn by reports of ready employment. She, too, had a brother in the colony, Thomas Young, who had "left the County Doney, Ireland about 17 years before" was "now about 46 years of age." The family had obviously maintained some contact with him, for Margaret knew that he had been "residing in Kingston, Upper Canada about 2 years ago."[114] Catharine Smith decided to emigrate from Letterkenny, Ireland, in the summer of 1844, and one of the factors that seems to have influenced her decision was that she had two brothers living in the colony: "James and John Smith, sawyers by trade" who had sailed from Greenock "about 20 years ago."[115]

A number of these young single emigrants seem to have had limited means. Well over 80 percent of the information notices in the colonial press were placed by individuals looking for family members who were labourers – working on the canals, on farms, or in local urban centres. But these brothers and sisters were not destitute. Either they or their families had paid for their passage; and they all expected to be able to get work in the colony. Some do seem to have expected assistance from those they were joining, however. When Mary Donnelly arrived in Kingston in 1835, she was "afflicted" and in some considerable distress; finding her brother Patrick, who had "sailed from Belfast twelve years ago last May" and was "supposed to be somewhere in the state of New York if not in the city" was a matter of some urgency.[116]

One wonders if Patrick Donnelly or James and John Smith even knew that their sisters had decided to join them or whether they wanted to be found. Like wayward husbands, these brothers (and, often, sisters) may have emigrated to escape familial responsibilities – to siblings and even to parents. Yet those at home did not assume that the Atlantic severed the webs of kin and community. Despite lengthy silences, most presumed that settler siblings, cousins, and even very distant kin would recognize and accept their responsibilities to kith and kin.

Not all the young and not so young men and women who left home were labourers. In 1839 Thomas and Catharine Traill urged Thomas's sister-in-law by his first marriage, Barbara Fotheringhame, to join them in Upper Canada. Barbara's sister Robina had just died, and Barbara was now without immediate responsibilities (her husband having deserted her shortly after their marriage) and was potentially in some economic difficulty. The Traills proposed that Barbara and Catharine open a small boarding school in the colony. This would provide Barbara with "a comfortable income," Thomas wrote, and would "open a way for others of your family" to join us. "I would not, dear Barbara," he said, "raise your hopes but if you cannot do anything better at home and are not venturing among us, I think as I said before you might find yourself comfortable and happy here."[117]

Barbara did not accept Thomas's and Catharine's offer. But others with skills and perhaps some capital, and certainly, confidence did decide that emigration to Upper Canada offered significant opportunities. Colonial newspapers frequently included notices from English, Scottish, and Irish doctors and teachers who had just arrived from the Old Country and hoped to parlay their training and experience "at home" into a secure position or lucrative practice. Young prospective emigrants with "classical training" or "experience in book keeping," or as clerks also anticipated that the colony would offer new opportunities. Despite the commonsense notion that emigration was best undertaken by young men and families, between 1815 and 1845 a number of apparently mature Scottish, English, and Irish women, many of whom may have been "gentlewomen in distress," began to consider emigration as a way to solve their dilemma. The colonial newspapers regularly included notices like that of a "Lady having lately arrived from England," who announced to the Kingston public in 1824 that she intended to open up a "seminary of respectability." This widow's advertisement indicated that students would receive the best of care and the finest of instruction, and she "solicited the patronage of the Ladies who [felt] disposed to place their Daughters where the most useful & polite Branches of Education are taught."[118] A few new arrivals offered colonists their skills as milliners or in other "womanly" businesses, having arrived with sufficient capital or credit to open their own shops. For these women, for whom marriage was either not available or desired, emigration seemed to promise both economic security and personal independence without a loss of respectability or rank.[119]

Thomas Langton, a retired businessman living in the outskirts of Liverpool, was looking for something else when he began to consider relocating to Upper Canada in 1833–34. His second son, John, had left home for the colony a year earlier and sent frequent lengthy letters about his adventures and his new home.[120] Thomas had experienced some financial reversals, and his household, which included his wife Ellen, sister-in-law, and adult daughter Anne, lived quietly and frugally. When he suggested to John that the family join him in Upper Canada, his son immediately replied, "Your company would add much to my comfort." But in the same letter, John expressed his concern that his father and the rest of the family would find emigrating and settling in Upper Canada difficult at their "time of life." He pointed out that his parents would miss the society of which they were fond, and he warned them that the climate tended to extremes and that for the first few years at least, the family's diet would be restricted to salt pork.[121] His father was determined to try the New World, however, and in 1837 the household packed up and set off for the colonies, leaving behind their eldest son, William, who was well established as a banker in Manchester.

John seems to have been ambivalent when his father first broached the subject of emigration. Certainly, he was lonely and life on a frontier farm, even with some capital, was hard work. At the same time, John had the resources to enjoy the company of friends – hunting, dining, and revelling – and he had no responsibilities other than to himself. The arrival of his parents, sister, and aunt would be a mixed blessing. Thomas may have been aware of this. Even before they left home, the family decided that they would set up their own household and live near to John but not with him.

The public discussion of emigration – and particularly that in the press – assumed that leaving home was an undertaking really suitable only for the young and healthy. In 1830 the *Manchester Guardian* was incredulous when it reported that a "venerable wedded pair" from Hernsea, "not much less than 80 years old each," were preparing to leave home for "the land of promise."[122] A report in the *Scots Times* two years later told of "a man of the name of Macdonald, said to be eighty four years of age," who had eagerly "bade farewell to his friends, neighbours and the land of his birth."[123] The report suggests that this was remarkable, not only because of Macdonald's advanced years but because of the implication that he was leaving family behind. Yet many "older" English, Irish, and Scots in similar circumstances to the Langtons seriously considered the proposition. Others, especially widowed parents, emigrated because they had to; with the children gone, this was the only way they could gain some security in their old age.

For many young emigrants, the question of "what to do" about Mother or Father had clearly been a factor in the original decision to leave home. John Langton had emigrated secure in the knowledge that his brother would look after their parents as they got older. Once settled in Upper Canada, other young people urged their parents "to come out here and live in comfort and happiness."[124] In his first letter home, the Petworth emigrant William Phillips was emphatic: "Dear Father, I would not advise you to come here if I did not know it would be to your advantage, even if you spend your last shilling to get here."[125] His parents arrived the following year. Colonist emigrants knew, from firsthand experience, that their parents might find the journey difficult. "The passage across the ocean may be tedious and attended with danger," a son told his mother, "but if it should please Providence to grant you arrive here safe, you will never regret the little inconvenience attending emigration."[126] There were others, however, who were just as emphatic that their parents would be much better at home. "I do not wish to see you come to this country, if you can live at home, for it is not fit for old people," Charles Moore wrote in 1833.[127]

Parents left home both at the behest of their children and, as in the case of some wives, because they were desperate. Like many other newly arrived emigrants, some discovered how difficult it could be to find their children. In 1822 "the aged parents" of Nathaniel Stein decided to join their son (whom they had not seen in three years) in Perth, Upper Canada.[128] In 1840 Lucy Chambers decided to emigrate to be with her sons Alexander Hughes and Henry Elam.[129] It was only after a few months that Elizabeth Hetherington, perhaps by pre-arrangement, followed her son Adam from Ireland.[130] For Catharine McCabe, the precipitating factor, as with a number of women, seems to have been the death of her husband. Alone and in some financial difficulty, she decided to join her son Patrick, even though he was the other side of the Atlantic.[131] Some parents, like Alan Elwin's mother, were desperate. Alan had emigrated to Quebec in 1840 and gone on to Montreal; in 1844 his mother was forced to join him, and on her arrival in Quebec she was "in distress and anxious to hear from him."[132]

For Lucy Chambers, Thomas Langton, Catharine McCabe, and many other parents, the decision about whether or not to emigrate was intimately linked to familial obligations and was made within a matrix of kin relationships. So, too, were the decisions of John and Ann Gemmill, Fanny and William Hutton, and the Scotts. And even for those apparently unattached young women and men who made their way to Upper Canada between 1815 and 1845, emigration was a family affair.

This is not to suggest that family members always agreed on an individual's decision to leave home for the colonies. Those same "information wanted" notices that attest to the underlying optimism of those who placed them – and their confidence that a brother, sister, son, daughter, or even husband was just waiting to be found and would willingly provide succour to the new arrivals – say little about the state of mind or the circumstances of those they were looking for. As noted earlier, it is likely that at least some of those already in the colony had left home to escape their responsibilities, or to flee a dysfunctional family or a relationship that had gone awry. There were also those who had left home having embezzled from an employer or defaulted on a debt.[133] At least some of those addressed in the "information wanted" notices did not want to be found, and one wonders how the new arrivals coped. At the same time, emigrants' letters illustrate the strength of the transatlantic world networks.[134]

When they began to consider the possibility of emigrating to the New World, individuals and families considered their own particular circumstances and expectations in light of the evidence they received from those who had gone before. John Scott's uncle, many of his cousins, and hundreds of thousands of other Irish, English, and Scots knew that this was never their only option. Those same letters that encouraged family and friends to pack up and join the writers in the colonies also attested to how difficult – physically, financially, and emotionally – the world of emigration could be. Those at home knew that some emigrants had returned bitter and disappointed. As young George Forbes recognized, many in the British Isles, including his former neighbours, friends, and even family members, had "a very poor opinion of the Americas"[135] and adamantly opposed the proposition, both for themselves and for others. And not all in the colonies were happy. A number of friends and acquaintances of John Langton wrote home "very despondently upon the subject of the country,"[136] and others abandoned the colony altogether and, like Fanny Hutton's neighbours, returned home.[137] Nonetheless, between 1815 and 1845, tens of thousands of husbands and wives, sisters and brothers, cousins and kin, obviously believed that they would succeed or, at the very least, that the uncertain promise of a foreign land was better than the predicted future at home.

This was a decision that was not taken lightly. Some young women and men may have become caught up in the moment and, infected with "America mania,"[138] joined a local emigration society or party of neighbours and left home eager for adventure or to escape an intolerable situation. Yet familial relationships and particular family dynamics influenced the thinking of even the most restless Irish, Scottish, and English youth. The matter was debated in family parlours and kitchens and at work, at church, and at play. Many prospective emigrants took years to make up their minds and then to gather the funds necessary to leave home. For a relative few – such as John Gemmill in 1821, the members of Peter Robinson's parties in 1823 or 1825, and the English labourers and artisans who were sent by the Petworth Committee – the offer of financial assistance perhaps hastened the decision.

The decision to leave home was only the beginning of the undertaking and only the first step from the imaginary world of public discussion and private letters into the more concrete world of actually leaving home. There were innumerable things to be done before prospective emigrants boarded a ship bound for Upper Canada – and longer still before they began to rebuild their homes. Over the next few months and sometimes years, as they worked their way through the complicated process of leaving home, many must have wondered if they had made the right decision.

CHAPTER TWO

The Bustle of Preparation

In April 1822 Frances Stewart wrote to her friend Honoria, "We are now emerged in the bustle of preparation for our departure which probably will take place about the middle of May – and you may suppose that all our ideas are in requisition to know what will be the most necessary provision as to food and clothing for so large a party & during so long a passage."[1] The Stewarts, along with their friends and business associates the Reids, had decided to emigrate. A manufacturing firm that Thomas Stewart and John Reid had been involved with in County Antrim had collapsed, and the two families had decided to use what little could be salvaged from the business to establish themselves in Upper Canada. Friends were dismayed by their decision; but the families, a party of twenty-two, including twelve children, three servants, and four unrelated young adults, were determined.

Frances had a hectic few months before the two families boarded the *George* at the beginning of June 1822. In addition to coping with the day-to-day affairs of her family, she had to organize the dismantling of her household and clean and pack bedding, kitchenware, and everything else that the family might need in its new home in Upper Canada. She and other members of the family also had to decide what precious personal items they would take – to remind them of home and of particular people and events. While Frances sorted provisions, medicines, clothes, and other things needed for the voyage, Thomas was winding up his affairs, making arrangements for the families' passage, and getting letters of introduction to well-connected officials in British America.

This was an exciting time for the Stewarts and the Reids. But Frances Stewart and her companions were always conscious that this would be their last spring in Ireland. Home and their lives as respectable gentlefolk were not easily abandoned. While the children played and eagerly anticipated the adventure, their parents were well aware that the Atlantic voyage would be long, tedious, and possibly dangerous. Thus, excitement was intermingled with apprehension as they wondered whether they had made the right decision. The bustle and confusion of packing was often interrupted by last visits with lifelong friends and family members, some of whom continued to remonstrate with the family not to leave. Two years later, Frances recalled, "I did suffer ... Who could not help dreading such a step – so very dreadful of its consequences, besides the idea of leaving so many I loved so tenderly & knowing how much the step was disapproved of by those I valued and respected most." She would have appreciated Fanny Hutton's resistance ten years later. But like Fanny and many other wives, Frances had concluded that her husband knew best: "I could not help feeling that Tom was right – & I plainly saw where Duty pointed so I tried to smother every other feeling – but no one can tell the pangs I suffered. Oh the bitter pangs when I last parted from you all so dear – & from dear dear Merrion St."[2]

Frances Stewart's "bustle of preparation" and the emotional upheavals that accompanied it were re-enacted in thousands of Irish and British households between 1815 and 1845. An individual's or family's decision to emigrate was only the first step in the long and sometimes difficult process of leaving home. There were myriad things to be done, affairs to be arranged, and farewells to be taken before the ship left the dock. For men and women who made the journey alone or in the company of friends or siblings or a new spouse, and for families with very little means, the bustle was relatively muted. Families with children, and particularly farmers, "gentlefolk," and skilled tradespeople, often had to make difficult choices about what household goods, tools of their trade, and personal items they would take and how to dispose of the rest. Then everyone had to work out the best way to actually get to America. Although most would sail from a port close to home, there was still the matter of what accommodation they could afford; whether to travel by way of New York or Quebec; and whether the family should engage an agent to make all the arrangements or whether they should do everything themselves, including their own provisioning. Just negotiating the lengthy maze of preparations to leave home could be physically exhausting. It was also emotionally trying.

As they gathered and packed and made arrangements for the voyage, prospective emigrants began to move into a world that set them apart from neighbours and friends who were staying home. Defending their decision to skeptical and resistant kin and neighbours probably heightened the feeling of separation from those around them; it also must have made the prospect of leaving home more concrete. Gradually, commitment to the familiar world of home, work, and community began to be subsumed by the growing anticipation of a New World and a new life. Yet in this intermediate period of preparation, familiar patterns and ways of doing persisted. Where possible, husbands and fathers usually tended to the "public" affairs of emigration – dismantling the household, sorting out the passage, and, if possible, gathering letters of introduction and recommendation that could ease their way in the colonies. Wives and mothers assumed the responsibility for the family's physical and emotional well-being, both on the voyage and after. As Frances Stewart and so many other wives and mothers knew all too well, there was much to be done before they mounted the gangplank and took that final step into the world of emigration.

While Frances was getting ready to leave Ireland in the spring of 1822, Ann Gemmill was preparing to join her husband John in Lanark, Upper Canada. We do not know precisely what this involved. As befitted the head of the household, John had sent Ann specific instructions. "Be sure to bring all your pots ... and also a large one for making Sugar in," he had written in March. She should also pack "a good quantity of tin dishes," the kitchen chimney and griddle, a few pounds of Spanish brawn, and some garden seeds. "Pack your crockery ware well up in a barrel," he advised. "With respect to the clothing you ought to bring as common wearing clothes, the Strongest you can get are the best."[3] His brother Andrew should pack some saws with frames, sickles, and a number of files. Such tools, John wrote, were available in Upper Canada but they were scarce and expensive.

Since John's letter did not arrive in Glasgow until months after the family had left,[4] Ann (undoubtedly with some assistance from her son Andrew and her brother-in-law) had to decide what the family would need and could afford to take. This may have been relatively straightforward. Although the Gemmills obviously had maintained their own household before John had left home, much of the family's furniture had probably been sold or dispersed when Ann and the children had moved in with John's brother Andrew. Ann still had to pack her crockery and housewares – those essential domestic items of home – so that they would survive the journey. She also had to gather clothes and perhaps make new outfits for the children that would be appropriate for those infamous Canadian winters.[5]

A decade later, Fanny Hutton received some – but not much – direction from husband William. "I do not know of anything in particular for you to bring out, but a warm suit of clothes for me and some blankets and better bring the carpets," he wrote. "Do not encumber yourself with much" because "everything can be had here quite reasonably," he said, adding that he would "procure a few plain things in the way" of furniture in the colony. At the same time, he told her that the cost of transport was low and (always conscious that Fanny was not enthusiastic about moving to America) that she "need not sacrifice anything" she had.[6] Such sparse directions were probably of little help to Fanny. She was left herself to decide what to take – both what the family would need and what personal treasures she and William would want to remind them of home. And while she was sorting through clothes and family keepsakes and considering which pieces of furniture were too precious to leave, Fanny (although herself still reluctant to leave home) was undoubtedly having to defend William's decision to family and friends, who were skeptical of the whole undertaking. In the end, Fanny and the children arrived in New York with "a good deal of luggage"[7] which William had to have transported to Belleville at some expense.

Most prospective emigrants could not afford to leave everything behind and replace goods once they got to America, as William had suggested, or to take almost everything they owned, as Fanny seems to have done. For those who were travelling alone or with a sibling, friend, or new marriage partner, the decision was moot. They travelled light, packing only what they thought they would need for the trip across the Atlantic and, if they had it, a few extra clothes. George Forbes seems to have had very little luggage and was thankful to borrow clean clothes from his cousin when he finally arrived at York. A year later, he told his family that if his brother Charles "come out next fall he should bring as little luggage as possible."[8] Mrs Murray packed what she thought Willy would need in a single small box, and this included a few extra provisions for the voyage and clothes suitable for the notoriously cold Canadian winters.

For labourers, the question was often not what to take but whether they had enough in the way of suitable clothes and provisions even for the voyage. In the 1830s and 1840s, parishes and aid organizations that sponsored emigration often provided clothing and food for those chosen to go, in addition to paying their passage. In 1832, for example, many emigrants sent from Frome left with "a separate bag and parcel well filled" with clothes and bedding provided by "the benevolent ladies and gentlemen" of the community.⁹ The Petworth Emigrant Committee provided parish authorities with a list of "the lowest outfit" labourers should have: "Single men must have ... a bed or mattresses, a metal plate or wooden trencher," a metal cup or mug, and a knife, fork, and spoon. Families were advised to take, in addition, a tea kettle and "working tools of all descriptions," and were told that "a large tin can or watering pot, would be useful." Each assisted emigrant was also given a Bible and prayer book.¹⁰

Families that were from well-established households and financing their own passage were in a somewhat different situation. Space available on emigrant ships was often limited, and the cost of transporting goods overseas and then into the interior of British America could be prohibitive. Prospective emigrants had to try to calculate the cost and trouble of taking various possessions (which could not be guaranteed to survive the voyage) against the unknown cost of replacing them in North America. The problem was made more difficult because, despite the advice they received from kin already there, most still had only a rudimentary knowledge of conditions in the New World and could only guess what things they would need.

Various guides, settlers' accounts, and government publications did offer some advice. But like the presentation of life in the colonies, the recommendations were often contradictory and confusing. As befitted the sensibilities of the time, they were also directed primarily to the head of the household. It was taken for granted that prospective emigrants would sell or otherwise dispose of their cottages or houses and stock (if they had any) before they left home. It was also generally accepted that would-be emigrants should dispose of all their furniture. It was "too cumbersome," as the emigrant enthusiast John MacGregor pointed out, and "could easily be procured in America" at less cost than transporting it.¹¹ There was a consensus that emigrants should take warm and serviceable clothes, bedding, and blankets; stout shoes and boots; and cooking utensils.

What else should be packed was a matter of some dispute. *Chamber's Information*, the guide which John Scott recommended to his uncle, advised the emigrant "to take a box of tools," including among other things an axe, hammer, handsaw, and augers "whether he be learned to use them or not."¹² Andrew Redford could have gone to his local shopkeepers, such as Russell and Clark of Glasgow, who had on hand what they considered the "necessary outfit to emigrants," including "an extensive assortment of TOOLS & OTHER IRONMONGERY ARTICLES."¹³ John

MacGregor was unequivocal that "if their means permit," families should take "as much clothing, bedding and linen as may be necessary for four or five years." In addition, farmers should pack their tools, some leather, a few door hinges, an assortment of nails, and, of course, cooking utensils.[14] William Catermole, an agent of the Canada Company who actively recruited prospective emigrants, stated in *Advantages of Emigration* in 1831 that "no heavy or cumbersome baggage ought to be taken." In advice that was widely reprinted in other guides, he explained, "Household furniture, iron utensils, implements of husbandry, in short all articles of considerable bulk or weight will cost, in freight and carriage, more that the expense of replacing them, besides the trouble of their conveyance, threat of damage and the danger of articles ... being found unsuited for use in America."[15] Clocks, books, and medicines were considered by some to be very important.[16] Others recommended that emigrants pack as little as possible. "People ought never to bring goods," one account stated in 1833. "Hard cash is the only substance worth bringing."[17]

It is likely that, as in other matters, emigrants relied on family and friends already in the colony for direction on what they would need. Most of those in Upper Canada suggested that emigrants pack basic personal and household items – "what you want for housekeeping,"[18] shoes, durable clothes, and bedding. In later years, many were advised to bring money and not goods.[19] Those who were emigrating to join households already established in America were often directed to pack specific items – tools for the farm or the workshop, for example. A son recommended that his mother sell her "pots, pans and fire irons" and bring only her "knives and forks and spoons, bowls, china and stoneware."[20] The possibility that a family member was coming out presented colonists with the opportunity to obtain things from home that they needed or wanted. For example, one of the Petworth emigrants, William Baker, wrote his father: "Be sure to bring me a hay cutting knife, but not other tools; for you can get them cheaper here." He also wanted "some tares ... and a little lucern seed. And all kinds of garden seed; and a gallon of bent grass seed and a little good barley and a little nonsuch seed." The last two things on William's list were a clock and "all the money you can get."[21] Charlotte Evans (another Petworth emigrant) asked her brother to pack some cloth "if [he] could," promising that the family would "refund the money" with thanks once he and the cloth arrived.[22]

Those who were preparing to emigrate still had to make some painful choices. There were very few families like the Huttons and Langtons, or even the Stewarts, who were able to take almost the entire contents of their households, including their furnishings and wine cellar.[23] Disposing of farms, livestock, shops, and homes that may have been in the family for generations must have been heartrending. Selling or giving away furniture and packing clothes and household items brought the world of emigration – which until then had for many been an abstract notion – into their homes and made it very real.

Even after disposing of most of their goods, large families could have an astonishing number of boxes, trunks, and casks to take to America. Local British newspapers sometimes reported families proceeding to local ports with "wagon loads of goods."[24] Catermole and others reminded prospective emigrants that they would have to carry their own luggage and that parcels should therefore be kept manageable. Items needed on the trip – clothes, bedding, utensils for cooking, provisions, and medicines – should be packed separately and be ready for use, and "articles not intended to be used on the voyage" should be sealed. And everything should be marked clearly with the owner's name.[25] Luggage often went astray and was tempting to opportunistic thieves. Even on board ship, as one colonist remarked, "I would warn you to look sharp, for sailors and passengers will sometimes make mistakes as to what is their own and what is not."[26]

For Ann Gemmill, packing up her household was only part of what had to be done before she and the children could join John in Upper Canada. As de facto head of the household, she also had to negotiate the often complicated matter of how to get to the colony. If Ann did join an emigrant society, as John had directed, many of the decisions about when to leave, which ship to take, and whether to go by way of Quebec or one of the American ports would have been decided for her. She might also, like the later emigrants from Petworth, have relied on the ship's captain for basic provisions during the voyage, and she would have been able to take only a few things to supplement the family's diet. Those who had to make their own arrangements were confronted with a bewildering number of options about when to leave, what ship to take, the accommodation available, the cost, and the destination; and these decisions were made amid varying degrees of pressure from ships' agents and captains and were, of course, subject to one's own financial circumstances.

The "emigrant trade" was a booming business between 1820 and 1845. As one traveller noted, by 1830 the connections between Great Britain and North America were "daily increasing," and for those who could afford it "the means of communication ... [were] daily improving."[27] Almost any ocean-going ship of any size could offer to transport prospective settlers to the New World. During the annual "emigrant season," British newspapers regularly carried notices of shipping companies, agents, and individual masters advertising passages to New York, Quebec, or other American ports, and between early April and September each year, hundreds of ships left Irish and British ports for America.[28] As a number of historians have pointed put, the availability of transport, both for the ocean crossing and for the journey from home to the point of embarkation, was a crucial but often forgotten factor in determining whether people could emigrate and when and where they landed.[29] This was particularly true for those who had limited means or who lived in relatively isolated communities.

Without exception, emigrant guides, government pamphlets, and private correspondence emphatically recommended that emigrants leave early in the spring. The Atlantic passage was particularly rough throughout the late fall and winter; by April, however, the weather had usually improved, and vessels leaving then "frequently took the shortest passage."[30] Leaving in the spring also assured families that once they arrived in America, they would have time to get settled – find work, buy or lease property, and build at least a rudimentary shelter and bring in a small harvest before the arrival of those infamous Canadian winters.[31]

When one left was also, to some degree at least, determined by how one chose to travel. The quickest but by far the most expensive way to cross the Atlantic was on packet ships, which regularly left Liverpool or Greenock for New York. "Nothing indeed can exceed the comfort of the regular packet," the Hon. E. Stanley wrote in his journal in 1824.[32] At the other end of the scale were the timber ships, which after unloading their cargo of wood from North America at British ports, made minimal conversions to take emigrants on the return passage. Throughout most emigrant seasons, the trade appears to have been quite competitive. Newspaper notices tried to entice custom by promising "superior cabin accommodation" or "comfortable berths in the cabin, second cabin or steerage." Often, a notice stated that the ship had been "admirably adapted for steerage passengers" or that the steerage was "spacious." Most advertisements promised that the ship "sails very fast," and many gave a definite date of sailing. Some enticed passengers by stating that the ship carried a surgeon. Without exception, the notices included the name of the vessel's captain, and sometimes they included a comment on his, and the crew's "excellent experience" or their knowledge of the St Lawrence River.[33] The cost of the passage varied, at times significantly,

"Irish Emigrants Leaving Home with the Priest's Blessing," *Illustrated London News*, 10 May 1851 (MCM)

depending on the ports of departure and arrival in North America, the accommodation (steerage or cabin), the size and quality of the vessel, and the changing government regulations.

Those who decided to travel as part of a large party avoided many of these decisions. The arrangements for John Gemmill's passage to Upper Canada were probably made by the local emigration society, which would have chartered the ship and arranged provisioning.³⁴ In 1842 John Hart of Glasgow organized a party of Scottish emigrants. He and a group of friends and associates chartered the vessel, the *Carlton*, and organized victualling for the trip. The committee also arranged the party's subsequent transportation to Perth, Upper Canada.³⁵ Like many other Scottish groups, the *Carlton* expedition was self-financed, and the group was made up of neighbours and friends who intended to settle together in America. More than four hundred emigrants were on the *Carlton* when it left Glasgow that April.³⁶

Between 1815 and 1845, the English, Irish, and Scottish emigrants who were able to take advantage of state or local aid had little to arrange. The organizers of such parties covered all or part of the cost of passage to Upper Canada and made all the arrangements, including provisioning, and often provided extra clothing; some even organized transport to the port of departure. Wardens or associations like the Petworth Committee also paid the various administrative fees and provided their emigrants with a small stipend on arrival in America.[37] After the passage of the new Poor Law in 1834, which officially sanctioned parish authorities to subsidize the emigration of local "paupers," an Emigration Commission began to systematize the process.[38] By 1837, some parish unions had begun to engage shipping agents directly. For a standard a fee, the agent undertook to provide emigrant parishioners with passage and provisions and to see that they arrived safely at their destination in Upper Canada.[39] All that the "industrious and steady characters"[40] who were chosen as members of a party had to do was to pack up their goods and board the ship.

The vast majority of those who left home for the colonies financed the undertaking themselves, and they had to work through the maze of emigration on their own. Sometime in the spring of 1833, a tailor from the Manchester area, George Pashley, and his family decided to emigrate to British America. We know very little of George's circumstances before he left home. His journal, which begins after his decision to emigrate, was written some months after his arrival in Upper Canada, based in part on notes made during the journey. At the beginning of July 1833, George "set out for Liverpool" to make arrangements for the family's passage. After a day of tramping about the city investigating various options, he engaged with a broker to sail on the *Reward* on 20 July. The family had to be ready to board the ship on the eighteenth. George returned home, made a brief tour to see friends "perhaps for the last time," and although his journal is silent on the issue, it is likely that he and his wife finished packing up their household. George then gathered his family, loaded their possessions on a cart, and together they made their way to Manchester and then by train to Liverpool. "We arrived [in Liverpool] tired and weary and wet to the Skins," he recalled. While his wife and children waited "at the top of Bond Street," he went to see about lodgings. "I tried several Times," and in the end he found a room with "very agreeable people."

To the Pashleys' chagrin, when George went to see the broker, he discovered that the *Reward* was still in dry dock for repairs and would not sail until at least the thirtieth. Apparently, the family had already invested all their funds in paying for their passage, and George was forced to apply to his father and friends for "a little Charity" to tide them over this "time of great need."[41] Meanwhile, he "set out in quest of another ship." The only one leaving immediately for America with space still available was too expensive. (The charge for steerage was eight pounds each with provisions.) George went on board another ship, which was bound for New York. "But I would not have gone with her for Passage free," he wrote in his journal. The problem was not the ship's destination. The Pashleys planned to make their way to York, the capital of Upper Canada – a community that was frequently mentioned in the emigrant literature and would be a good place from which to start looking for work and a new home. Since the family had no personal connections in the colonies and thus no fixed final destination, landing in New York instead of Quebec would have made little difference if the price was right. But George objected to this ship because it was already overcrowded. Moreover, "the Smell was abominable," a condition he attributed to its "Chiefly Irish" passengers who were, in his view, "dirty" by nature. As a devout Methodist Yorkshireman, he had no desire to spend weeks with foreigners. The family decided to wait for the *Reward* to come out of dry dock, and George found work to help cover the family's expenses in the interim. In the end, they almost missed their sailing. On 1 August, George discovered, while in conversation with another passenger, that the *Reward* was to sail that day. Alarmed, he "hasted home to inform his Wife." After confirming with the broker that the *Reward* would be out of dry dock within the hour, the Pashleys hurriedly gathered their possessions and "arrived at the Dock as soon as possible." They would have been "to late but thro' a Kind Providence," which delayed sailing by another day.

For George Pashley and thousands of his compatriots, journeying from home to port, then negotiating the intricacies of arranging passage to the New World, and then finding lodging while waiting to board the ship separated them emotionally as well as physically from their friends and family who were staying behind. The world of emigration, which even as they were packing their belongings had still been part of their imagination, was now very real. It was a world with its own rules and customs, and for those in transit it was often bewildering and sometimes overwhelming. It is not surprising that many, like George Pashley, clung to the familiar vestiges of his old life. He continued to rely on family for support and was determined, if at all possible, to make this all-important journey in the company of others of his "own kind."

The Pashleys' experiences were not particularly unusual. During the peak years of emigration in the 1830s and 1840s, British and Irish ports were flooded with emigrants looking for passage to the New World. William Catermole commented in 1831 that in major ports, such as London, Greenock, Hull, Plymouth, and Liverpool, "vessels are scarcely advertised to sail for Quebec than more passengers are offering their ship (although they have ample room) can possibly take."[42] The British press reported that the quays were "crowded to excess" with both those "who had fortunately engaged their berths early" and others "lamenting that they had not been more timely in their application."[43] During the season, the docks were always "scenes of the greatest bustle"[44] as emigrants searched for the best passage and then prepared to embark. In much of Scotland, the emigrant trade was "decentralized," and "ships left from any place where a demand existed."[45] In Ireland, as in Scotland, the emigrant trade was also part and parcel of larger trading networks that linked ports and communities on each side of the Atlantic. Captain Neil, who took Willy Murray under his wing in 1833, had carried his brother Tom to Montreal some years earlier, and Mrs Murray trusted him. The Irish ports of Derry, Belfast, and Cork were "conjoined" with Quebec, as well as with Saint John and Halifax.[46]

Feeding, housing, and entertaining the hundreds and sometimes thousands of prospective emigrants as they waited to take their passage was an industry in itself. And it is not surprising that enterprising and often unscrupulous individuals took advantage of unsuspecting emigrants. Brokers sold passages for ships that did not exist or were not scheduled to depart for weeks rather than days. Emigrants were regularly grossly overcharged for provisions and lodging; or when they came to claim their berths, they found that the broker had disappeared and the captain had no record of payment. One newspaper reported, "It is notorious that ships are advertised to sail upon a particular day, and are kept in port many weeks after the time ... When emigrants arrive with their families [they are] waylaid by agents of these vessels, are conducted to lodging or public houses ... and in the end are generally plundered for every farthing they brought with them."[47] As an English emigrant wrote in 1823, many were caught in the trap of "compleat swindlers."[48]

Captains and shipowners were often implicated in these frauds. In 1834 the Montreal Special Sanitary Committee – which often had to cope with the results of the "common avarice and desire for gain prevailing over every other considerations" – noted that many captains, owners, and agents were party to "a most horrible traffic in human life."[49] Emigrant guides warned of "men of broken fortune or unprincipled adventurers" who enticed prospective emigrants with false accounts of the New World and then crowded them into "a ship of the worst class, ill founded with materials and most uncomfortably accommodated."[50] It was, as John MacGregor and others noted, "a traffic long known by the emphatic cognomen of the 'white slave trade,'"[51] and emigrants always had to be on their guard.

The Bustle of Preparation

"Emigrants Arriving on the Quay at Cork, Ready for Their Departure,"
Illustrated London News, 10 May 1851 (LAC, C3904)

In response to growing public pressure in the late 1820s, Parliament took a few tentative steps to regulate the trade and stop the worst abuses. New regulations were introduced which, among other things, specified minimum standards for emigrants' accommodation aboard ships and required captains and brokers to deal honestly with their customers. Government agents were appointed at some British and North American ports to enforce the regulations and to provide prospective emigrants with advice and assistance.[52] In their advertisements, private agencies began to offer "respectable references" concerning their good character and saying that "the strictest attention [would be] used to prevent the imposition too often practiced upon strangers."[53] Nonetheless, there continued to be reports of "great frauds" daily practised "upon persons who were about to emigrate."[54] One settler told his countrymen that they had to investigate carefully how best to proceed and should find "a good convenient vessel commanded by a sober, experienced man."[55] After he had taken passage with a questionable broker, George Pashley discovered "the plan he ought to have taken." Echoing advice found in some guides (and after 1830 in government publications), he wrote in his journal: "An emigrant ought first to go to the Government Agent for Emigration by him he will be directed to A Ship, when he has seen the Broker (if there be one employed for the Ship) he should go to the Ship and see the Captain, enquire of him, then of men or Mate of the ship, by doing this he will perhaps be able to ascertain something about the time she will Sail."[56] When in 1838 William Knox decided to join his cousins, the Scotts, he received "very good" advice from Lieutenant Lowe, the government agent at Liverpool.[57]

The confusing and often frustrating process of determining which captains and brokers could be trusted and therefore on which ship to book one's passage was compounded by the dilemma of how much one could afford for accommodation. In the 1830s and 1840s, the cost of a steerage passage varied, from about £2 (without provisions) to £10 to £15 (including provisions) for each adult on the better ships. Cabin passengers paid between £12 and £20 for individual fares, and a single passage on one of the regular Liverpool-to-New York packets cost thirty to forty guineas.[58] In 1827 Thomas Magrath, a gentleman, secured an entire cabin, containing six berths and two staterooms, and the services of a steward for his party of nine, at a cost of £50, with an additional £20 for provisions.[59] His subsequent passage to Quebec was quick and uneventful.

In his letters home (which soon afterwards appeared in print), McGrath stated that in his view, the best route was by way of New York. The journey to the American port was, he believed, shorter and the vessels of superior class. Magrath was clearly writing for a select audience, for he observed that merchant ships (or packets of the first class) "had every accommodation that the most luxurious person could desire." Such a passage "could be engaged for twenty guineas," he wrote, and included "each delicacy of the table, spirit of all kinds, ad libitim." Indeed, he concluded, "What is called and considered a <u>cheap</u> passage should be avoided by those who are not generally straightened in means ... It is bad management to make one's self miserable for the sake of a few pounds, during perhaps a long and boisterous voyage; shut up, it may be during six or eight weeks, with all the inconveniences of breakfasting, dining, sleeping and <u>getting sick</u> in the same wretched apartment of a crazy merchant vessel."[60]

Robert Pengelly, a gentleman from Guernsey, had obviously heard similar advice. Shortly after his marriage to Harriet in September 1834, he decided to emigrate to Upper Canada. The following spring, the couple were ready to get underway. Just getting to the port was a strenuous undertaking, at least for Harriet, who began a new diary when the couple left home. After three and a half days of travelling by steamer, stagecoach, and mailcoach, they arrived at Plymouth "half dead with fatigue."[61] While they waited for their luggage, Robert investigated how best to travel to America. The *Cosmopolite*, which appears to have been his choice before he had arrived at Plymouth, was already full – and anyway, he discovered, it was "not a ship at all adapted for a lady." He and a friend then boarded the *Louis* "to look at her accommodations." In the end, as Robert noted in his own journal, he "gave up the idea of going in any vessel but the regular packet," and he wrote to his agent "to take places for ourselves and servant."[62]

Robert Pengelly appears to have been particularly concerned that his young wife should be as comfortable as possible. The couple could afford the seventy-five guineas it cost to go by packet, and they had friends to stay with in Plymouth while they waited for the ship to leave. Robert and Harriet were removed from much of the bustle and chicanery of port life. During the two-and-a-half-week wait, they received and visited friends, attended church, and made an extended trip to see Salisbury Cathedral. Only once did Harriet remark in her journal on the seamier side of life in Plymouth. On a walk one day "about the town," she "was shocked to see such a number of bad girls about the streets" and commented, "Alas! what depravity."[63]

For the Pashleys waiting to board the *Reward* at Liverpool, such "bad girls" were undoubtedly their neighbours. So, too, were the beggars and the numerous hawkers who were selling provisions; and so were dozens and sometimes hundreds of farmers, artisans, mechanics, labourers, families with young children, single men and women, grandparents, and maiden aunts who arrived daily with parcels and chests and boxes and barrels, looking for a ship to take them to America and needing lodging while they waited. Most, like the Pashleys, had limited means and were seeking the best bargains from brokers, agents, and ships' captains.

Emigrant guides and government publications did offer some advice on how to secure as comfortable a passage as possible for the lowest price. Part of the calculation was whether it was more economical to provision oneself or to pay extra and have food for the voyage provided. Those bound for Upper Canada also had to weigh the benefits of landing close to their intended destination (at Quebec or Montreal) against the possible discomfort of a longer and rougher voyage than they would have by going by way of New York. And what was a few extra inches of space in a berth worth? And how did one know if the ship would be overcrowded?

Robert and Harriet Pengelly, like William and Fanny Hutton and many other gentlefolk bound for Upper Canada, appear to have chosen to travel by way of New York as a matter of course. That passage was the

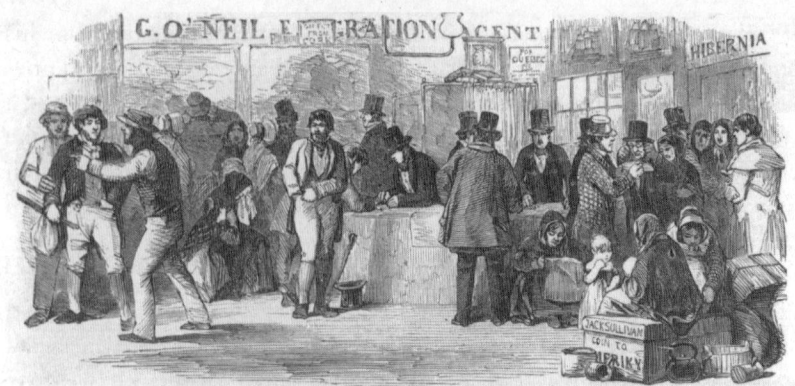

"At an Emigration Agent's Office, Paying the Passage Money to Upper Canada," *Illustrated London News*, 10 May 1851 (LAC, c6556)

quickest and was believed to be safer and less subject to the legendary Atlantic storms. Many published accounts and private letters argued that when one considered all the costs of travelling to the interior, this route was also the least expensive.[64] But others, including the author of the *Counsel for Emigrants*, believed that travelling by way of Quebec was "the least expensive upon the whole," because passengers could avoid paying duty in New York.[65]

Certainly, in the late 1820s and 1830s, the terms of the new Passenger Acts ensured that the basic cost of passage to British America was significantly cheaper than to any U.S. port, and most British and Irish emigrants landed in Quebec (including many who immediately crossed the border to join family or friends in the United States).[66] MacGregor and others noted, however, that emigrants saved "much expense and inconvenience" if they embarked on a "ship bound for a port nearest to [their] point of destination."[67] Each route clearly had "its advantages and disadvantages," and *Counsel for Emigrants* suggested that "intending emigrants should deliberately weigh these and choose which he thinks will suit his own particular circumstances best."[68] As the editors of *Chamber's Information* noted, in the end, many were probably "governed by the convenience of shipping and other considerations."[69]

For George Pashley and many others, the cost of passage and the state of accommodation on board a particular ship was a prime consideration. Most emigrants could only afford to travel steerage. By definition, this meant that their quarters would be cramped, and passengers would have to share berths. It was possible, as John Scott's cousin discovered, to pay a little extra "to get a good ship" that was "not so crowded."⁷⁰ There were undoubtedly many who, like George Pashley, wanted to travel with their own "kind." Emigrating in the company of members of an extended family or with friends and neighbours offered a sense of stability and comfort. When this was not possible, emigrants tried to find like-minded travelling companions who shared their concerns (perhaps their religious beliefs) and at the very least, shared their cultural and ethnic sensibilities. If one chose wisely, some of the problems associated with steerage could be avoided. William Catermole recommended that all families or parties of emigrants, including those of some means, take steerage passage rather than engaging a cabin. "The cabin is all very well for single ladies and gentlemen," he wrote, "but with families it is an expensive place." Far better to "arrange with the captain to have a portion of steerage" partitioned off. In this way, families or groups would "possess all the comforts of the cabin," with its relative privacy, "and at one fourth the expense."⁷¹ The savings could subsequently be used to defray some of those inevitable costs that would mount up when one arrived in Upper Canada.

In the 1830s and 1840s, emigrants were frequently reminded that by law "the bed should not be narrower than three feet."⁷² They were advised to avoid berths opposite or near the hatchway; otherwise, they were likely to become soaked, because "when at sea, the water often rushes in."⁷³ They were told that it was better to take an upper berth and, if possible, to get one as "near the stern of the ship as you can, [where] you will not find so much motion."⁷⁴ Such matters did not affect the cost. William Catermole advised emigrants to examine other aspects of the accommodation carefully. They should determine the number and location of the water closets, find out what access they would have to the quarterdeck, and "at what time lights are expected to be put out." He concluded, "These cautions may prevent bad feelings on the passage."⁷⁵

A more important part of the calculation was the question of provisioning. For those who could afford a cabin, the fare included provisions. When Mrs Radcliffe and her family emigrated in 1832, they were in the "second cabin" – accommodation that was not as expensive as a cabin but did provide the family with some privacy and additional space. They also brought their own provisions. "We thought it prudent to do so," she wrote her father-in-law, "but are now convinced we were wrong." She explained that this had "excluded [them] from the attention of the captain or his steward." Just as important, she continued, was that "your stores [are] useless while you are sick; and before you are well, either spoiled or stolen."[76]

The fare for a berth in steerage almost doubled if provisions were included. Even so, for those emigrating on their own, this was often the most economical and convenient way to travel: "With the few extras they might provide themselves, this answered their purpose better than having the trouble of laying in and cooking their own provisions."[77] The extra £2 or £3 for each emigrant over the age of fourteen could nonetheless be a significant drain on a family's resources. Many determined to bring their own victuals. *Chamber's Information* commented that "in ships sailing from Scotland and Ireland, it has mostly been the custom for passengers to find their own provisions; but this practice has not been so general in London."[78]

Emigrant guides and letters home provided considerable advice on what and how much food emigrants should take. "You must find provisions for sixty days," they were usually advised.[79] Although one commentator stated that "no person need take other than oatmeal or potatoes, and may be if they could afford it, a little butter, sugar and treacle," at a total cost of sixteen shilling for a man,[80] most recommended that emigrants pack a variety of basic foods: a combination of potatoes, salted beef or pork, cheese, eggs, dried fish, flour, root vegetables, bottled beer or cider, and if possible some apples, oranges, or lemons.[81] William Catermole suggested that parties travelling together could also "arrange to take a pig or two and if they will look after it a sheep." Fowls he rejected as being "much trouble and often very sickly."[82]

After 1828, ships' captains were expected to ensure that passengers had sufficient stores for the voyage and to provide "fifty gallons of pure water, and fifty pounds of bread, biscuit, oatmeal or breadstuff for each passenger."[83] This frequently did not happen. Moreover, the quality of the water was notoriously bad, and prospective emigrants were often advised to pack vinegar or a little wine to make it drinkable. And even if the passage was all found, as with the Petworth project, many who had gone before advised family and friends that they would still need to supplement the ship's stores. "Bring a good ham or bacon; some pickled onions; bake some seed cakes hard, they will keep better," George and Lydia Huton told his mother and siblings in 1836. Their own experience had also taught them that the family should regularly "draw [their] allowance of everything except biscuit" from the ship's store and "take care of it." Then, when their own stores ran out, they would have enough food to see them to the end of the voyage, and some provisions for the journey up the St Lawrence beyond Quebec.[84]

For John Gemmill, a greater concern seems to have been that Ann should pack "a little mercurial ointment." He told her, "Be sure of keeping it at hand as you will want it before you were long in the ship."[85] Everyone knew that on the Atlantic seasickness was inevitable, and everyone offered advice on how to prevent it – or at least how to alleviate the symptoms. Most guides and personal letters recommended that passengers pack "a few medicines ... and those chiefly of the purgative kind."[86] A number suggested that Epsom Salts, magnesia, or other emetics were essential sea kit.[87] One of the Petworth emigrants told his family to make sure to pack pickles, because they were good to eat after one had been seasick.[88]

Preparing for future seasickness was only one of Ann's concerns in the spring of 1822. There was much to be done before she and the family took leave of friends and family. In addition to packing the things they would need or want in their new home, families and particularly wives packed the bedding, clothes, and kitchen items (a kettle, cups, spoons, plates) that they would need on the voyage. For days and probably weeks in advance, emigrating wives such as Ann baked enough flatbreads, scones, and hard biscuits either to supplement the ship's fare or to last the family for at least four or five weeks. They cured, dried, or salted meat, eggs, and fish. Many who left in the early spring before gardens were ready to be harvested must have found it difficult to find fresh fruit and vegetables. But whatever they could find (together with other staples, such as flour and cheese) was carefully packed into boxes or tins for use on board ship. If at all possible, families guarded their "sea stock" and hoped not to have to open it until after they were actually on board and underway. But when the Pashleys and undoubtedly many others encountered unexpected delays, they were forced to rely on their sea provisions while they waited. Those who could afford it replenished their victuals just before they left, but the goods sold by shopkeepers, ship agents, and the hawkers who had set up business along the docks were often overpriced. This was too expensive for many, and countless emigrants ran short of provisions on the voyage.[89]

While their wives tried to find room for one more piece of clothing or a few biscuits or that small, special token of a remembrance of home, the husbands were visiting friends, former employers, or the local squire to get that promised testimonial or letter of introduction. They may well have offered to take a parcel to friends or acquaintances overseas, in exchange. For those without friends or family waiting for them in the colony, such references could be invaluable when looking for work, seeking a loan, or just asking for temporary shelter and assistance to get settled. For gentlemen emigrants, a letter of introduction was evidence of their status, as well as their respectability. In Upper Canada, such testimonials, particularly if signed by a ranking member of British society, opened up the world of colonial patronage and the doors to colonial society. Even for farm workers, labourers, and "ordinary" emigrants, the ability to claim some personal connection to an established settler could bring immediate benefits. When Isaac Wilson, a settler who lived just outside York, was presented by a newly arrived emigrant with a letter and a parcel from his brother at home, he felt obliged to do what he could to support the family.[90]

As George Pashley and his family, Ann Gemmill and her children, and thousands of other families sealed the last box and locked up their chests full of crockery and other precious items, worries about the end of the voyage were probably overshadowed by the immediate anxiety of leaving friends, family, and home. George Pashley, like Thomas and Catharine Parr Traill, the Moodies, and many others, visited friends and family and old haunts for the last time. Frances Stewart later recalled "the bitter pangs when I last departed from you all so dear."[91] Such pilgrimages were an important part of the rituals of leavetaking; they were also a way to mark the ending of one life and the beginning of another.[92] Then, accompanying wagons or carts laden with goods or awkwardly carrying an assortment of packages and boxes, families were ready to leave home.

The first entry of Harriet Pengelly's 1835 diary was "Left my happy home."[93] The entries over the next month, until she and Robert boarded the *Montreal* for New York, chronicled her distress. Rather than setting up a new household in England – where, as a half-pay officer, Robert would have had difficulty maintaining his status and middle-class lifestyle – he had decided to seek his fortune in the colonies. Harriet seems to have had little say in the matter. As a young (and, her diary suggests, innocent) new wife, she was unable and perhaps unwilling to object to Robert's plans. While she waited anxiously for her luggage to arrive in Plymouth, she was "in very low spirits," and when it did arrive, she was heartbroken to find all her "dresses and bonnets" soaked and ruined: "Very sad day, oh! more than sad!" To pass the time and to help herself cope with her impending departure, Harriet read and reread letters from

"The Embarkation, Waterloo Docks, Liverpool," *Illustrated London News*, 6 July 1850 (MCM, M993X.5.1530.1)

family and friends. Her diary indicates that she was very apprehensive about the future. Yet even in the privacy of her diary, Harriet never questioned Robert's decision.

Others making their way to Plymouth or waiting to board ship at Liverpool, Greenock, Dublin, or one of the smaller ports shared Harriet's apprehension and sense of loss. For John Colquhoun, who waited in Liverpool for his ship to sail in 1841, sorrow was mingled with apprehension. "At present," he wrote to his mother, "my heart is almost broken at the thought of those I leave behind me – My Wife and You, My sister and my poor Children – I may never see any of you again." John Colquhoun, like John Gemmill twenty years earlier and many other husbands, appears to have been going ahead to find work and begin to make a home before the family joined him. He knew that even in the 1840s, crossing the Atlantic could be dangerous. And once in the colony, any number of things could prevent the family from being reunited. "I hope for the best," he wrote, "but who can tell."[94]

As emigrants moved ever closer to actually boarding the ship, many must have been anxious whether they would survive the trip. By the

"Emigrants by the Ship Ganges Departing for Canada," *Illustrated London News*, 6 July 1850 (MCM, M993X.5.694-R1)

time John Colquhoun left home, the British government was beginning to enforce its regulations under the Passenger Acts concerning the captain's responsibility for the safety and well-being of his human cargo. But in the 1840s, as in the past twenty-five years, the world of emigration was dangerous, and no one could guarantee that a ship would not founder on the rocks or become the casualty of a violent storm. As the British and colonial press regularly reported, such "melancholy events" inevitably resulted in the death of some or all of a ship's company. Steerage passengers were at particular risk, for if locked in the hold as a ship was going down, they had little chance of survival.[93]

Some who were just about ready to embark decided that the trip was too dangerous. Harriet's maid Emily, for example, was so fearful of the voyage and so wretched at the thought of never seeing home again that after ten days waiting with the Pengellys in Plymouth she changed her mind. "Emily cried and said she wished to go back to Guernsey," Harriet recorded in her diary. The prospect of going without Emily made Harriet "very miserable all day." But Emily's ties to Guernsey were clearly stronger than her commitment to her employer. Robert was

"The Departure," *Illustrated London News*, 6 July 1850 (MCM, M993X.5.1528.1-R1)

forced to try to get the fifteen guineas he had already paid for Emily's passage refunded and to find another maid.[96]

Having come this far, most people were determined to proceed, however. And poets and contemporary commentators were often lyrical in their depiction of "the departure." They presented romantic images of friends and relatives gathered along the shore, waving goodbye while emigrants crowded on deck for "One last long look, till the tear-drops start / To ease the load of a busting heart."[97] In "Songs of Emigration," a poem reprinted widely in both the British and Upper Canadian press, poet Dorothea Hemans told of the "song of the chiming sea, A mingled breathing of grief and glee."[98] A number of colonists fondly remembered that "never-to-be-forgotten day" when they left home.[99] Frances Stewart was rather more prosaic in her description of leaving home. "Our family, accompanied by some of the Reids and our dear friend Mr Mitchell, left White Abby, in the barge; our dear friend Mr Quinn was also with us," she wrote in her diary. The party soon reached the *George*, but there was some concern because Mr Reid, who had gone to finish some last-minute arrangements, had not arrived when the captain "gave orders for sailing immediately." Reid boarded as the ship was pulling up the estuary; at the same time, Frances's friends made their farewells. It was "a sad trial," she recorded.[100] In Scotland, sometimes an entire community would gather to bid their neighbours goodbye. Those departing from smaller ports were often waved off by crowds of curious wellwishers, who had "collected" along the river or at the dock and sometimes "followed the vessel along the bank as long as they could keep it in view."[101] The Pashleys and Pengellys took their leave at home, and there was no one to wave them off as they boarded the ship.

John Thompson, an English emigrant who left home in 1818 or 1819, recalled that the sense of loss and apprehension was often mingled with barely suppressed excitement: "Our feelings when we entered on board ... not knowing when or where we should land & our Friends bidding farewell not knowing that we should ever meet again in their world these things with a many more that crowded in upon the mind was almost ready to counterbalance the desire we had to see America." But after he and his companions had boarded and "the bustle a little subsided & the ship got on her way and a few reflections pressing through the mind," he noted, "we became a little more composed and a desire sprang up that we might through the blessing of God be wafted safe through the maritime element & land safe on the shore of America."[102]

Others were not so sanguine. Harriet Pengelly recorded that when boarding the *Montreal*, she had been "disappointed when [she] saw the ship." Frances Stewart, Fanny Hutton, and perhaps Ann Gemmill also must have wondered whether they had made the right decision as they shepherded their children on board. Yet many were undoubtedly distracted by the last-minute bustle and confusion. As emigrants hurried along the crowded docks, often with children in tow, and tried to keep track of parcels and boxes – or, like George Pashley, fearing that they would miss the ship's sailing altogether – there was little time to wonder whether they had made the right decision.

In 1835, as Harriet climbed up the rope ladder and as others balanced precariously on a narrow gangplank, she and her fellow passengers were entering a new world. The time for decision making was over. The Pashleys, Pengellys, Huttons, and Stewarts had prepared for months and in some cases years for this moment. What had once been an abstract idea being discussed and debated – one that could still be put aside as a plan for the future – was now a reality. These families had passed a threshold in the emigrants' world. Boarding the ship bound for new worlds and new homes did not sever all their connections with those they were leaving behind. Indeed, they were still intimately tied to and often dependent on them, both emotionally and financially. But they were already thinking of the possibility of new friends and of reuniting with family who had gone before. The Atlantic voyage was the means of bridging the two worlds. For the next few weeks or months it was also its own world, one that was apart from both the Old and the New, and that had its own dynamics and rhythms. Certainly, it was a transitory community. But it was one that confirmed and reinforced a sense of identity and community that set them emotionally as well as physically apart from home.

CHAPTER THREE

A Nether World on the Atlantic

Two weeks into their voyage, Harriet Pengelly was in "wretched spirits." Although the Atlantic was almost calm and she was not seasick, her journal entry for 20 April 1835 ended: "Guernsey, my beloved spot – my heart is with you day and night – oh! Nature never intended me to roam. I am so very, very dull, till I came on board I feel as if I was in a dream, I had no time to think alas! It was fortunate for me, and I dare not look sad on my husband's account it makes him so unhappy."[1] Three years earlier, William Radcliffe had remarked to his father after arriving in Upper Canada, "I do not feel at home here yet – my former home, my sea voyage and traveling some seven hundred miles to a new country appear more like a dream than a reality ... My very existence in these drowsy woods appear doubtful."[2]

Many of those who emigrated to America in the first half of the nineteenth century may have wondered if the whole experience had been a dream. For some, like Elizabeth Peters, who left Plymouth with her husband and three young sons and travelled to Upper Canada in 1830, it was a surprisingly pleasant experience. Harriet Pengelly, on the other hand, appears to have moved through her dream into a nightmare of seasickness, homesickness, and fear for her life. And the passengers of the *Wallington*, which went down at Cape Rosier in the St Lawrence in 1832,[3] and those aboard the *Lady of the Lake*, which sank in the ice off Newfoundland a year later, lived their worst nightmares.[4]

The dreamlike quality of emigration was usually associated with the Atlantic voyage. As soon as they boarded the ship, emigrants entered a nether world that was, to a large degree, out of time and place. For the next few weeks and even months, they were isolated from the familiar world of their former homes and the new world that they were seeking.

"Embarking with Your Family for America – taking leave of Albion's white Cliffs – <u>No More Taxes</u>," in C.J. Grant, "Emigration, Detailing the Progress and Vicissitudes of an Emigrant," 1833 (LAC, e000943150, PWC, R.9266-P1044)

This world "in between" had its own rituals and rhythms. During the long, often tedious, and sometimes dangerous voyage, the emigrants created a community that recognized and to a degree respected rank and authority. They also recreated patterns of daily life which, in some measure, resembled those of home. Family continued to be the emigrants' foundation. Emigrant women cooked and sewed and, as much as possible, maintained the daily routine of the family. Some men tended their livestock; others talked politics and business. Children played or followed sailors around as they went about their tasks. Cabin passengers, as befitted their rank, were waited on; those travelling in steerage did for themselves. Living in a confined space, cut off from other human contact for an indeterminate period of time and being subject to the vagaries of the weather was often a tremendous strain, however, both on individuals and on relationships.

Emigrants readily recorded their experiences of life aboard ship. During a time when they had little control over their future and depended on the forces of nature, on the skill of the captain and crew, and on the beneficence of God to reach their final destination, the very act of keeping a journal seems to have been a way to make sense of the experience and to bring order and familiarity to a foreign and potentially chaotic world.[5] Journals of the voyage helped to recreate this world into manageable tidbits and routines. Emigrants regularly recorded the weather, the health of their companions, and the events that helped to mark the passage of the days and weeks, and each journal also reflected the particular concerns and activities of the writer. Various emigrants' experiences of the voyage and what they chose to record was influenced by their gender and age, as well as by their class and familial circumstances. Women's and men's journals reflected differing world views. Even husbands and wives who travelled together and shared a berth with their children recreated this in-between world in different ways and with different sensibilities. At the same time, when read as a piece, shipboard journals and diaries, like emigrants' letters, offer a window into the rhythms and complexities of this part of the emigrants' world.

After waiting days and in some cases weeks for their passage, emigrants were anxious to be off once their ship was finally ready to board. Many quickly discovered that even then they had to put up with further delays. For instance, George Pashley's departure was anticlimactic. His scramble to get his family and their luggage aboard the *Reward* before she sailed was unnecessary, for the Pashleys discovered on arriving at the dock that the *Reward* "could not sail till the next day." "So," George wrote, "we got our things on board in the afternoon and had a good night lodgings in our Temperance Residence." Even after the ship set sail next morning, there was a further delay. "We have gone in the River and the Sails spread," George recounted, but the ship was becalmed when "the Wind changed." Not until the following evening did the *Reward* pass the mouth of Liverpool harbour, and another two days passed before they "could not see land."[6]

William and Elizabeth Peters and their three children had to wait a week after they boarded the brig *Friends* at Plymouth before it sailed at the beginning of May 1830. They had spent the previous day "very busy getting things for the voyage" and had what they thought would be their last night on shore with Aunt Denham. But while they and their travelling companions were finding their berths and stowing their belongings, it was announced that the mate had been injured and the captain had to find a new one. After another night on shore, Elizabeth Peters recorded that she "felt peculiarly tired getting up the side of the vessel," and the family decided to stay in their berths until the *Friends* sailed. For the next few days, William, a Methodist minister, carried on with his daily routine. His journal recorded how he organized and led daily prayer meetings and visited friends in town. Elizabeth, who stayed on board, was kept busy cooking and looking after their three children – Thomas, age six, William four, and Nicholas almost two. As Elizabeth noted in her diary, she found the wait trying. During the day, the ship was noisy, and although she found the nights "as comfortable as when on shore," the motion of the ship often made her feel "indisposed." By day five, she and everyone else "were anxious to be off." At the end of a week's delay, she recorded, "We have been in full expectations of sailing. I hope it will not be long. Having parted from our friends, we feel anxious to get on." The captain finally came on board on 3 May, and suddenly "all appear[ed] hurry and bustle on deck, the chains rattling and the ropes drawing sails, etc." Elizabeth missed the actual departure. As the *Friends* pulled away from the dock, she was below with the children, having "great difficulty" keeping them amused.[7]

John Hart's party of about four hundred emigrants had to wait for four days before the *Carlton* weighed anchor at Greenock in April 1842. Part of the delay was the result of new government regulations. The ship and its passengers had to clear customs before departing; in the meantime, no one was permitted to leave the ship or open their sea stores. While they waited, the passengers depended for their provisions on local merchants, who came alongside in their boats. Not surprisingly, many in the party became restive. The boredom was periodically relieved by daily prayer meetings and the arrival of various visitors. On Sunday, a minister from Port Glasgow came aboard to conduct a service. When the *Carlton* finally sailed two days later, on 19 April, all were much relieved. "The first thing we did," John Hart recorded, "was to serve out 2lbs of Biscuits to each and 3 oz of Tea" and other provisions.[8]

Emigrants who travelled first class were usually able to avoid such waiting. In 1822 the *George* sailed shortly after the Stewarts boarded, and it was actually underway when Mr Reid finally boarded. When Edward Talbot left home in 1823, the "emigrants" boarded the *Brunswick* first. Cabin passengers boarded just before the ship sailed.[9] In 1834 John Reilly, a young English traveller, and a number of his cabin mates hired a steamer to take them to their ship after it had left the dock.[10] Others, such as the Pengellys, knew exactly when the packet would sail. Robert had time to help Harriet up the rope ladder and safely settled in their cabin and then go ashore to ensure that all their luggage was aboard before the *Montreal* sailed just after noon on 6 April 1835.

Whether travelling steerage or in a cabin, most emigrants viewed the bustle of departure with satisfaction. They had been preparing for this day for months. William Peters recounted with relief, after more than a week of waiting, "About 4 o'clock this morn weighed anchor." The *Friends* "got underway with a fair wind down channel" where "soon, almost all passengers, got sick." Neither he nor his wife expressed any regret at leaving home. He did note, however, "Last sight of English land this day, which perhaps I will see no more."[11]

Many emigrants remarked on their last sight of land. The passengers on the *Carlton* lost sight of Scotland after two days at sea. "I was going to make some remarks upon the last sight of the land that gave me birth," John Hart wrote, "but again when I thought that it was a land that denied me bread and forced me to leave it for another their impression soon left me." A day later he noted, without any further comment, "We saw the last of Ireland this morning away in the distance."[12] On the other hand, a somewhat elderly Mrs Langton, who was sailing with her family to join her second son, John, in Upper Canada felt bereft as her homeland receded over the horizon. Writing to her eldest son, William, in Manchester she observed that with the last sight of land she had also had her "last sight and touch of [her] first born."[13] Even though he was preoccupied with looking after his family, George Pashley, too, took time to record the passing of Wales, Ireland, and, lastly, the lighthouse at Cape Clear.

Yet even before home disappeared over the horizon, the Pashleys, like most other emigrants, were already occupied with the realities of life aboard ship. There were new routines to be established and new relationships to be made. Just getting one's sea legs and learning how to negotiate around berths, up and down hatches, and around the deck took some practice. Almost immediately after sailing, most on board succumbed to seasickness. Meanwhile, there were still children to be watched and people to be fed. The last sight of land did heighten the realization that one was cut off from the rest of the world, however. Joseph Wilson, who together with his wife Jenney and their two sons set sail for Quebec from Whitby, England, in early April 1831, recorded after eleven days, "Last sight of land ... We are now fairly upon the long talked of and much dreaded Western Ocean."[14]

For the next month, the Wilsons had to endure seasickness, storms, bad food and water, and boredom. The Peters family's five-week voyage appears, on the basis of their individual journals, to have been relatively uneventful. George Pashley's, on the other hand, was marked by personal tragedy when his youngest daughter died and was buried at sea. And John Hart's account of the voyage of the *Carlton* reflects his preoccupation with the welfare of the party that he had been instrumental in organizing and his efforts to make his family as comfortable as possible, despite storms and difficulties with the water. Emigrants' experiences of their Atlantic crossing varied considerably. The size and condition of the vessel, whether they were travelling cabin class or steerage, the weather they encountered, and the predisposition of the captain and crew, all had an impact on life on board. So, of course, did the personal circumstances of the emigrants themselves.

At the same time, all passengers shared many of the trials of life aboard a sailing ship in the nineteenth century. "A ship has been compared to a prison with a chance of being drowned," John Reilly cryptically wrote in his published account of his journey to America in 1835. He personally did not think the comparison correct, because on board ship the company was more select, the air freer, and "the wonders of the deep" were "not to be seen in jails." But he conceded, "The resemblance holds true in one particular importance, for the sailor and the prisoner may both exclaim with the bird in the cage, 'I can't get out, I can't get out.'"[15] On even the most comfortable, modern vessel, space was limited and passengers' movements restricted. Emigrants of all classes were periodically thrown together and obliged to live in one another's pockets; and almost everyone had to cope with the ravages of seasickness and the terror of storms. By the end of the voyage, all were as anxious to get off the ship as they had been to embark.

Some likened the ship's community to a family.[16] Perhaps a better comparison would be a small village. Shipboard society, like that in small British and Irish communities, was differentiated by rank and occupation. At sea, distinctions of class and authority were reflected by how the limited space was divided and used, and also by the differing day-to-day activities of the passengers. A social and economic hierarchy was recognized and respected by all on board. At the same time, a community of interests and experiences quickly developed aboard each emigrant vessel; and although relatively short-lived and transitory, this world of emigration had its own internal rhythms and rules. Certainly, there were times during a voyage when the accepted notions of appropriate behaviour were strained. But as much as possible, passengers tried to maintain or to establish relationships and daily routines that mirrored those at home.

At the head of this emigrant community was the ship's captain, and his authority was rarely questioned. All on board recognized that they depended on his skill and his ability to see them safely to their destination. Many also appreciated that the captain's personality and his level of concern for their welfare had a direct impact on their daily lives. Frances Stewart seemed to have quite liked Captain Thompson, who commanded the *George* in 1822. He was cautious and competent and "what you might expect to find" of one who had graduated "from the position of common sailor." He was "rough," she conceded, but he was "anxious to pay us every attention in his power and very good to the children."[17] William Knox (John Scott's cousin) reported to his uncle that the captain of the ship that took him to America in 1838 had been "a very steady and active man" who had, to Knox's approval, run "a Temperance Ship."[18] Elizabeth Peters found that Captain Butters of the *Friends* "could not be a more pleasant or kind man."[19]

It was the captain who established and maintained order on board. He decided, among other things, where passengers could go and when they ate and slept, and he determined basic rules of conduct. He was responsible for making sure that the passengers' daily rations were potable, edible, and adequate, and were distributed fairly. And in the 1830s and 1840s, he was expected to oversee the health of his human cargo by maintaining a basic level of cleanliness. When passengers became ill, some captains provided medicine and advice, and some, like Captain Butters of the *Friends*, organized and led the Sunday service.[20] A good captain (and crew) could make a rough crossing bearable. A bad captain not only could make passengers' lives miserable but could endanger all.[21]

Most on board had little direct contact with the captain. Although on some vessels the captain personally inspected passengers' quarters or, conditions permitting, mingled with families on deck, this was not possible on vessels carrying hundreds of emigrants. On such ships the captain controlled activity and enforced his regulations through intermediaries – the ship's mate or an appointed committee of emigrants. Only cabin passengers, such as the Pengellys and Stewarts, had regular contact with the captain, who sometimes joined them for meals and conversation. For all others, the captain was an impersonal though powerful symbol of authority.

Access to the captain was only one indication of a passenger's rank and place in this Atlantic community. Another fundamental and ever-present representation of status was how the limited space on board ship was allocated and used. When John Reilly decided to tour America in 1834, he booked a berth on one of the "transient ships" that sailed out of Liverpool. "We had on board in all 245 souls," he wrote, of whom 222 were passengers.[22] He was one of about 20 who had cabin accommodation; there were another 20 or so in what was called the second cabin, and about 180 in steerage. Despite "boisterous weather"[23] and various bouts of seasickness, Reilly appears to have had a relatively com-

"Quarterdeck of an Emigrant Ship," *Illustrated London News*, 6 July 1850 (MCM, M993X.5.1528.2)

fortable passage. The cabin had a fireplace and its own water closet, and the meals, cooked by one of the crew, were wholesome and sometimes very good. Reilly and his companions had complete freedom of the ship, and when the weather was fine they spent considerable time on deck.

Women travelling in "cabin class" were usually given separate accommodation. Mary Gapper (O'Brien) and her mother, who travelled to Upper Canada in 1828 to visit Mary's brother, were assigned berths in an "inner" cabin, which Mary found "close" and cramped. The more public room that was reserved for "the ladies" was "much airier, with the windows open" and was good for reading.[24] Frances Stewart appreciated the "little cabin" that she and the little girls shared. "I am very comfortable here," she wrote, "and quite independent; and though I have only just room to stand up and dress myself, I am much happier than if we were all together." She added, "It is very nice to have this cabin to which I may retire whenever I like."[25]

Men, women, and children travelling in "second cabin class" and steerage were not so comfortable. Second cabin accommodation did offer some privacy from other passengers. Located in the "afterpart of the vessel" and separated from steerage by boards "about an inch thick," some of the families in the second cabin on board Reilly's ship had arranged, for an extra fee, to have a separate room each with a door that locked. Although they had slightly more room than those in steerage,

Reilly considered the accommodation "very little different from the latter."[26] The Scottish families who were willing to pay up to £2 extra each obviously found the difference significant, however.[27]

In steerage there was no room or any semblance of privacy. "About 180 men, women and children" lived for the duration of the voyage "in a space not larger than a large drawing room" and (as Reilly noted after "popping his head down the hatch") with no air or light "but what come down the hatchway."[28] Whereas Reilly had his own berth in a stateroom, with space to unpack some of his luggage and to store the rest, and with a separate water closet for his ablutions,[29] those in steerage slept as many as six to a berth and had to stack their luggage and sea stores as best they could in the aisles and under the berths. What for Reilly was an interesting adventure was for most other passengers a forty-nine-day trial. Not only were steerage passengers crowded together, but they were restricted in their movements – confined below in bad weather, often with the hatches closed, and at other times limited to when and where they could go on deck.

The ship's company did periodically come together – for worship, to mourn the death of a child, and to play. But the distinction between the few privileged members of the community and the rest was clear as soon as they came on board. Reilly and others who had paid a considerable price for their quarters actively maintained the distinction. Not only was cabin accommodation physically separated from steerage, but life in the staterooms was often set apart from that in the rest of the ship, and it had its own rituals and rhythms.

One of the first things that cabin passengers had to decide was when they wanted to dine. Aboard the *Napoleon* in 1833, Patrick Shirreff and his colleagues were served breakfast at eight, luncheon at twelve, dinner at four, and tea at eight in the evening. At other times, the passengers just had to call "for what they wished."[30] Cabin passengers on the *Resolution* travelling from Liverpool a year later had two formal meals – breakfast at nine and dinner at two – but had access to the cook's provisions as desired.[31] Even though Mrs Radcliffe, travelling in second cabin, was not one of the most privileged passengers, she could enjoy (when not dining or afflicted by seasickness) the company of some of her "respectable and refined companions." And when the weather was fine, she wrote, "We remain on deck to a late hour," marvelling at the appearance of the sea.[32]

It appears that as at home, gentlemen and ladies often spent much of their time and took their amusements separately from one another.

Male cabin passengers gathered to smoke, drink, and wager on the ship's daily progress, when they would first see land, and when they would dock. The lottery was "a usual amusement ... on many voyages," Anne Langton reported to her brother William. Tickets, each indicating a different date and time of arrival, were sold to passengers, and the winners, "whose ticket most closely corresponded to when the pilot came received the proceeds."[33] While men walked the deck and conversed with new-found friends, their wives, mothers, daughters, and female companions read, sewed, took tea with other ladies, and wrote letters home.

Harriet Pengelly spent much of the voyage in her berth, ill and indisposed. At other times, she wrote letters home or listened to one of her fellow cabin passengers play the piano and sing, and in fine weather she walked the deck with her husband. Robert Pengelly appears to have adjusted to life on board more easily. In addition to looking after his dog (who, to the discomfort of other passengers, accompanied him everywhere), he spent a good deal of time walking the decks, reading, or conversing with other gentlemen.[34] Anne Langton reported that life aboard the *Independence* was "uncomfortable." The noise and confusion were tiring, and she recommended that if her brother William ever made the journey across the Atlantic, he should bring lots of books and a small mattress, "for the aching of the bones when obliged to toss upon a hard, uneven surface for many days is no trifling inconvenience."[35] Frances Stewart seems to have quite enjoyed her voyage. She had a maid to help look after the children, and when the weather was fine she sat on deck and watched the whales and birds. A few cabin passengers were surprised at how quickly the days passed "with conversation with ... fellow passengers – reading, writing and meals."[36] Most, however, found the voyage long and tedious.

Part of the problem for many cabin passengers was their self-imposed isolation from others on board. The "ladies" travelling with Robert and Harriet Pengelly objected strenuously to the presence of their servant in the cabin – to the point that the Pengellys and the captain had to find other accommodation for her.[37] Others watched but did not participate in the shipboard games and dances in which steerage passengers participated. Most guarded their society jealously; they were nonetheless intrigued by the life in the steerage. In some ships the captain inspected the steerage as a matter of course, and sometimes clergymen "went below" to conduct services; or a doctor might be called to attend to an injured or ill passenger in the hold.[38] But for most cabin passengers, steerage passengers were the subject of considerable curiosity. John Reilly recorded, for example, that he "popped his head" down the hatch "for a minute or two" just to see what it was like.[39] He and his companions were appalled at the conditions "the poor things" had to endure. "The emigrants," as some in cabin class referred to those travelling steerage, were obviously from another world, and Reilly and his new-found friends quickly returned to their own temporary home.[40]

With such visits, cabin passengers were asserting their right – and, for some, duty – as elite members of the shipboard community, to view and attend to the less fortunate. As they returned to the light and relative spaciousness of their cabins, they were also implicitly acknowledging the gulf that existed between them and "the other." There was little that those in steerage could do to assert even a limited right of privacy or proprietorship over their quarters. And it was only in very exceptional circumstances – as when a seriously ill child was brought into Reilly's cabin to try to save his life – that passengers even in the second cabin saw inside or were admitted to the first.

The difference between life in the cabin and that in steerage was often startling. On many ships, steerage accommodation was unimaginably cramped, dark, and badly ventilated. With rows of two and sometimes three tiers of bunks, which accommodated up to six adults a berth, steerage was not only a place to sleep but was also an eating hall, living quarters, a play area for the children, and a place to store all the occupants' possessions. Yet what from above appeared to be a chaotic "other" world was, for those who inhabited it, a community with its own order and rituals. Aboard the *Carlton* in 1842, for example, the Harts and other families appear to have had their own space for sleeping and, when the weather was inclement, for eating. Lit by a lamp, each small partitioned area also housed the family's "pots and bags and baskets and tubs." As John and Jean Hart discovered to their chagrin, everything had to be firmly lashed down. One night when "the ship gave a lurch," not only was the whole family thrown out of their berths, but all their possessions "came tumbling down" on their heads.[41] Aboard the *Reward*, the Pashleys had an open berth in a "room" they shared with at least two other families.[42] Individuals travelling on their own often shared a berth with a stranger of the same sex. Although William Knox appears to have had a berth of his own, he was surrounded by other single men.[43] And it is likely that any woman travelling without a male companion would be in another part of the steerage, often separated from the men by groups of families, as befitted British sensibilities.

"Scene Between Decks," *Illustrated London News*, 6 July 1850 (MCM)

Steerage accommodation was almost always crowded, however, and as Elizabeth Peters noted, the "close habitations" made it "trying for all, the children in particular."[44] Depending on the weather, on an individual's health, and on the ship's regulations, steerage passengers could seek relief from their cramped quarters by staying on deck. Some captains restricted where they could go. The cabins were obviously off limits, and "on some vessels, the Steerage Passengers [were] not aloud to go behind the main mast," William Knox explained to his uncle in 1838. On other vessels, steerage passengers were permitted on deck only at certain times. William Knox was fortunate; he was one of only twenty-five who occupied a space which, he judged, could have housed one hundred. "We have plenty of room and accommodation," he reported and "could go wherever we pleased."[45] The Peters, too, seemed to have had free access to the deck, which served, Elizabeth noted, as "a drawing room and thither we repair, to dine or tea in fine weather."[46] The deck often doubled as a children's playground; and it was at the galley on deck that steerage passengers cooked their meals.

But when the seas ran high or during a storm or if there was an altercation between passengers, steerage passengers could be ordered to their berths and confined. In particularly bad weather the hatches, the only source of natural light, were closed, and then emigrants had to rely on precious candles or oil lamps to attend to their business or help those in need. Even during good weather, many captains imposed regulations on when lamps in the steerage were to be extinguished each night, and they forbade residents to smoke or cook below decks.

Cabin passengers looking down the hatch frequently commented on the smell that emanated from "below." John Reilly found it was "too powerful for his olfactory nerves,"[47] and it prevented him from actually going below. There were reports of ministers who visited the sick or tried to hold a service in the steerage being "overcome by the foul air and stench" and falling senseless "on the deck."[48] The offensiveness of "the heated noxious atmosphere" was compounded by the apparent confusion. John Reilly recounted that "the mess they are in beggars all description." While the seas ran high, most of the 180 steerage passengers were sick; moreover, he wrote, there were "children crying, women screaming and all tossing from side to side as the vessel pitched, butter, biscuits, treacle, herrings, beef and potatoes all lying higgildy-piggildy or rolling from side to side all together made up a scene of misery and confusion such as I never saw before."[49] Reilly was undoubtedly sensationalizing his account for the benefit of an audience of respectable middle-class readers. Certainly, his often detailed and lurid descriptions reflect as much about his own middle-class sensibilities as they do about life aboard ship. But even Joseph Wilson, himself a steerage passenger in 1831, found the confusion and the "mighty din" below decks distressing. It was "a complete pigstye below," he recorded, and he was so distracted that he could neither "reed or think."[50]

Certainly, thousands who travelled steerage between 1815 and 1845 barely survived what were often appalling conditions.[51] But many other steerage passengers did not share these experiences. They were not passive victims, living in squalor. Although within this world many emigrants had few privileges, life in steerage had its own order and its own informal and formal regulations. An account of a voyage that appeared in *Blackwood's* in 1821 described how, although the steerage had been "divided into various small compartments" on the assumption that "families ought to be separated to each other," the "novelty of the situation," initially at least, "created a community of feeling among people who had no connection or acquaintance with each other." For the first few days of the voyage, noted the author, the Scottish emigrants talked "freely about their private affairs, confided to each other the causes that had respectively induced them to leave home and mutually offered to use their endeavours to alleviate the inconveniences and uncomforts which they expected to encounter during the voyage."[52] Life aboard most ships was not so idyllic and mutually supportive, however. The "inconveniences and uncomforts" of steerage often led to dissension. Order did need to be maintained.

Two days after the *Curler* sailed from Greenock in 1828 bound for New York, John Steele, a steerage passenger, recorded in his journal, "This day received the Captain's regulations for the government of the steerage when the following committee was appointed to carry the regulations into effect."[53] Among other things, the committee of ten passengers led by Steele distributed daily rations of water, ensured the water closets were cleaned out, tended and supervised use of the communal galley, and generally made sure that "the people [were] attended and ... all things arranged."[54] The committee was particularly determined that the quarters below decks be kept as clean and healthy as possible. Steele's journal recorded periodically overseeing "a general cleaning out of the berths" and regularly "getting all passengers on deck" while "the lower deck was washed" or sprinkled with vinegar.[55] Although its authority came directly from the captain, a steerage committee needed the confidence of other passengers to be effective. In one instance, Steele reported about three weeks into the voyage that there was "a quarrel about Wilson's [one of the emigrant's] bed." The committee persevered, however, and "for overhauling the same, the committee secured the thanks of the passengers."[56]

Steerage committees not only maintained order, they also gave passengers a voice and an avenue through which to express their concerns to the captain. In the second week of their voyage, Steele and his fellow committee members presented a formal petition to Captain Jones. "In consequence of your positive refusal to furnish clean pails for lifting water from the hold for the use of the passengers, and we knowing it to be your duty to furnish us with fire and water," the committee wrote, "we request that henceforth you will order your people to put the water on deck and light the fire and furnish coal for the same and supply us with clean pails."[57] The matter was apparently resolved so well that by the end of the lengthy voyage, the committee presented the captain with a medal to express its appreciation "for his general conduct, especially for his humanity to our brother passengers during illness."[58]

One of the most important responsibilities of shipboard committees was to oversee the distribution of water and provisions. The committee also often assumed responsibility for maintaining the fires in the open-air galleys and establishing daily schedules for cooking. Not surprisingly, John Hart, who had been the principal organizer of the party that chartered the *Carlton* in the spring of 1832, led that ship's committee. Throughout the forty-one-day voyage, Hart regularly distributed provisions to the company, served out daily rations of water, made sure the

"Searching for Stowaways," *Illustrated London News,* 6 July 1850 (MCM, M993X.5.1592.2)

fires were kept stoked, and when the "galleys fell down" or were washed away by successive storms, he supervised their reconstruction. During one particularly bad storm, when "the hatches were all down" and Hart predicted they might "stay all week," the passengers "were completely starved" and had little water. Although few ventured on deck, Hart and his son Jamie got themselves "two or three times wet all over" when they went to fetch water, which they "served ... in small quantities and made it go far." When the storm had passed, Hart got the galleys rebuilt, and the company of the *Carlton* resumed its fair-weather routines.[59]

A large part of each day revolved around the preparation of food. Whereas cabin passengers sat down at a formal table and were often served elaborate meals, steerage passengers usually cooked all or a large part of their own meals. Arrangements for cooking and feeding dozens (and often hundreds) of passengers varied from ship to ship. Emigrant ships had at least one and sometimes two communal galleys – "a little house between the masts,"[60] with fires that were continually lit. Often, the captain or the committee assigned a member of the crew or a couple of passengers as "cooks," to tend and supervise use of the fire and to make large pots of soup, porridge, or gruel. When Joseph Wilson was back on his feet after a serious and lengthy bout of seasickness, he discovered that there was "a great deal of mischief about getting anything done in the cook's galley." He noted in his diary that the cook was "an old snarly curmudgeon unless you bribe him with spirits. This we will not do."[61] Gordon Sellar, who emigrated to Upper Canada as a boy in the 1830s, remembered that the cook on their vessel was an old whaler. Although he made good soup and porridge, his abilities were limited and he did not take suggestions well.[62] On some ships, emigrants who had taken passage all-found were divided into groups, both for the distribution of food and for particular times at the galley.[63] The cook provided the basic fare, and then either "everyone cooked their own provisions" or passengers organized themselves, with families or groups of two or three, "or as many as may agree," preparing and cooking meals together.[64]

Aboard the *Friends* and the *Curler*, women did much of the cooking. Elizabeth Peters initially found that providing meals for her family was easier than she had expected: "We cook just as at home." If anything, cooking for the family on board ship was less taxing, she noted, for she did not have to tend the fire: "The cook keeps the fire and keeps it well." Although once underway, she discovered that seasickness and the rolling of the ship sometimes made cooking difficult if not impossible, in fair weather she appreciated having all her things at hand: "We have not the trouble to run for milk or butter to the dairy or to the parlor for our best things, where we'd have it all common."[65] Preparing meals and eating in cramped quarters with children always underfoot was difficult, of course. Weather permitting, Elizabeth sent the children on deck "while the next meal [was being] prepared,"[66] a process that began almost immediately after the last was eaten. The Peters ate quite well on the voyage. "Sometimes we have ham and water for tea and potato cakes etc," Elizabeth wrote. "Pudding we make as we like it better than the ship biscuits. We make stews, and pasties, and baked pudding. It is generally done well."[67]

One thing Elizabeth regretted was not having brought sufficient herbs as a substitute for tea. "Now it is all gone, I am obliged to have recourse to gruel," she recorded about two and a half weeks into the voyage, for "the [ship's] tea I cannot let down nor the coffee." Elizabeth was able to supplement the family's diet by trading with her neighbours, exchanging her surplus goods for items she had not packed. She exchanged flour for "pease, which we like very much,"[68] and obtained oatmeal from the captain. Indeed, she wrote, "Many things that I had I've been able to sell on account of the length of our voyage such as butter and bread, figs, sugar, etc." Nonetheless, by the time they reached the Grand Banks, when provisions were getting low and trade between passengers diminishing, the Peters had become tired of shipboard meals. "Our appetites are such that most of us are longing for what others had got, and what we have on our own we cannot touch,"[69] Elizabeth commented cryptically after about three weeks at sea. The addition of fresh fish to their diet once they were on the Grand Banks was most welcome.

Other families did not enjoy such meals. Aboard the *Carlton*, the Harts' diet consisted primarily of bannock, biscuits, porridge, stews, and gruel. Jean Hart seems to have found the voyage very difficult, and during her frequent bouts of seasickness, John and his son Jamie did much of the family's cooking. Moreover, in bad weather or when the seas were heavy, cooking was "hazardous and disagreeable." Then, as John Hart commented, it was often considered "too dangerous for a female to walk on deck,"[70] and any member of the family who was able prepared meals.[71]

Frequent storms seem to have prevented the Wilson family from cooking any proper meals for the first three weeks of their voyage. Moreover, Joseph and perhaps others were "very ill" for much of this time. "Everything is quite bitter in the mouth," he recorded, and usually all he wanted was "a little ale or porter."[72] By the time the weather improved and Joseph had his sea legs, much of the family's food had become tainted. But Jenney Wilson had prepared for the journey well. Although on day twenty-two of the voyage Joseph remarked, "We are scantily supplied," he also noted in his journal, "Our preserves are now useful." And two days later, Jenney still had sufficient provisions left to make biscuits, which were "quite a treat to us as they are so thick and well made and well baked."[73] Jenney Wilson's ability to make good biscuits and, later, warm cake[74] was clearly appreciated. But Joseph seems to have taken her efforts for granted along with other domestic arrangements. While Joseph read his Bible, led prayer meetings, and talked with his neighbours, Jenney – like Elizabeth Peters, Jean Hart, and other wives and mothers – assumed primary responsibility for looking after the children, doing the cooking, washing, and repairing and making clothes.

The day before the *Friends* sailed, Elizabeth Peters remarked, "My time seems to be as much taken up as on shore." In particular she noted, "The children must be taken care of, or they are much in danger."[75] A little more than a week later, after the Peters had weathered two gales, she commented, "We have many times said to each other how little did we know about our voyage. Our friends thought we should have nothing to do but to make observations and write them, but I assure you so far the contrary that we have as much as we can well do, all of us, even those without children."[76] Apart from preparing meals, a considerable portion of Elizabeth Peters's time on board was devoted to caring for the children. A ship could be a dangerous playground, and children needed to be supervised carefully.[77] In bad weather, when passengers were confined below decks, the children had to be amused and often comforted. And few voyages escaped having children (and, indeed, adults) come down with colds, the ague, or one of the "childhood diseases," particularly measles.

John Hart reported two weeks into their voyage, "The Measles have got in among the children and there is four or five of them poorly with them." In the close quarters aboard ship, he feared that his youngest child, William, would contract the disease. Although William escaped, at least seven children became seriously ill, and one died and was buried at sea.[78] Nursing ill children was, as George Pashley recounted, time consuming and worrying, and was made all the more difficult by the crowded conditions and rolling of the ship. The Pashleys spent a number of restless nights and days tending their youngest daughter, who "threw her head and arms about ... in such a manner as indicated much pain." After two weeks, "her happy Spirit took its flight," wrote George. "My dear wife and I had to perform the last office for the remains of our Child. I think we bore our Bereavement in such a place as well as could be expected."[79] Few voyages were made without the death of one or two young passengers.

In the early 1830s, many shipboard communities were also devastated by cholera. No one was immune from the disease, which spread quickly in the cramped conditions of emigrant vessels. By the summer of 1832, ships were arriving at Quebec having lost as much as 10 percent of their passengers. In 1834 cholera again accompanied many emigrants to the New World. Although once in Quebec, those stricken with the disease could receive some rudimentary medical attention, in mid-Atlantic there was little anyone could do other than tend the ill and quickly bury the dead at sea. It was not unusual for children to be orphaned or for parents to arrive at Quebec childless. For prospective emigrants at home, reports of the toll cholera was taking must have given some of them cause to reconsider their decision.[80] Most were not deterred, however.

News of the death of a passenger spread throughout the ship's company quickly. So, too, did news that an expectant mother had safely given birth to a child. On his first day aboard the *Carlton*, John Hart recorded, "About twelve o'clock James Hay came to me and told me that there was a wife on board that was crying out and he wanted a wife to bring home the child and Mrs Hay was the howdie, the child was born about one o'clock after that we had a very comfortable sleep."[87] Hart's relief that he and others on board could now get some sleep starkly belies the concern that this woman and her family (and other women in the party) must have felt.

Childbirth was always dangerous for both mother and child in the nineteenth century; giving birth in the cramped quarters of steerage, with dozens in sight and sound of the event, only made it more stressful. A woman on board John Reilly's ship who went into premature labour was fortunate that there was professional help on board. "She was safely delivered of an ocean child," Reilly recounted, "before as large as a company as ever was present at a ceremony of the kind."[82] On the Reverend William Bell's voyage in 1819, a young woman went into premature labour, and Bell found the whole experience "embarrassing." What for him seems to have been particularly worrying was that during the delivery the surgeon was thrown down a number of times "by the pitching of the ship"; and at one point, the berth on which the woman was lying collapsed into pieces. Yet Bell reported that within a few days both mother and child were "as well as before."[83] Many women in labour had only the assistance of family members or someone met only recently. Just being pregnant and manoeuvring between rows of berths and up and down the ladders from the hold to the deck must have been difficult; bearing a child and caring for a newborn was emotionally as well as physically draining.[84]

Elizabeth Peters, to her discomfort, had still been nursing Nicholas when the family left home. "I wish he were weaned," she wrote almost at the end of the voyage. "The milk does him no good nor me either."[85] She had two other young sons to keep track of, but even with a child at her breast and two others underfoot, she was distressed that she had little time to wash the children's clothes or maintain basic standards of cleanliness. Not until the *Friends* was off the coast of Newfoundland and the passengers "now allowed to use some fresh water" could she report a day "very busy washing." "Our sewing," she recorded "has been little ... nothing worth mentioning" (though this included a new hat for Nicholas, a cloak for Thomas, knitting a pair of stockings, and "fitting up a few [other] things.")[86] Mary Steele (John's wife) aboard the *Curler* appears to have had more time for sewing and even did a little drawing. At least three of her eight children were old enough to look after the younger ones, and on a voyage somewhat longer than that of the Peters, Mary managed to make a number of shirts for the children as well as some trousers and waistcoats for her husband and for one of her sons, and she "drew a number of drawings and paintings."[87]

While emigrant wives, mothers, and daughters coped with the daily demands of their families, their husbands and young children seem to have spent considerable time on deck. "Our children have been so well and enjoy themselves as much as on shore there being so many boys to play with," Elizabeth Peters commented.[88] John Steele's son John followed the sailors about and "learned a great deal about casting knots on ropes etc."[89] Life aboard ship offered children adventure and playmates. Many men found the voyage less satisfying. Joseph Wilson, like William Peters, kept busy preaching, organizing prayer meetings, and reading the Bible. John Hart and John Steele seem to have been fully occupied overseeing the welfare both of their families and of the passengers generally. John Reilly and his companions spent their time "walking on deck – standing or sitting in groups telling long stories – shouting at seagulls or any other sea birds that venture within shot – playing at cards, draughts, or backgammon – and if a fine evening, dancing on the quarter deck and poop."[90] But many men, without farms to tend or shops to run, found the enforced "holiday" tedious.

Men's shipboard journals, like those of farmers, regularly recorded the weather. They also frequently noted the condition of the sea and sometimes the ship's position and progress. The sighting of birds (whether at the beginning or end of the voyage, or "Mother Carey's chickens") and marine life was also cause for comment. Some men had livestock to look after,[91] and the arrival of a "fine young lamb" during Joseph Wilson's voyage was a welcome diversion and was "viewed with pleasure by all the passengers."[92] Others walked the decks, discussed the ship's progress, read and wrote letters, or wrote up their journals; and as they reached the Grand Banks, some had the opportunity to fish and watched with interest the native birds and marine life.[93]

Various shipboard journals suggest that, as at home, women and men assumed distinct but overlapping responsibilities while on the voyage; but all were delighted when another ship came into sight. Journals were peppered with such notations: "Saw a ship sailing in the West"[94] or "Saw a ship in the distance."[95] As they peered out from the deck, the pas-

"Emigration Vessel – Between Decks," *Illustrated London News*, 10 May 1851 (MCM, M993X.5.1529.3)

sengers tried to identify the ship's port of origin and destination. Frequently, ships came close enough for the passengers to exchange shouted conversations and get some account of the other ship's progress. Even Elizabeth Peters, who was busy with her children, hurried up on deck when two ships drew near to the *Friends*: "We spoke with two vessels, one going to America & an other from Avanna going to Spain. They accosted us in a different language and could scarcely understand our Captain when he spoke."[96] Her husband recounted that some of the passengers were "attacked with fear" because the Spanish ship was a man-of-war. But as Elizabeth recorded, that ship's captain "made the inquiry whether we wanted anything on board." Somewhat ruefully she noted, "We did not want anything as much as fresh water, and that they wanted most likely as much as ourselves."[97]

Sightings of other ships breached, for a time at least, the passengers' sense of isolation. As a traveller to the United States remarked, when a sail hove "in sight at a distance," it was "a messenger sent from another world."[98] It was reassuring to know that one was not completely alone on the Atlantic and that others were experiencing similar dilemmas with bad water and storms. John Hart noted just after the *Carlton* had weathered another storm, "We saw a ship today in the same condition as ourselves" with the sails in shreds. "Sometimes we saw her masts and sometimes nothing and at other times we saw the whole of her. It was truly awful and fearful and at the same time the appearance was grand."[99]

Most of the time, however, those aboard the *Carlton* were alone on the Atlantic, and passengers had to find other diversions. One way to pass the time when all the domestic affairs were completed was to gather on deck to play or worship. Sometimes, when the weather was fine, the

"Dancing Between Decks," *Illustrated London News*, 10 May 1851 (MCM, M993X.5.1530.2)

captain organized games and activities for the passengers. Joseph Wilson described "many kinds of diversions going on under the sanction of the captain, who seemingly enjoys a lark such as diving for oranges, boxing, races with legs tied together, which owing to the motion of the ship created a lot of fun."[100] John Hart wrote of an entertainment in mid-May: "We have had the band on deck tonight and they played us a great many tunes. We had some reels. It was such a fine night and a fine wind. We had songs likewise. We went all to bed as happy as we would have been on a Saturday night in Glasgow."[101] Ten days later, as the *Carlton* approached Cape Breton, he wrote, "We had the musicians on deck tonight and all in good spirits."[102]

Despite dances, games, and songs, living in such confined quarters for any length of time inevitably led to tensions and sometimes rows between passengers. What at home might have been overlooked often became a major grievance. Robert Pengelly was incensed, for example, when some of his fellow cabin passengers objected to his dog roaming the ship, and one threatened to throw the dog overboard because "his wife had stepped in something not very agreeable."[103] It was not unusual for "fighting and quarrelling" to break out in steerage, where disputes

"Scudding in a Gale" was exciting and terrifying. Pen and ink by an anonymous officer, ca. 1830 (LAC, C150001, PWC, R9266-554.9)

were often fuelled by alcohol.[104] Elizabeth Peters complained of "losses" – of cider and a bottle or two of wine that had mysteriously disappeared. She and others aboard the *Friends* did not trust the sailors, and she believed that "the forecastle passengers," who appear to have been pauper emigrants subsidized by their respective parishes, were "not all honest."[105] Sometimes, even the members of the crew became involved in an altercation. After more than seven weeks at sea, John Steele reported, "Sailors having got liquor, a riot nearly took place." The captain confined two of the worst offenders, and that evening some passengers had to take turns on watch.[106]

One published account of a voyage noted that within a week or so, "most of the emigrants had become reconciled to a sea life, and those who still disliked it consoled themselves with the prospect of soon reaching the termination of their voyage." But still, "day after day passed in monotonous routine" and "no one seemed ever to wish for the arrival of the morrow, experience having taught us that nothing new was to be anticipated or looked for while we were on board."[107] When a stowaway was discovered aboard the *Carlton*, the captain and John Hart were concerned. Other passengers were intrigued.[108] When a passenger fell overboard on John Reilly's ship, all came on deck to watch his rescue. The diversion created by such incidents was short-lived, however, and emigrants turned to other ways to fill their days.

Aboard the *Carlton*, the *Friends*, and Joseph Wilson's ship, a number of passengers found comfort in daily prayer meetings. On the *Carlton* there was "prayer and praise every evening," and on one occasion, John Hart put off writing in his dairy until the service was over, "for there was no time for doing it through the day."[109] For the first few days of his voyage, Joseph Wilson preached and led his companions in prayer, and he resumed his work after he had recovered from seasickness. "Prayer meeting tonight as usual," he recorded on the Saturday the captain had organized games on deck.[110] He and his fellow communicants also led Sunday services. The Peters were pleased that the captain of the *Friends* encouraged passengers to attend prayers on Sunday. "The Captain ordered one of the sailors to ring the large bell to announce the time of service," William Peters reported, and he was gratified when, a little more than four weeks into the journey, "almost all on board, cabin as well as steerage passengers and sailors attended" the service. William viewed the voyage as an opportunity to bring the unredeemed to the Lord, and he was pleased when "Great attention prevailed" to his preaching from his admittedly captive audience. Towards the end of the voyage, he recorded, "We have reason to hope that our labour is not in vain in the Lord."[111] Only violent storms or his own indisposition interrupted William's work.[112]

Regular prayer and Sunday services were important events in the lives of many on their transatlantic voyage. They created a sense of community, which in some ways transcended class or gender. When passengers and sailors, cabin and steerage, came together to worship, they were affirming their common humanity and their shared faith in an omnipresent God. Daily prayers also reaffirmed their connections to home and to those they had left behind. Many, like John Gemmill, took comfort in knowing that their future was in the hands of God; even if they never saw home again, family members and friends of the faith would be reunited in another world.

Shipboard services could also divide the community, however, by denomination and ethnicity. And even at a common service, the distinctions between cabin passengers and those in steerage were often maintained. John Reilly described how his captain arranged the service, at which attendance appears to have been obligatory. The captain sat at the front, and the minister "was placed with his back to the captain." Then "the genteel passengers sat on stools and the Irish rag-tag and bobtail made up the background of the congregation."¹¹³ The Methodist minister on the packet boat, *Samson*, which left Portsmouth in February 1834, was pleased to see that steerage passengers at least acknowledged the Sabbath by appearing on deck in "their best coats and all cleaned." But he was disconcerted when the time came for worship. Although the cabin passengers were attentive, many others were too "intent upon their dinners & others remained forward smoking, so that the attendance was rather thinner" than he would have wanted.¹¹⁴

On some ships there were two services – one for Catholic passengers and another for Protestants. On the *Reward* there were no services at all; despite valiant attempts, George Pashley found "no friends to join him in the worship of God." On the first Sunday at sea, he "read a sermon, a Psalm or two and a Chapter" on his own. But "my mind very low," he noted, "and so it always is without proper exercise." It was only when his daughter was buried at sea that all gathered "with Hats off" and listened to a service conducted by the captain.¹¹⁵ George clearly missed the fellowship and rituals of faith that provided a crucial link to home and to community. For many on the Atlantic, Sunday worship also helped mark the passing of the weeks and offered solace and hope for safe passage.¹¹⁶

The sense of a community that encompassed all on board was often sporadic. For much of the voyage, those in steerage and in the cabin – like the friends and relatives they had left behind who lived either in cottages or in the big house – had little sustained, personal contact. Certainly, passengers could not help but see each other on deck and would rub shoulders as they watched whales or birds. Sometimes, individuals struck up a conversation or would point out to each other a passing ship; or they would come together to help the crew – with setting or lowering the sails or taking the watch. Although William Catermole, who recommended that even gentlefolk travel steerage, asserted that "when you get to sea the distinction of cabin and steerage, if respectable, cease,"¹¹⁷ such "levelling" seems to have been more apparent than real.

Aboard the *Resolution* in 1834, for example, the cabin passengers watched but did not participate as "the sailors and emigrants" had "fun and amusement."¹¹⁸ John Reilly delighted in "a regular Irish row" among the steerage passengers and later observed them dancing.¹¹⁹ Elizabeth Peters was conscious of the gulf that divided her from those in the cabins. "The cabin people take notice of us," she commented in her journal towards the end of the voyage. Like most wives and mothers who inhabited the world below decks, she had little time to socialize with anyone but her immediate neighbours. Elizabeth did not regret her situation; she seems to have enjoyed the company of new-found friends, and she almost felt sorry for those in cabin class. Their lives were much more regimented and restricted than hers. Indeed, as Elizabeth perceptively noted, it seemed that the ladies "sometimes almost wish they were like us, as we are able to get anything our appetites are to when we like."[120]

The ladies and gentlemen aboard the *Friends*, and all others who travelled "first cabin," were more like Elizabeth Peters and her compatriots than they would have wished. The weather on the Atlantic had no respect for affluence. And although cabin passengers had their own berths, could enforce to a certain degree their personal privacy, and had servants to attend them, they too were obliged to cope with many of the trials of life aboard ship.

One constant complaint from all was the quality of the water. Elizabeth Peters felt, "If we could get fresh water, I should not at any time dislike a sea voyage." Government regulations notwithstanding, by the time their ship was approaching the Grand Banks, the water aboard the *Friends* was "so bad that it [was] a punishment to drink it."[121] Mrs Radcliffe, travelling in the second cabin, found the water disgusting.[122] John Reilly reported, "The stench [is] so great that I am obliged to hold my nose with one hand whilst I bolt it."[123] Sometimes, crew members put out barrels to collect rainwater. Passengers also added vinegar (or, if they had it, wine) to the water to disguise the taste. Cabin passengers did have other beverages available – beer, wine, and so on. But even on the most exclusive packet, the water used for cooking, baking, and making tea and coffee soon became dank and foul tasting.

The problems with the water were, for many, secondary to that which inevitably came with travelling on the Atlantic – seasickness. The vast majority of passengers "suffered (with short intervals of relief) the most torturing seasickness."[124] Emigrant guides and published travellers' reports all alluded to that "sensation of seasickness," which Joseph Wilson described as "the most curious I have ever experienced."[125] Many, like Elizabeth Peters, felt "indisposed" with the motion of the vessel as soon as they boarded.[126] This was nothing, however, compared to the wracking sickness that exhausted most passengers once they were well underway. For days and in some case weeks, passengers took to their berths, unable to eat, and drinking only weak tea, gruel, or whatever was readily available. Joseph Wilson graphically described the sensation. It was "as though the blood in the extremities of the feet was urged up by a certain jerk with the bowels and the bowels altogether pushed into the

"'On the wide and boundless Sea' – Rolling mountains high, a month on the Atlantic. Provisions nearly exhausted or spoild, but no lack of hard Tack and Putrid Water," in C.J. Grant, "Emigration, Detailing the Progress and Vicissitudes of an Emigrant," 1833 (LAC, e000943151, PWC, R.9266-P1044)

head and then returning back again into the feet."[127] For Mrs Radcliffe, "the parching thirst of seasickness" had no comparison.[128]

A few passengers were fortunate. John Gemmill was apparently never ill on his trip to Lanark. Another young emigrant recounted that despite "a very long and rough passage of eight weeks and three days to Quebec," he had had "a great deal of fun on the passage ... instead of only being sorry and sick."[129] Many gained their sea legs quite quickly and like George Pashley, who was sick once and then "not troubled so bad," were able to help those who were not yet recovered.[130] John Connel, who left home in the spring of 1845, reported to those at home: "I have not enjoyed better health these number of years back that I have done for the last six weeks" of the voyage. His family was not so fortunate. Once they had cleared the coast of Ireland, "all on Board, with very few exceptions got sick and remained so varying from 2 days to 3 weeks." John's "cargo" – his family – "was seized all at once which kept [him] Busey for some time."[131] Children often recovered quickly;[132] many adults were not so fortunate. Jean Hart and George Pashley's wife were the last of their families to gain their sea legs. In the Peters family, Elizabeth recovered first and nursed the two eldest boys and her husband

William for another week. In extreme cases, a passenger never really recovered. Two weeks into the voyage, a steerage companion of Joseph Wilson was still so seasick "that he was obliged to be let blood," a procedure which "two or three bungling fellows" had difficulty performing. The man survived, but he was bruised as well as weak.[133]

Passengers' recovery from seasickness was often short-lived. An approaching storm or an outright gale forced many back to their berths. On those days, only the most hardy and intrepid ventured on deck or wanted more than weak gruel to eat. Two weeks into their voyage, the Wilsons awoke to "a terrible gale." The passengers were confined to their bunks: "Sickness was again renewed amounst us and we found ourselves very ill for we could get nothing to eat and consequently were very strained by throwing." For the next two days, although the winds abated, Joseph continued to feel ill: "We cannot eat anything for meat of all kinds is loathing. Everything is quite bitter in the mouth after the sickness."[134]

The torment of seasickness was compounded by fear of the storm. Emigrants making their way to North America knew all too well the danger of an ocean crossing. Reassurances from family and friends and in the press that very few ships ever went down in the open sea meant little to those restricted to their cabins or confined in steerage as the wind increased. One Methodist minister going to Upper Canada by way of New York in February 1834 recorded "the days of anxiety and the nights of horror" during one storm as "wave after wave broke over the ship," the mast broke and was carried away, the cookhouse was smashed, and no one "expected to see the morning."[135] Four days later, he judged that "'Tempests' indeed is the Lord revealing Himself to us," teaching us that "we must be kept mindful of our place in the hollow of his Hand."[136] To this minister, the terrible voyage confirmed "the Course of the Lord to destroy to the wisdom of the wise and teach men to trust not in the discoveries of Science nor the certainties of Calculation but only in God."[137]

Many recognized that crossing the Atlantic in winter was particularly hazardous. Even in spring and summer, however, few emigrants escaped storms and gales; and particularly for those in steerage, the experience was terrifying. "The storm now at its greatest fury," Joseph Wilson recorded on the fourteenth day of his voyage. "The water breaks over the bulwarks and pouring down our hatchway in torrents. The people in the lower cabins were almost flooded out of their beds, articles of all descriptions flying almost like shuttle cocks."[138] As soon as the wind picked up, most captains ordered steerage passengers below and closed the hatches. With the seas rolling high, the Harts took to their beds. "If they were to come out," John Hart wrote, "they would be tumbled about."[139] But even then, passengers were tossed around, bruised by flying luggage, and many were very sick. After a particularly fierce roll of the *Carlton*, two weeks into the voyage, Jean Hart ended up with "black lumps on the arms."[140] A few days later, the *Carlton* encountered swells "the like of which we never saw,"[141] wrote her husband. Even with "the hatches all down" the sea "still ran down among us. Our bed was all wet." The next day, John believed that they were in "a perfect hurricane." The ship was badly damaged, and its passengers were left battered, bruised, cold, and miserable.[142]

The noise of the wind and rain, the creaking of the ship's timbers and flapping of the sails, and the pitching and rolling in high seas could be terrifying. An account in *Blackwood's* in 1821 described the "tumult, anxiety and confusion" that often prevailed during a storm: "Every time the ship rolled more violently than usual, a host of ejaculations, shrieks and screams burst from the mouths of men, women and children." When one added the sound of the "rolling of casks, the crashing of earthenware and the noise of articles of furniture tossing from side to side," it was a "terrifying combination."[143] Even the most organized passengers, who had done their best to secure anything that could move, did not escape injury. Water continued to leak into the hold, the high seas broke cabin windows and soaked beds, papers, and passengers,[144] and sometimes floated luggage and the lower berths in steerage.

As each storm abated, passengers carefully left their berths and tried to bring order to their tumbled luggage. And while the crew unreefed the sails and repaired the rigging, the passengers began to repair what they could of the damage. On board the *Carlton*, the galleys "fell down" or were washed away at least three times during the voyage. Before the emigrants could cook their meals or just boil water to make gruel or tea, the galleys had to be rebuilt and the fires lit. Calm weather did bring "a great comfort to all."[145] But for many, their anxiety that they might encounter another storm persisted. Their only satisfaction was that the winds might have taken them closer to their destination.

For many emigrants, the Atlantic voyage was something to be endured – a trial they wanted to end as quickly as possible. Two weeks into his voyage, Robert Pengelly, who was travelling in considerable comfort, was already "heartily tired of the voyage."[146] After twelve days, Joseph Wilson prayed that "Lord send us a speedy passage."[147] As days became

"The Life-Boat of the 'Tagus' Taking a Rope to the Wreck 'Martin Luther' Emigrant Ship," *Illustrated London News*, 2 May 1857 (MCM, M993X.5.678)

weeks, everyone was increasingly anxious to arrive, and many were frustrated at their inability to hasten the ship's progress. Journals not only recorded the weather; they also began to be preoccupied with the ship's position, its speed, and its course. Within a week or ten days of sailing, passengers came to realize that though "a very fine morning" offered a respite from sickness, it was often cause "to lament the little progress we make on our voyage."[148] And contrary winds that stalled progress or blew a ship off course were noted with impatience, particularly as one got nearer to America. One passenger on the *Resolution* noted wryly when the ship met head winds as it approached the Grand Banks, "When you are 1000 miles or so from *any* land you care little to hear in the morning 'wind right ahead sir.' you feel as if you have plenty of miles & time to spare – but when anxiously looking out for land, to know but one evening that you are but 65 miles from it – & to hear the next day you are 200 – makes a person feel as if they were robbed of their just right."[149] Aboard the *Curler*, John Steele and his family reached the coast of North America in four weeks. Two weeks later, after heavy rain, fog, and westerly winds, Steele's journal recorded, "*Now Six Weeks at Sea*. This appears to be a very tedious voyage."[150] At seven weeks, Steele was becoming increasingly frustrated and commented, "*Curler* will not do well for carrying passengers."[151] It was another week before the *Curler* finally anchored in New York harbour.

Passengers began to look eagerly for signs of land after three or four weeks at sea. "We had a very good day's sailing," John Hart recorded on day twenty-six of the *Carlton*'s voyage. "I think we are very near those long looked for Banks of Newfoundland. They have been long talked of."[152] John's prediction was confirmed two days later when the captain began to take soundings and the *Carlton* found itself among "a very great many vessels" – French fishing boats harvesting the Banks.[153] Other signs that they were approaching the coast was the beginning of "Bank Weather."[154] Hart and many others commented on the heavy fog that "wet you to the skin" and the persistent rain and much colder weather, which sometimes forced passengers to remain in their berths.[155] Although it was early June when the *Friends* approached the Grand Banks, William Peters remarked, "From the coldness of the air we should have thought in England it was the commencement of March."[156] Many vessels encountered icebergs, which both intrigued and concerned those on board. But almost nothing could dampen the passengers' enthusiasm as they anticipated their first sight of land.

"This morning at 6 o'clock the cry got up that there was land seen on our lee bow. At 8 o'clock it was quite visible." For the rest of the day, Hart and his companions waited anxiously to see if the *Carlton* would manage to round Cape Ray. The wind died, however, and at 11 o'clock that night Hart disappointedly recorded, "Still where we were." When he came on deck the next morning, he was gratified that the ship had "cleared the Cape" and they were "fully into the Gulf."[157]

Just the sight of North America was cause for celebration. "Saw land early this morning," Joseph Wilson recorded in mid-May 1831. After briefly describing the distant hills and rocks of Cape Breton, Cape North, and St Paul's Island ("a black and dreary looking place"), his diary entry concluded, "This was a very refreshing sight after having nothing but water around us for so long a time. We all rose early and got upon the deck to enjoy the prospect."[158] Aboard the *Friends* in 1830, "all hearts were cheered and ... spirits enlivened"[159] when the Peters and other passengers knew that Newfoundland was to the north and they could see the coast of Cape Breton. Certainly, Elizabeth Peters and her companions were aware that Quebec was still a considerable distance and could be weeks away. But as George Pashley commented, once on the Grand Banks, "We frequently looked for the Gulf" with "Longing Eyes and Rejoicing hearts."[160] Many ships' companies marked their safe arrival on the other side of the Atlantic with impromptu festivities. On board some ships there was "dancing and singing and capering about the Captain."[161] On the *Carlton*, passengers laughed and sang and took the opportunity to fish. William Peters and his companions thanked God: "Blessed be God, we are all well and they that love God are happy."[162]

As soon became apparent, the first sight of land did not mean that the emigrants' journey was over. Particularly for those bound for Quebec, there was still a considerable distance to travel through the Gulf and up the St Lawrence River. As John Steele discovered, contrary winds could mean it would be days or even weeks after arriving on the Grand Banks before passengers bound for New York docked. There may have been some comfort in knowing that they were no longer completely alone on the Atlantic. Sightings of fishing ships, coastal steamers, and other emigrant ships were now quite frequent. Moreover, there were still meals to be prepared, children to be watched and amused, and the ill to be nursed. On board the *Carlton*, measles continued to infect the children, and after one youngster died, Hart organized a burial at sea, despite the mother's wish "to keep" the body "till we went ashore."[163] In addition to the daily chores, women now took the opportunity, afforded by having a regular supply of fresh water, to wash clothes. In preparation for landing, many brought out needle and thread. Elizabeth Peters "prepared the frills" for her children and "a cap for herself."[164] John Hart "had a new coat made ... a first rater, a real good shooting coat, made in the top of the fashion."[165] Captains sometimes hove to and gave passengers an opportunity to fish.[166] Passengers were also often pressed into service to take a regular watch to ensure that the ship did not run aground or collide with the growing number of ships in the river. Male passengers aboard the *Resolution* helped the crew to take down the sails when they unexpectedly encountered a storm.

The arrival of the pilot to guide the ship safely upriver was a sure sign that the end of the voyage was in sight. Life on board now took on new rhythms. Emigrants took every opportunity to stand on deck and marvel at "any wonder," of which, as Elizabeth Peters commented, "there have been many." She found that "even a bird or a fly has been a object of surprise or wonder."[167] She and the family and neighbours gazed delightedly at what Joseph Wilson called "a very romantic country."[168] John Hart was pleased with the evidence of prosperity along the river's banks: "You never saw so fine a shore ... It is all houses and very fine spots." But Hart continued, six days after sighting land, "We are tired now lying all day doing nothing and so near our journey's end." He was therefore relieved when "the Captain called in the Committee and told us we were so near the Quarantine Station we would require to clean all our berths and wash all 'tween decks."[169]

In the 1830s and 1840s, all vessels bound for Quebec with fifteen or more passengers had to stop at Grosse-Ile for inspection. As the Langtons and Huttons discovered, U.S. authorities, too, had instituted a system to quarantine incoming passengers. In preparation for their inspection, passengers frantically washed bedding and clothes, cleaned berths, and generally made themselves presentable. Aboard the *Carlton*, there were still three children sick with the measles when they dropped anchor at Grosse-Ile. To the party's consternation, although they "had tumbled all [their] beds and bolsters and straw over board that all would be clean ... expecting to be in Quebec that night," the doctor, apparently not satisfied with conditions on board, ordered all ashore. "Well you may guess what kind of night we put in lying on the hard boards from the berths ... put up the same as they were in a ship."[170] The three families with ill children were placed in hospital, and the next day everyone else from the *Carlton* "commenced washing." After two nights on the island, the passengers were finally permitted to get underway again. Two days later they reached Quebec.

Not all passengers bound for Quebec had to participate in the general clean-up and inspection. Cabin passengers usually watched as "the steerage passengers were landed on the island to clean their clothes and bedding."[171] Some, like Susanna Moodie in the early summer of 1832, were invited to tour the island while they waited for the inspection to be over.[172] Catharine Parr Traill and her cabin companions – who arrived a few weeks later, when the colonial authorities had begun to appreciate the seriousness of the cholera epidemic – were not allowed ashore. "Nothing can exceed the longing desire I feel to be allowed to land," she wrote. "To all my entreaties the visiting surgeon who came on board returned a decided negative."[173] When the *Curler* arrived at New York in the middle of July 1828, John Steele and his family and the rest of the company were inspected by a surgeon who came on board. Steele reported with relief, "All well."[174] When Fanny Hutton and the children arrived in New York in mid-September 1834, the quarantine authorities "ordered" them "into the hospital" on Staten Island. Two of the children, Anne and Mary, were very ill with a fever.[175]

While Catharine Traill and her companions waited for clearance to proceed, three "emigrant ships" docked at Grosse-Ile. From the deck of the *Laurel*, Catharine and Thomas thought the scene was quite "pictur-

Quebec City, John Henry Walker, 1853 (MCM, M930.50.8.163)

esque." "You may imagine yourself looking on a fair or a crowded market," Catharine wrote. But even the Traills realized that a "nearer survey" revealed misery and want. As John Hart's party discovered, conditions at the quarantine station were sparse in the extreme, and it was often very crowded. Although emigrants could buy supplies from local merchants, Hart found that the provisioners took "advantage of you in the prices of everything" and many "cheated in weights and prices."[176]

Once released from quarantine, the *Carlton* took two more days to reach Quebec, and everyone on board was busy with last-minute preparations. As the river became increasingly crowded, with timber ships bound for Britain, steamers taking mail and goods to and from the Maritimes and south to the United States, and dozens of ships carrying emigrants to Quebec, the passengers became increasingly anxious to arrive.[177] "We expect to be in Quebec tomorrow," Hart wrote the day after leaving Grosse-Ile. "We are only ten miles from ... that long looked for place."[178] A few aboard the *Carlton* planned to disembark at Quebec to join friends, to try to find work and shelter, or to make their way south to the United States. Most were going on to Montreal and thence to the upper province, where they hoped to find friends or relations and to take up land or get work, which reports in the British press had promised was plentiful and lucrative. For everyone, however, Quebec was anticipated "with joyful expectations."[179]

"Weighed anchor this day at ½ past 9 o'clock," John Hart announced on 3 June. Then, rather prosaically, he recorded that the *Carlton* was "7 weeks from Port Glasgow." He continued: "The officers came on board and examined us all, we passed and all well. Went ashore brought in some fresh meat. Got the offer of a job. Did not take it. Went aboard."[180] Hart's journal entry belies the excitement, confusion, and often the bewilderment that emigrants experienced when first landing at Quebec. Many had dressed "themselves in full fluff for shore"[181] and were determined to take advantage of the opportunity to escape the constraints of the ship. Joseph Wilson spent his first afternoon ashore looking for friends and visiting a tavern.[182] George Pashley looked for work. When John Steele finally arrived at New York, he "wandered about for some hours" before returning to the *Curler* for one last night. He was obviously still concerned to maintain order among the passengers, and at one point he stepped into "a squabble (rather than a fight)" between two emigrants who "had got drunk" while on shore.[183]

Whether arriving at Quebec or New York, for most Irish, English, and Scottish emigrants, this was only their first stop in North America. Shortly before she landed, Elizabeth Peters looked forward to a new home. "I feel thankful to the All-Wise Disposer of Events," she wrote, "and I trust that God, who has brought us so far across the sea, will settle us on that part of the land which may mostly advance his course and glory and our interest."[184] But she still had a considerable distance to go before the family was settled. The Peters, like the Harts, Wilsons, and many other emigrants from Great Britain and Ireland, were bound for Upper Canada. Once John Hart had sorted out various administrative matters with the emigrant agent, he returned to the ship to get ready to take a steamer upriver. Joseph and Jenney Wilson also arranged passage on a steamer, the *Independence*, which would take them to Montreal. The Langtons and Huttons, who arrived in New York, had rather more to sort out. A steamer would take them to Albany, whence they would travel overland and by lake steamer to York, and from there move on to their final destination. George Pashley was not sure what he intended to do. He "did not much like the appearance of the Upper or Lower Town"[185] of Quebec, he recorded in his journal, and without friends or relatives in the colonies, he had to find work to support his family. But he had arrived in the New World, and at least this part of the journey was over.

The experiences of the ocean passage would continue to shape George Pashley's life and that of his companions for some considerable time.

"The Government Inspector's Office," *Illustrated London News* (MCM, M993X.5.1529.1)

For weeks, he and his family had lived in an isolated nether world; they had survived storms, bad food, cramped quarters, fear for life and limb, and considerable emotional tumult, including the tragedy of losing their daughter. It would be some time before the sharpness of these memories would recede and it would all seem "like a dream." Moreover, as George Pashley stood on the dock at Quebec, although that often terrifying physical isolation had been breached, the sense of being cut off, emotionally, from all that was familiar and dear remained strong. He and the thousands of others who left home between 1815 and 1845 were still emigrants when they arrived in the colonies. Although the transatlantic crossing marked an indelible transition in their lives, they were still attached to the world on the other side of the Atlantic, and this feeling would persist for months and often years. Moreover, as they tried to decide what to do next – and many eagerly anticipated reunions with family and friends – they carried with them identities that had been forged in cottages, workplaces, and villages and towns "at home." George Pashley, for example, was still a Yorkshireman and a devout Methodist. He was also a husband and father. Certainly, he and other emigrants had made new connections on board ship and could not help but be conscious that the experiences they had all shared set them apart from those they had left behind. But this new-found identity rested on old sensibilities and understandings of themselves and the world around them. Both would be essential in successfully negotiating this last part of the emigrants' world. And as many soon discovered, they still had a long way to go, physically and emotionally, before they could feel that they had finally "arrived."

CHAPTER FOUR

Into the "Strange Land"

The day after he arrived in Quebec, George Pashley recorded, "Perhaps it was kind Providence for us that the Ship was not reported Yesterday." Because the customs office had not examined the *Reward*'s cargo and thus passengers had not been able to unload their luggage, everyone had one more night on board. For the Pashleys, this provided them with an opportunity to decide what they would now do. The family had no money, and apart from their new-found friends from the *Reward*, they knew no one in Quebec. George needed to find work, but he soon discovered that "as the Winter Season has not set in," there was nothing to be had in Quebec. "I was at a loss what to do," he recorded, "but I believe the Lord put into my mind to ask one of our fellow Passengers (an Irish Protestant)" who had a brother in the Canadas, for a loan to cover the fare to Montreal. This "learned and cheerful, but kind dispositioned young man" agreed, to the Pashleys' "great joy," and once the *Reward* passed customs, George shepherded his family, along with their belongings, aboard the packet *Canadian Eagle*.

The *Eagle* drew into Montreal harbour a day and a half later. It was so late in the day that they "were permitted to remain on board another Night." George and his family were much relieved, for they were in a "strange land" without family to call on, and this one last night aboard ship provided them with a temporary haven from an unknown future. As George later recalled, "We had comfortable Births and were also safe at that strange to us and busy place."[1] The next morning, "the goodness of God" again intervened when their friend's brother took them to his home. George immediately sought out "our English Missionary" stationed in Montreal, who put him in touch with a member "of the Committee of the Emigrants' Relief Society." The Pashleys were judged to be

The Port of Montreal, 1830, Robert Auchmuty Sproule (MCM, M303)

"fit subjects of relief," and the committee agreed to pay for their passage to Prescott, Upper Canada. From there, they would have to make their own way into the colony. Since the family did not yet have the funds to repay their debt or to cover the cost of transporting their luggage to the upper province, they took temporary lodgings in Montreal and George found work. Ten days later, they had earned enough to proceed, and they took the next opportunity to sail to Prescott.

George Pashley's dilemma does not seem to have been unusual. Between 1815 and 1845, having spent almost all their resources on their passage, many emigrants who landed at Quebec or Montreal left the ship virtually penniless and not sure what to do next. While one part of the journey was complete – they had left home and were now in the New World – they had yet to find a place for themselves in this strange land. From their journals, it appears that the Pashleys and the Wilsons (who also seem to have had no immediate family in the colonies) had decided the best thing to do was to make their way to York, the capital of Upper Canada, to find work and a new home. For many others, the first priority was to try to track down family members or friends. When the Traills landed in Montreal – and when, a few years later, Thomas Langton and his family arrived in New York, for example – they knew where they were going and had the means to get there. The same is true of Ann Gemmill and Fanny Hutton. Others were not so fortunate.

View of the Harbour, Montreal, 1830, Robert Auchmuty Sproule (MCM, M21764)

Many had only the vaguest idea of where their kin actually lived, and as they began to appreciate how vast this new world was, and the difficulties of travel and communication, the euphoria of having survived the transatlantic crossing must have quickly given way to anxiety and dismay.

The first priority was to find a way to sustain themselves during their first few weeks in the colony. As George Pashley discovered, in some years the local labour market was inundated with new arrivals, and finding work in Quebec, Montreal, or settlements in Upper Canada could be difficult. Some turned to their travelling companions for help. Many sought out some connection to home – a local church that offered a familiar liturgy or a local ethnic organization whose members spoke in the same dialect, came from the same region, and offered fellowship and often material support. A growing number of emigrants received assistance from benevolent associations that had been established specifically to help "strangers in distress"; and, beginning in the 1830s, there were state-sponsored agencies that provided new arrivals (especially families with children and the old and infirm) with temporary lodging, food, and assistance to proceed upriver.

The liminal space between emigration and settlement – of having arrived but having not really yet arrived – was confusing and often frightening. Everyone who landed at Quebec, Montreal, or New York could not fail to realize that there was still a long way to go, physically and emotionally, before they would really reach the end of their journey. George Pashley – and many and perhaps most of those who left England, Ireland, and Scotland for the New World – relied on their faith in an omnipresent God to carry them through the uncertainties and fears for the future. George Pashley also discovered fellow travellers and settlers who, as Methodists and Yorkshiremen far from home, shared a common cause amidst the sea of strangers. And, of course, he and other emigrants continued to find reassurance and a sense of belonging in their identity within their families – as husbands and wives, fathers and sons, mothers and daughters, sisters and brothers.

"Fanny and the children arrived on the 17th after a most uncomfortable passage of 44 days," William Hutton reported to his mother in September 1834.[2] He had been waiting in New York since mid-August and must have been growing anxious. The family's reunion was anticlimactic. Two of the children, Mary and Anne, had taken a fever ten days before they landed, and Fanny was frantic with worry. Not only did his daughters, "both delerious, not know me at first," but William was dismayed that the whole trip had been a miserable experience. Fanny and the children had had "an abominable cabin," the food had been "very deficient both in quantity and quality," and the weather had been terrible. Although Fanny had not been "so tearful as I expected," he told his mother, she was still not reconciled to the family's move. "Every person thought I was mad not to return" to Ireland, Fanny had told him. Moreover, "her friends [had] pressed her very much to allow the children to remain home and she was sorry she did not." William was upset by Fanny's distress, but he remained determined. "I acted to the best of my judgement," he told his mother, and it was too late to change one's mind. "We ought to make the best of it and not judge too hastily," he continued. "The thing is done and it is nonsense to repine."[3]

In the short term, the Huttons' greatest concern was the health of their daughters. Both Mary and Anne were admitted to the emigrant hospital as soon as they landed in New York, and Fanny was provided by the authorities with lodgings close by. William took rooms "for the three other children and servant" and himself. It was expected that the two girls would not be well enough to travel for weeks, so William decided that he would go ahead with the luggage and most of the family; Fanny, with Mary and Anne, would follow later "in the most expeditious way." It is unlikely that Fanny had much choice in the matter. Having the whole family stay in New York was too expensive to contemplate, and the girls could not be left on their own. Thus, once again, Fanny had to cope alone. She had to negotiate the final stage of her journey – up the Hudson River, overland to Lake Ontario, and then by boat to Kingston – without her husband's help. It was not an auspicious beginning.

Despite Harriet Pengelly's difficulties with the voyage, she and Robert arrived in New York in 1835 in good health and anxious to proceed. Harriet's introduction to the New World was not particularly encouraging, however. To her dismay, she and Robert had to remain on their ship for another night after it docked, because "all the houses were full."[4] The couple spent the next day walking about the city, and that night they boarded the steamer for Albany. Although Harriet found the scenery "enchanting,"[5] and although they were travelling in relative comfort in the cabin, the two-and-a-half-week journey was a trial. She found the people "dirty and uncouth"; the accommodation on the steamer and later on the canal boat and at Albany and Oswego was, at best, "disagreeable"; and on the canal boat, "the Captain and crew abused us and we abused them, remained in the cabin, played cards & etc."[6] For Harriet, who was not yet reconciled to Robert's decision to emigrate, it was a journey "of misery and insults," and she was very lonely.[7] The only consolation was the companionship of some new friends (Miss Matthews, the Roys, and the Scobles) for part of the journey, and of her husband, "dear Robert."

Mary Gapper (O'Brien) and her mother, brother, and sister-in-law had quite a different experience after their arrival at New York in the summer of 1828. This may partly have been because Mary and her mother were not emigrants; they were visitors, and the trip was, from the beginning, an adventure. They intended to return to England after an extended stay with Mary's brothers in Upper Canada. "After coming to anchor and making arrangements with the custom house, we left the 'Warrior' with feelings of regret," Mary began her New World journal.[8] As they made their way along the dock, Mary was very conscious that she was in a foreign land: "I now felt for the first time that I was far away from home and all that makes home dear." Within a few hours, however, "the feelings of strangeness" disappeared. "Everything and everybody" in New York "looked so perfectly English,"[9] she declared.

After three and a half days in the city, during which time Mary and her brother got their luggage through customs and walked about town, the party commenced its "land journey."[10] A steamboat, with two hundred passengers, took them up the Hudson River to Albany; they then proceeded by stagecoach and canal boat to Lewiston, on the American side of Lake Ontario. It seems to have been a pleasant week's journey; but by the time they reached Lake Ontario, "which is my pathway to Bill [one of her brothers]," Mary was anxious to get on. The very next evening, they were "all seated around" her brother's fireplace, and her sister-in-law was "contriv[ing] without fuss to prepare beds for her sudden influx of guests."[11]

Thomas and Ellen Langton and their family followed the Gappers' path about ten years later, though they took considerably longer to reach their new home. First, they were delayed in New York because Ellen needed time to recover from the twenty-two-day voyage. After two weeks, the family began a leisurely journey by steam packet, railway, and canal boat to Lewiston. Although their various lodgings were, in Ellen's judgment, reasonably comfortable, she found the journey tiring. There was no rush, however. Their son John had written that their new home at Sturgeon Falls was not yet ready, so there was time to stop at Niagara Falls for their daughter Anne to do a little sketching, and once in York, to visit a new friend they had made on the Atlantic voyage.[12] The family still had to take the Lake Ontario packet to Port Hope and then travel to Rice Lake by coach. When they finally arrived in Peterborough, John was waiting for them.[13] Once again they were delayed; this time, it was Anne who was ill. After a pleasant eleven days in Peterborough meeting John's friends, it was with some trepidation that Ellen got into a small boat for the last part of their journey. It took two more days before John proudly led his parents "to his little habitation." The family's new house was still not ready. "All certainly look wild," Ellen Langton wrote, "but his little cottage ... promises snugness, but with primitive simplicity." She concluded her journal and the account of her journey: "If God in his mercy grant us health, we may be happy, free from many cares in this quiet retreat and may profit by it, waiting the next change with humble hopes of it being a blessed one."[14]

Catharine Parr Traill's journey into the interior of British North America was decidedly more uncomfortable. The Traills, like most emigrants from Great Britain and Ireland, had taken passage directly to the colonies. More significant was the fact that as the *Laurel* made its way up the St Lawrence in the summer of 1832, British North America was being ravaged by an outbreak of cholera. Health authorities advised the Traills not to disembark at Quebec, "as the mortality that still raged in

The St. Lawrence, at Montreal, William Henry Bartlett, 1841 (MCM, M16634)

the town made it very hazardous,"[15] so Catharine did not set foot on North American soil until they reached Montreal. She and her husband took rooms in the Nelson Hotel, intending to leave for Upper Canada the next day. Catharine had contracted cholera, however, and it was several days before she "was at last pronounced in a sufficient convalescent state"[16] to begin her journey. Over the next three weeks or so, the Traills made their way to Peterborough by coach, schooner, and wagon. At the end of most days, the couple found beds in a local inn or hotel, and Catharine sometimes was "dreadfully fatigued"[17] by the day's travel.

Catharine's diary often reads more like a traveller's or adventurer's account rather than that of a new emigrant. She frequently described in detail the characters she met along the way and "the bold forests" and "well cultivated settlements."[18] And the last leg of her trip to Peterborough is told as a journey into the wilderness – alone in the darkness, for a time "almost in despair."[19] The rich description and often romantic illusions are not particularly surprising, since only Catharine's published account has survived, rather than the original diary. But the personal journals of other well-heeled emigrants, like the Langtons and Frances Stewart who travelled by batteau from Montreal to Kingston in 1822, included lengthy descriptions of "the scenery," which they described as "most sublime and magnificent."[20] Although Frances Stewart found much of the journey upriver "monotonous" and the heat trying, she took the time to comment on what she considered the relative

Many emigrants would have shared C.J. Grant's sentiments about "Sailing up the St Laurence in an American Boiler – stored in a hold very like the black hole of Calcutta – all got a fit of the American Ague – Thermometer at 100," in "Emigration, Detailing the Progress and Vicissitudes of an Emigrant," 1833 (LAC, e000943153, PWC, R.9266-P1044)

prosperity and pleasing cottages of "established emigrants."[21] And like the Langtons, each time they arrived in a largish community, such as Kingston or York, the Stewarts took time to recover from the latest leg of their journey. They presented their letters of introduction to various local officials and spent a few days in a hotel or, at York, in a vacant house at the local barracks before proceeding.

Most new arrivals did not have the inclination or the financial resources to make this last leg of the journey a leisurely sojourn or to take the time to reflect on the scenery of this new world. Once they had landed in British North America, Joseph Wilson and his family were impatient to get to Upper Canada and start making a new home. Thus, Joseph organized a passage to Montreal within hours of arriving at Quebec, and the family, with all their luggage, boarded the steamboat, *Independence* the next day. To his dismay, Joseph discovered that in the rush, one "barrel of pots" had been left behind on their old ship. The family would need the pots when they finally arrived in Upper Canada, and Joseph "was at a great loss as to how to get them." Finally, "after a great deal of difficulty in the dark & a strong wind" against them, he and a new friend, who was also an emigrant, took a small boat and retrieved the barrel.[22]

The Wilsons spent less than two days in Quebec, and as the *Independence* made its way to Montreal they quickly discovered that the trials of the Atlantic voyage accompanied them. The *Independence* was crowded and the two-day trip from Quebec to Montreal was "uncomfortable." They had "a crew of dirty looking Irish" who were "a thievish set," according to Joseph, and he was "obliged to watch [their] goods upon deck all night."[23] Moreover, the steamer's progress was slow, and before it reached Montreal a child had died from fever. The day-and-night stay at Montreal offered little respite. Most of the time, Joseph was busy unloading luggage onto the wharf and then reloading it onto the smaller durham boats that would take the family to Prescott. It was tiring work, made more difficult by the confusion of hundreds of other emigrants milling about – and also by the weather. It became very hot, and by the end of the day, many in the party "suffered very much having the skin burned off their faces, noses and their eyes swell[ed] like the sting of a bee."[24] But the fine weather was an advantage once they finally cast off, because the open boats ("an extremely tedious mode of travelling") would have offered no shelter in a rainstorm.[25] Once the Wilsons arrived at Prescott, their luggage again had to be unloaded and the family had to wait for the Queenston steamboat to arrive.

Joseph was not particularly impressed with his first encounter with Upper Canada. Prescott was "a very shabby nasty place," he thought, and many of the residents were "a pack of sharpies ... & a drunk beastly set of people."[26] The two days aboard the Lake Ontario steamer, which was "so crammed full that [they] could not rest either night or day," was a further trial. But they finally "entered the bay" and arrived at York. "I never saw such confusion as attended our landing," Wilson recounted. "People from the shore rushed in ... so we could not get our luggage landed without the greatest hazard and difficulty. The sailors in the boat and other superiors were the most uncivil and disobliging scoundrels we had met with in all our travels." For the Wilsons – tired, bewildered, and in need of work – the only redeeming feature of their arrival in the Upper Canadian capital was when "a gentlemen on the wharf very kindly presented us with a ticket for lodging in the emigrant buildings."[27] The family had a comfortable night in the sheds. Joseph found work the next day, and the Wilsons were able to rent two rooms of their own. The voyage was at last over, and Joseph ended his journal with the

Lachine Canal, Lachine, QC, James Duncan, ca. 1850 (MCM, M984.273)

words: "Here we are resting comfortably after a long and fatiguing journey, having traveled almost 4100 miles. End."[28]

George Pashley encountered rather more difficulties finding his place in Upper Canada, and his journal illustrates how changing circumstances and chance encounters often determined where new arrivals ended up. Like Joseph Wilson, Pashley and his wife were skilled artisans, but like so many other emigrants they quickly discovered that work was not as easy to come by as they had expected. The Pashleys were forced to rely on "the goodness of God," the advice of new-found friends, and the assistance of local emigrant organizations to ease their passage. During the five days and nights it took them to reach Prescott, they were in the company of almost sixty other emigrants who hailed from all over the British Isles. The cosmopolitan nature of the passengers was not lost on George Pashley, who carefully recorded his companions' places of origin. There was a second family from Yorkshire as well as families from Scotland, Nova Scotia, Nottinghamshire, and Lincolnshire, he noted in his journal. The rest were "from Ireland," which George did not find particularly pleasant. Some of them were "filthy enough," he commented, including "an old man of 81 years of age by his own account, but almost lost in filth and dirt."[29] Given George Pashley's sentiments about the Irish, he was not surprised by the state of these emigrants. He was, however, concerned: "It was impossible for us to escape getting some of the Greybacks on us." Like many new emigrants, the Pashleys' sensibilities of the Old World accompanied them to the New.

Throughout the journey upriver, each night the family slept either on the shore or on the bateau. It was a "tedious journey," which George and some of his fellow passengers tried to hasten by periodically helping pull the boat upstream. It took almost a week to reach Prescott, and there the family boarded a steamer bound for Cobourg. This part of the journey was "a fine voyage," but because of the head winds, they did not reach their destination until after 10 PM.

The Pashleys had made the decision to stop at Cobourg only after they had left Montreal. "We had always intended to make York our landing place, or starting point for to seek out a resting place in Canada," George noted in his journal; but their plans had changed when, at Prescott, the family had struck up an acquaintance with a Mr Hancock, a painter and Methodist, who "gave a favourable account of Cobourg." Although Hancock had himself been in the colony only three weeks (having arrived from the United States), the Pashleys obviously trusted his judgment. Hancock offered to share his accommodation until the family could get settled.

The Pashleys' first few weeks in Cobourg were difficult. George had problems finding work and was forced to accept another loan, and the family became increasingly uncomfortable with their shared lodgings. Mrs Hancock did not seem to have approved of her husband's arrangements; moreover, George was upset by her behaviour. Mrs Hancock had become a member of the Methodist Church before leaving the United States, but George judged that she "was a Misrable Backslider." He commented: "The Backslider in heart shall be filled with his own ways and the state of that man is worse than the first." After two weeks, the Pashleys took a single room let by a fellow Yorkshireman, the local baker and confectioner, who was from Whitby. "We had little of the Comforts of life, as it regards food," George wrote. "I have very little work, but the Lord whom I serve can supply all Our need and tho he suffered our Patience to be tried He did in his own good time grant us necessary food."[30] Gradually, George and his wife found some piecework and were able to repay their debts. George was asked to preach at a local meeting. Here again, "the Hand of a Kind Providence" intervened.[31] Connections made at the meeting provided George with more customers, and he soon had steady work tailoring. He and his family were quickly integrated into the local Methodist community. "We were welcomed by all our new neighbours and encouraged," he remarked. And even though, in his judgment, many members of the class "were in a low state of grace," he and his wife clearly appreciated their new friends' "cheerful and welcome reception and the Right hand of Fellowship as Christians, Friends and Neighbours."[32] After their more than three-month journey from Manchester, the Pashleys had begun to re-establish ties of friendship and faith and to build a new home.

The difficulties confronted by the Traills, Wilsons, and Pashleys pale in comparison with the troubles many new arrivals encountered on their way to the interior. During the height of the annual emigrant season, new arrivals landed in the midst of chaos. The docks were always crowded; lodging was sometimes difficult if not impossible to find; and as at home, there were any number of locals who were willing to take advantage of the newcomers. In 1831 and 1832, and again in the early 1840s, the local press reported emigrants sleeping on the streets, surrounded by their luggage. Periodically, the press condemned "the impositions" perpetrated on emigrants by unscrupulous colonists. Innkeepers and provisioners regularly overcharged for their services, petty thieves preyed on the unwary, and forwarders tried to entice new arrivals to take passage on their boats with promises of cheap fares and an impossibly quick passage. Others simply absconded with emigrants' funds or intentionally misdirected emigrants about where to go and how best to get there. It was not unusual for new arrivals to find themselves in Upper Canada but hundreds of miles from their intended destination and having to backtrack at considerable cost.[33] By the early 1830s, the colonial authorities had appointed a number of agents to assist emigrants and had established a rudimentary network of state aid for "worthy" recipients, including women and children. But their resources were limited, and many new arrivals had to manage on their own.

Once emigrants had negotiated their arrival, they soon discovered that the trip upriver could be dangerous and debilitating. Individuals were injured or died as a result of accidents on the durham boats and lake steamers. Newspapers frequently reported the "melancholy death" of youngsters who fell overboard and drowned or individuals who were injured by rolling cargo or hurt while trying to get off a pitching ship. Precious luggage was often lost, stolen, or inadvertently left behind.[34] More seriously, family members were often separated, and their companions had to carry on as best they could without them. As the "information wanted" notices illustrate, many new arrivals had considerable difficulty coping with what they presumed was this last leg of their journey. It must have made many wonder, yet again, if they had made the right decision.

Henry Anderson, with his wife Elizabeth and their children, emigrated from England in the summer of 1828. When they landed in Montreal, they needed to purchase supplies for the rest of the journey to Upper Canada. Having arranged with a Mr Fanning that he would take the family to Belleville, where they intended to settle, Henry and Elizabeth went to find provisions, leaving their two oldest children at the boat. For some reason, Fanning decided to set off with the children on board before the Andersons had returned. Henry "pursued on foot," overtook the boat at Lachine, and "got on board." But Elizabeth, with a baby in her arms, could not keep up, and she was "left behind." There was nothing for her to do but take the next available boat to Prescott, and from there she "made her way to Belleville." To her dismay, the family seemed to have disappeared. When she found Fanning, he told her he had left the family in Kingston, and she immediately returned there, expecting they would be waiting for her. A month later, Elizabeth, was "in a distressed situation," and as her appeal to the public stated, she was "anxious to hear from" her husband or where he might be.[35]

Robert Rumsby, of Reland in Suffolk, found himself in a similar situation a few years later. He and his wife and six children had been making their way to Kingston when the steamboat *Queenston*, on which they had taken passage, ran aground. The family went ashore and somehow were separated. When Robert returned to the vessel, "expecting to find his wife on board," he was startled to discover that the vessel had already got underway. He made his way to Kingston, but there was still no trace of them. "She is supposed to be with the family of Dusenetts, who also went ashore at the same place," he explained in his notice to the public. And he proposed "to remain at Kingston until he obtain[ed] some information about his wife and children."[36]

Such mishaps may have been quite common. More frequently, however, it seems that families consciously decided, for one reason or another, that one or more of them would go ahead and the others would join them later. Many, like the Huttons, were reunited without any particular difficulty. Others were not so fortunate. In 1819 Mrs Graham was frantic. She and her husband had left Ireland that summer for Upper Canada. When they got to "La Chine," John Graham "sent his wife forward" by coach to Kingston, intending to "follow by water." Perhaps Mrs Graham was finding the journey particularly trying; or perhaps the couple were concerned that their luggage would be lost if it was not attended, and it was too expensive to ship by land. For whatever reason, Mrs Graham went ahead and waited for John to arrive. But after a month she was getting desperate, and she placed a notice "to request any person who may be acquainted with the circumstances" of her husband to write to her in Kingston. She had "long been anxiously looking for" him, she wrote, and needed to know "whether he is still living or where he is to be found."[37] In 1832 Mrs Huston and her child "lost" her husband. When the family arrived in Prescott, for some reason – perhaps the child or its mother was ill – Mrs Huston had stayed for a time at Mr Boss's, and her husband Samuel went ahead. When she finally arrived in Kingston, Samuel was nowhere to be found.[38]

Such scenarios or variations on this theme were replayed time and again in the 1820s, 1830s, and 1840s. The trip from Quebec or Montreal to the upper province could be costly. It appears that one of the primary reasons why emigrant families became separated after they arrived in the colonies was that, like the Pashleys, they did not have sufficient funds to cover the cost of the last leg of the journey. In such cases, one member of the family, usually the head of the household, would look for work while the rest of the family either joined relatives already in the colony or took cheap lodgings and waited. But as the information notices and the records of emigrant agents indicate, those left behind were often in a difficult situation, and sometimes a family member was "lost." When the Hanagan family, who had just arrived from Scotland, reached Prescott in July 1834, Patrick Hanagan decided to go and find work and sent his wife and children up the lake to join her cousins. The couple arranged that Patrick would soon join them. But by the end of August, Mrs Hanagan still had had no word of him, and she anxiously asked the public for its help.[39] Similarly, Richard Thomson and his wife and three children, who landed in Montreal from Bedfordshire, England, three years later, decided that once the family reached Prescott, Mrs Thomson and the children would go on to Bytown and Richard would try to find work. When Mrs Thomson became very ill two weeks later, some newfound friends in Bytown were forced to ask the public to help find Richard or at least to inform him of his wife's condition.[40]

The situation could become even more complicated when one or more members of a party fell ill on the journey. If it was during the Atlantic crossing, family members and friends did what they could to nurse those who came down with measles, smallpox, ague, or cholera. On arrival at the quarantine station at Grosse-Ile, the colonial authorities intervened. In the 1830s and 1840s, any new arrival with a fever – or, during the height of the cholera epidemics in 1832 and 1834, with even the slightest symptom of an infectious disease – was refused entry into the colonies.[41] If it was a child who was ill, often the whole family (like those who were part of John Hart's party in 1841) were separated from the rest of the group and isolated in an attempt to stop the spread of infection. If it was an adult, she or he was admitted to the emigrant hospital, and usually the rest of the party would carry on. Most new arrivals had calculated the cost of their trip carefully and could not afford to break their journey before they reached their intended destination. Being forced to leave a family member or friend behind was often unavoidable. Some, like the family of Rachel Bell, who arrived from "the Parish of Faun, County Donegal" in 1836, did not seem particularly concerned. Rachel arrived in the colonies in the company of her sister and brother-in-law but was placed in quarantine at Grosse-Ile, and the rest of the party carried on without her. Not until seven years later did the couple try to re-establish contact with Rachel![42] For most, however, such a separation was heart-rending, and they were faced with the dilemma of how and when they would be reunited in this strange land. As the "information wanted" notices illustrate, a number of emigrants became lost in the shuffle.

For example, when Timothy Marrah and his wife and two sisters, all from Killarney, landed at Grosse-Ile in July 1837, Johanna, Timothy's wife, was ill and was immediately placed in the hospital there. Timothy and his sisters went on to Montreal and then upriver to Upper Canada. Johanna followed later, expecting to join them. To her dismay, she "could learn no tidings of" Timothy after the rest of the family had left Montreal. Undeterred, she went on alone to St Catharines, in the western part of Upper Canada. A month later she was still looking for her party or for information of where they had ended up.[43] Elizabeth Halton was in a somewhat different situation in 1832. Soon after the family's arrival in British America, she and her children fled Quebec "in consequent of cholera." The family arranged that her husband would join them once his business was complete. Nine months later he still had not appeared, and Elizabeth was growing increasingly fearful. As a last resort, she "appealed" to the public for their assistance in finding him.[44]

For the Cameron family of Scotland, the 1832 cholera epidemic brought disaster. Hugh Cameron and his family had left Scotland that summer, apparently intending to join his brother Alexander and his family, who had emigrated earlier in the season. Although it was the height of the cholera epidemic when the Camerons arrived in Quebec, all seemed well until the family reached Prescott. Then Hugh "was unfortunately seized with cholera while coming up the Lake" and died. Since his wife and children were "totally unprovided for," all she could do was try to find her brother-in-law, who she thought had planned on settling "somewhere in the Township of Cavan." And to do this, she asked the public for their assistance.[45]

John Whelan found himself in a comparable situation a few years later. In 1836 he, his wife Ellen Clancy, and their infant children had left County Cork to join her two brothers, John and David, who had emigrated to Upper Canada "some four years past." Ellen died on the voyage; the family had little choice but to carry on. When John and the children arrived in Kingston, he was desperate. According to the notice placed some months later by the local emigrant agent, John Whelan had been destitute, and without a wife to care for his infant children he could not leave them to look for work. John had gone to the emigrant agent, A. Manahan, to ask for assistance, and Manahan had engaged a local woman, Mary Daly, to care for the infants while John went to find work. This was supposed to be only a temporary measure, but two month later John still had not come back to retrieve his children. He, too, may have succumbed to an illness; or he may have absconded, deciding to leave the children behind. Manahan's notice was silent on this issue. It did, however, declare, "The children are destitute" and "the uncles are requested to come speedily to their assistance."[46]

Many emigrants turned to local authorities for help when they arrived alone and desperate. For the most part, Upper Canadians welcomed their compatriots from England, Ireland, and Scotland; and most communities of any size in British America – especially those that received emigrants on their way into the colony – had set up committees or organizations to help them and in some cases had build facilities to meet the needs of the new arrivals.[47] In the early part of the period, assistance was rather ad hoc and was provided by private benefactors. As the number of emigrants grew, local resources were often overwhelmed, however, and colonial legislatures, with assistance from London, began to subsidize and formalize the assistance.[48] By the 1830s, a network of societies and government agents had been put in place to help emigrants move onto the land, find work, and be reunited with family and friends. Emigrant societies also began to provide new arrivals with temporary shelter, provisions, medical assistance, and the cost of their passage upcountry.[49] When the Wilsons arrived in York, their one night in the emigrant sheds gave them the opportunity to recover from their journey and gather themselves before looking for work. And George Pashley and his family were certainly not the only new arrivals whose passage to Upper Canada was subsidized by the Montreal Emigrant Society.

For a number of new arrivals, such assistance seems to have been viewed as another form of parish assistance. John Whelan certainly took this view. So did Alexander McDonald, a Scottish tailor. He and his father-in-law, Donald Calahan, arrived in Upper Canada in July 1832. At Prescott, the pair decided that Alexander would go on ahead "with the intention to settle on lands" and Donald, who apparently was "a very old man," would stay behind at the emigrant sheds. After a month relying on the local agent for shelter, Donald may have become restive. Certainly, the emigrant agent grew concerned when there was still no word from Alexander. To facilitate the pair's reunion (and undoubtedly to free up space in the shed), the agent asked the authorities in the colonial capital for their assistance in finding "any information respecting the said Alexander."[50] When David Little and his wife and six children arrived in Montreal a few years later, they too turned to the colonial authorities for assistance. The family had exhausted all their resources, and Mrs Little and the children stayed in the emigrant sheds while David went ahead "to seek employment in Kingston." Soon after David left, the Montreal Emigration Society decided to send the rest of the family to Kingston. But when they arrived, David was not to be found, and Mrs Little and the children again relied on the local emigrant agent for shelter and to help find her husband.[51] When Mrs Redman stopped in Kingston after she and her husband had been separated at Grosse-Ile in July 1840, she contacted agent Manahan for help in finding him.[52]

Sometimes, emigrants turned to a local agent for assistance months after they had first arrived in North America. Michael Hennesey and his family emigrated to Upper Canada in the summer of 1836 and made their way to Cornwall. Michael then went off to find work, leaving his wife and three children behind. It is not known how Mrs Hennesey coped throughout the following winter. Perhaps she took a position as a domestic; perhaps the family had arrived with enough to keep her and the children for a time while they waited for Michael's return; or perhaps, in the company of other women and children, she remained in the care of the local emigrant society. Whatever the case, by the following summer she was becoming desperate. On her behalf, the agent at Kingston placed a notice in the local paper stating, "His family ... are in absolute want and it will be deemed a charity of any person knowing" Michael Hennesey "if they inform Mr Manahan, Emigrant Agent at Kingston, of his residence."[53]

One can only wonder how Mrs Hennesey, Donald Calahan, and Mrs Little coped and what they thought as they waited for husbands, sons, or other family members to come and collect them. Certainly, for some, having one member of the household go ahead was a conscious strategy of settlement. In many ways, it was a variant of the arrangement that families such as the Gemmills had made back home in Scotland, whereby one member went ahead to "spy out the land" or find work, and the rest of the family relied on either relatives or local charity until the family could be reunited. As a report in one Upper Canadian newspaper stated in 1828 (and as is intimated in some of the "information wanted" notices), wives were often given little or no choice in the matter and "were in absolute ignorance of the movements and actual sojourn of the husband."[54] Being abandoned while at home, surrounded by other kinfolk or friends in a familiar setting, was one thing; to be abandoned in a strange land, without any network of support other than the charity of strangers, was quite another. Even women who had agreed to what they assumed would be a temporary separation must have been anxious; as the days passed into weeks and, in many cases, months, anxiety turned to dismay and then to despair.

Although one report stated that it was "an extremely common practice" among emigrants for husbands to leave their families to the care of others ("trusting that a deserted and helpless family [would] be regularly provided for" by local charity groups), Mrs Hennesey, Mrs Little, and others in such circumstances could not have been happy about the situation. They knew that although colonists willingly offered assistance to the "worthy," this was only temporary. It was assumed that new arrivals would stay in the emigrant sheds for only a short while, and they were then expected to find work and lodgings of their own. For emigrant women with young children, this was often difficult or even impossible. In the 1830s and 1840s, government agents had a mandate to assist widows, wives and children in such circumstances, but for those whose husbands had absconded and who had no other family in the colony, the consequences could be devastating. Often, children were bound out to local families while their mothers tried to find work. Some emigrants ended up begging on the streets; others stayed as long as they could in the emigrant sheds and then, in the late 1830s and 1840s, took shelter in a local "house of industry."[55]

Many, and perhaps most, new arrivals were more fortunate. They had family members or friends already settled in the colony to whom they expected to be able to turn for assistance. Many, like Ann Gemmill or

Entrance to Toronto (Ontario) (LAC, C1023)

Catharine and Thomas Traill, arrived with detailed instructions about where these connections lived and how best to proceed once they had landed at Quebec or Montreal. For example, when George Forbes, that young Scotsman who arrived in Upper Canada in 1845, landed in Quebec, he immediately headed for York and the home of his cousin, Alexander Forbes (though he took a circuitous route by way of Montreal, Kingston, and Bytown). George seems to have had no problem finding Alex. But by the time he arrived in Toronto some weeks later, he was very pleased to be able to "stop" with his cousin. "I got out of my clothes for the first time since I left the St. Lawrence [and] got a sound sleep," George reported to his parents. "Alex and his wife have been very kind to us," he continued, and he obviously appreciated the welcome.[56]

A fortunate few were actually met at the docks as they disembarked. George Pashley's shipmate and friend "GA" (who had initially lent Pashley the fare to Montreal) was concerned when his brother was not waiting for him when the steamboat landed in Montreal. He was "readily found" the following day, however, and carried his brother and the Pashleys off to his house.[57] Finding a waiting family member amidst the confusion of the docks was made all the more difficult when family members had not seen each other for some time. When John Counel arrived in Montreal in 1845, he almost missed his brother altogether. It had been so long since John had seen him, he admitted, "I would not really have recognized him."[58] Colonist Patrick Shirreff, who travelled on Lake Ontario with a party of Scots, remarked that their meeting with friends in York was "an interesting sight": "A group of Scotch-Highlanders, consisting of old women and half a dozen innocent looking girls, incapable of speaking the language, appeared in ecstasy at joining their friends on the pier."[59] In 1833, when the Petworth emigrant James Rapson's brother William and his family joined them in Upper Canada, their reunion was cause for celebration. As James reported to his father, "They came all unexpectedly, as I have not had a letter for a long time." He had not known "any thing of it," he said, until he "saw William coming, now a quarter of a mile before he came to our house; and he held up his hat." James knew him right away, he told his father. "But I could not believe my eyes for some time: but I was highly pleased to see them and especially as they are all so well."[60]

Not all new arrivals had such happy reunions. For example, in July 1843 Thomas Wilson went to Bytown to meet his wife and children, who were arriving from County Donegal. Somehow they missed each other, and Mrs Wilson and the children ended up in Pembroke. As their notice in the local paper explained, they now had no idea where Thomas was and asked the public's assistance in finding him.[61] Given the difficulties of communication and transportation once emigrants had arrived in the colony, it is surprising that this type of situation did not occur more often. When it did, anxious colonists often began their own search. In August 1832, for example, Jane and Margaret Magee were bewildered when their cousin Andrew did not arrive. They thought he had landed safely at Quebec, but then he seemed to have disappeared.[62] Mrs McNally was "extremely anxious" in August 1831 when two friends from home, Mary Ellen and Robert Lowden, did not appear in Newcastle. Somehow, Mrs McNally knew that the couple "had landed in Quebec June last." Her "information wanted" notice was directed to the Lowdens themselves, who were "earnestly requested ... to inform their friends of their present situation." Mrs McNally added, "Should they be detained by want of money, it shall be sent to them."[63] In 1839 Mrs Phillips of Cobourg was initially surprised when her sister Catherine Burns did not appear at her door. She then became increasingly "anxious." Since Catherine had landed at Quebec "about a year ago and has not since she arrived there been heard of," Mrs Phillips finally decided to turn to the public for its assistance in finding her.[64]

More frequently, it was the new arrivals who appealed to the public for help in locating family members who were already in the colony. In 1842 Susan Whitcraft, who was "supposed to be living in Kingston," was told in a public notice that her sister Jane and her brother-in-law had just arrived and were waiting for her at the emigrant shed.[65] Once he got to Kingston in the late summer of 1841, Michael Riordan announced in the press that he would stay put until he heard from his brother John, who had left home "some years before."[66] When Mrs Robert Morris and her three children made their way from England to Cornwall, Upper Canada, in the summer of 1837, they were in a more difficult situation. They expected that Robert, a schoolteacher, would be waiting for them. But as their information notice stated, they were disappointed to discover that he "had left that place in July last": "It is supposed that he is now living somewhere in the London District." All they could now do was find lodgings and wait "to hear from him as they do not know where he resides." Mrs Morris's notice to the public concluded, "Any person knowing him will please inform him that Mrs Morris is now at Lane's Hotel, Cornwall."[67]

It appears from the notices in local newspapers that many new arrivals were "expected" by husbands or siblings who had gone to look for land. In 1819, for example, a card in a local York paper asked Robert Happer to "take note" that his wife Ann had arrived.[68] In 1843 Thomas Wright's family were surprised when he was not at the wharf to meet them, as they were "expected from Ireland."[69] A year later, Mrs Thomas Wilson arrived to "meet" her husband, who had left Ballysuggart, County Donegal, in 1842. She was "disappointed" that he had left Pembroke the previous July, and she stated in her notice that she would be "greatful to any persons giving any intelligence of him."[70]

When a reunion was unexpectedly delayed, emigrants coped as best they could. In 1832 Ellen Fleming probably looked for work soon after her arrival in York while she looked for her sister Margaret, "who emigrated last year" and was "supposed to have come to" York "or somewhere near it."[71] Sarah McCulloch left home in Ireland in 1833 to join her sister Esther, who had left home three years before. The family had obviously kept in touch with Esther, and Sarah knew that her sister had lived for a time in Belleville and had then "moved on to the Trent." When Sarah arrived, she immediately made her way to Cobourg, and when she could not find her sister, she may well have taken a position in the community. She anxiously asked the public and specifically "housekeepers in the village and vicinity" to "please make enquiry among their Irish domestics" for news of Esther.[72]

Emigrants with some means sometimes took lodgings in a local boarding house or hotel while they waited for a husband or other family member to arrive. Mrs Michael McKeny took a room in Mrs Pearson's National Hotel in Kingston in September 1843 while she looked for her husband Michael, a turner by trade, who had sailed from Liverpool the previous year and was now "supposed to be in Kingston or its vicinity."[73] Mrs Kent stayed at the Red Lion Inn in Toronto while she looked and waited for her husband William. She hoped that her "notice [might] meet his eye, or that of some person who can give her some information respecting him."[74]

Many new arrivals did not have the resources to stay in a hotel or were determined not to expend precious funds that could be better used later. Instead, like families separated on the journey, they called on the assistance of local emigrant agents to find husbands, brothers, sisters, or friends. In 1837 Mrs Neil Horkan, for example, turned to the agent in Kingston to help her find her husband.[75] In 1840 Mrs William Banks and her four children sought shelter from the Kingston Emigration Committee while they tried to find her husband William. Part of Mrs Banks's problem was that she was not really sure where he was. He had left home three years before and was "supposed to be near Toronto."[76] That same year, Mrs Barker and her three children sought help in finding their husband and father.[77] Between 1836 and 1845, one of the priorities of local emigration was to assist "widows, orphans or women and children who [had] immigrated with the intention of joining their relatives or friends" and who did not have the funds to proceed.[78] For many emigrants who arrived bewildered, often exhausted, and without financial resources, such assistance was invaluable.

Not all – and perhaps not even most of – the Irish, Scottish, and English emigrants who arrived in Upper Canada between 1815 and 1845 relied on the colonial authorities for assistance. Moreover, it is likely that many arrived unannounced, especially in the case of a brother or sister who had decided to join a sibling in the New World. In 1831 Norry Shorancy wished to "obtain information of a relative of hers," John Dosman, "a Carpenter and Wheelwright, who left Limerick County about five years since."[79] Ann Bleakney arrived from Cloyn, Ireland, in 1832, looking for her sister Margaret, who had left home about eleven years earlier. Ann knew that Margaret had married a man who had been in service in Quebec, and she believed that Margaret was "living on a farm in Upper Canada."[80] Charles McCarty began to look for his brother John and his cousin Dennis Driscoll soon after he arrived in Cobourg in 1842. The pair had left the parish of Skibreen, County Cork, "about 23 years ago." Charles asked editors in Canada and the United States to "please give the above a few insertions," adding that "any information respecting [them] will be thankfully received."[81] For young and single Scottish, English, and Irish men and women, the presence of a brother, sister, or distant kin in Upper Canada probably provided them with at least an initial destination, and it was undoubtedly one of the factors that had influenced their decision to leave home in the first place. But the tone of their "information wanted" notices suggests that although most of them clearly wanted to resume the relationship, their expectations were quite low. Mary Dwyer, for instance, who arrived in the colony in 1836, began to look for her brother Richard only after she had established herself in Newmarket. Richard, she explained to the public, had left Tipperary some time ago; more significantly, the family had not heard from him in five years. Mary was "anxious to find out where he is."[82] She may have wondered if he was still alive.

For many new arrivals, the search for family members had a tone of urgency. By the time Mary Duffy and her five children arrived in Upper Canada in 1829 from County Kerry, they were "in a distressed situation" and dismayed that John, "who had emigrated to Quebec" two years earlier, was not there to meet them.[83] Mary Donnelly seems to have used all her resources just to get to the New World. When she arrived in Kingston in 1835 to join her brother Patrick, who had sailed from Belfast "twelve years last May," she was "afflicted." Her problem was compounded by the fact that all she knew was that Patrick was "supposed to be somewhere in the state of New York, if not the city."[84] Benjamin Booth was "anxious" to find his sister Elenor, who had emigrated three years before.[85]

Wives arriving to join their husbands often seem to have been in financial difficulties when they arrived. In 1831 a notice appeared in a Kingston paper from "the distressed wife and family" of William McIndoe.[86] Three years later, Mary Jane Machogan and her infant son were "disconsolate" and "in a very destitute state" when she could not find her husband.[87] And Mrs Flin was at her wits' end when she arrived looking for her husband William, a cooper, in September 1843. Her notice to the public was "the last resource of his dejected wife,"[88] she said. Parents who had followed their children also were often dejected when they could not find them. James Pickering's "aged" father John arrived in 1820, and all he knew was that James was supposed to be "in the vicinity of Kingston."[89] When Michael Carey's parents arrived in 1841, they were "most anxious" and "distressed" when they could not find him.[90] Elizabeth Hetherington was dismayed when she could not find her son Michael, whom she had followed to the colony in 1832. "Any person acquainted with him," she announced, "would serve the cause of humanity by letting him know that his mother is at the house of Mr James Botfield, Matilda, U.C. and wishes him to write or come to her immediately."[91]

We have no idea if most of those who sought the public's help – or those who turned to an emigrant society or local agent for assistance – found their friends or kin. It is likely that at least some of those named in the "information wanted" notices did not want to be found. The world of emigration had offered many the opportunity to escape familial obligations, and some were not about to assume responsibility for someone – even a brother, sister, or parent – whom they had not seen for years. Others were quite willing to have others assume responsibility for their wives and children. What is clear, however, is that for a great many people, the anticipated reunion was an extremely important part of the process of emigration, both for those who were leaving home and for those whom they hoped to join. To those who were already relatively settled in the colony, the arrival of family and friends from "home" was a vitally important link to their "old" lives, and it helped assuage some of the "strangeness" which many continued to feel as they established themselves in Upper Canada. For those just off the boat, knowing that even a very distant family member lived on this side of the Atlantic (and perhaps was waiting for them to arrive) provided a measure of reassurance as they made the last leg of that difficult trip to Upper Canada. It also confirmed that they had a place in this strange land, one that rested on their ongoing relationship to kin and old communities.

Whether their arrival ended in a joyous reunion or in the disappointment and dejection that accompanied the realization that, for whatever reason, family members and friends were "lost," or whether it culminated in the uncertainly that must have haunted those, like the Pashleys, who on the face of it were "alone" in the New World, the physical journey of emigration did come to an end. Gradually, emigrants became settlers. The Pashleys and the Wilsons found work and became part of a new community; the Gemmills, Andrew Scott and his family, the Huttons, the Traills and even the Pengellys took up land and began to "settle in." Eventually the experiences of the journey, including that last very difficult few weeks (or months) into the strange land, did begin to seem like a dream – though often one with decidedly nightmarish qualities that were not soon forgotten. However, the realization that one had finally "arrived" in Upper Canada did not mean that an individual had left the emigrants' world completely behind. For many, the sense of being an emigrant – of living in two worlds yet in neither – persisted for some considerable time. These new emigrant settlers took their experiences of the journey with them as they gradually became integrated into new communities; and they continued to rely on relationships made during the journey to help them negotiate the future. And while they looked forward to a better life for themselves and their children, they continued to look back to "home." Emigrant settlers consciously depended on their identities as Scots, English, Irish, and Welsh. Although some were determined to reinvent themselves, most of them determinedly clung to their status as gentlefolk or skilled workers. Many clung to their faith, and as the "information wanted" notices attest, they still identified themselves with a specific village or town in the Old Country. Most importantly, emigrant settlers saw themselves primarily as husbands and wives, parents and children, siblings and cousins. The world of emigration rested on and helped to sustain these familial and community networks. It also created vital transatlantic communities, ones that both new arrivals and well-established settlers were determined to maintain.

CHAPTER FIVE

Transatlantic Webs of Kin and Community

When young Harriet Pengelly finally arrived in Upper Canada, she was exhausted, bewildered, and miserable. The difficult voyage from Plymouth to New York had been followed by a slow and disagreeable journey by way of Albany and Oswego to Toronto and then west to Flamborough. "Alas! What am I come to! My heart is breaking with grief," she wrote at the end of May 1835.[1] She was almost overwhelmed by "the dirt and misery"[2] of their new lodgings; and while Robert travelled about looking for land, she was desperately lonely. "I feel very low in spirits, would I were home," she cryptically reported after a week in the colony.[3] The arrival of the first letters from home was bittersweet: "I am still very low. Wept when I read Sophy's and Uncle Irving's kind letters, such prayers for my happiness, dear friends may God bless you all."[4] To help her assuage her sense of alienation and, when Robert was away, her feeling of being "all alone in this second Siberia,"[5] Harriet reached across the Atlantic. She frequently wrote to sister Sophy and to other friends and relations in Guernsey. When not writing, she was thinking of her "absent friends";[6] and when letters arrived from home, she "felt happier than [she] had done for some time."[7]

Harriet's correspondence with home provided an emotional lifeline. It is clear from her journal that, from the beginning, she had been hesitant about emigrating to the colonies. Married in September 1834, in the space of six months she had had to adjust to life as a newlywed and to leaving her "happy home" and "dear Guernsey friends," along with all she loved "so dearly," for a foreign land.[8] Letters home were a way of maintaining contact with the familiar world of her youth. They also reaffirmed the emotional, if not physical, proximity of friends and family. On the very day the couple boarded the packet at Plymouth and also on the day they landed in New York, Harriet sent letters home.[9] Especially in the early months of her journal, Harriet's notations that she had written home often appeared in entries that recounted some disappointment, whether it was the abrupt decision of her maid Emily not to accompany the couple to America or the failure of the luggage to arrive; or, once they were in the colony, the realization that their original choice of land "was mistaken."[10]

Even after the Pengellys had bought a farm and built a home on Rice Lake and had begun to settle into the rhythms of their new lives, Harriet maintained an active correspondence across the Atlantic. She was "truly miserable" when anticipated letters from home did not arrive.[11] One "disagreeable" day in August 1835, for example, she recorded, "No letters from home, could eat no dinner – very, very unhappy."[12] Even after the couple had decided to return to Guernsey for a visit after two years and Harriet's sense of exile began to abate, letters from home remained a vital part of her daily life, something to be cherished and read "over and over."[13] As she read of the comings and goings of kith and kin in Guernsey and England, she was able to maintain a sense of belonging to a community that was far removed from her daily round of housekeeping and visiting neighbours, and at times "the awful silence of the woods of Canada."[14] Letters like that from her sister Sophy, which arrived in November 1835 and reassured her about the continued good health of those at home, brought "tears of heartfelt joy." She "wept over it like a child," she wrote: "My heart thanked heaven for the happiness it gave me."[15] Even letters that brought news of illness and unhappiness at home were welcomed, despite the fact, she said, that they "gave me too much joy & sorrow, I cannot sleep."[16]

Until her death a little more than a year after she arrived in the colony, Harriet remained emotionally rooted in a world that lay more than three thousand miles away. Although she had "the smiles and love of a very dear husband," on New Year's Day 1836 she longed for her mother's smile and "a kind mother to wish me many happy returns of the day."[17] Letters provided Harriet with the means of participating, at least vicariously, in the community of family and friends "at home" even while she was forging new friendships and becoming part of a new community at Rice Lake. For Harriet, letters were also tangible evidence that she had not been forgotten and had not lost her place in the family circle. As was the case for many around her, letters from home were a touchstone, an affirmation of who one was and, for a time at least, where one continued to belong.

Certainly, not all or even most emigrant settlers maintained such an active transatlantic correspondence. Like her husband Robert, a former British officer and a gentleman of some means, Harriet was a member of the "letter writing classes."[18] The couple could afford to travel in a cabin on a packetship, and Robert had the capital to buy land and hire neighbours to help build his house and clear his fields. And when they arrived in the colony with their letters of introduction to the lieutenant-governor, they became part of a society that was directly tied to London and the Colonial Office. Harriet was determined "to do without" a servant after she had sacked, for insolence, the one they had brought from Guernsey; she hoped, she said, that work would keep her "alive in this dull disagreeable country." But the young wife obviously had considerable time on her hands.[19] She had no children to attend to and was often alone when Robert worked in the fields.

Most new arrivals had not the time, the means, or perhaps the inclination to write home so often or at such length. As George Pashley recorded in his diary, his first letters home – one to his father, a second to a friend, and the third to his "dear partner's" father – were not sent until three months after he landed in British America: "I could not get Money to Pay the Postage till then."[20] Of course, some emigrants may have chosen not to write. They wanted to sever ties with home – whether because they were fleeing from particular responsibilities (as in the case of absconding husbands) or from the court, or because they were determined to grasp the new opportunities of America and, in the process, reinvent themselves. However, it is clear that for many, re-establishing contact with home was an integral part of the process of making a new life away from home. As the new arrivals joined kin, former neighbours, and even just acquaintances who were already settled in Upper Canada and were integrated into or helped to create new families and communities and gradually become residents, the desire to maintain contact with those at home persisted. Frequently, the responsibilities attendant on kinship – coping with the needs of an elderly parent, providing aid to a young sibling or cousin, or settling disputes over parents' estates – continued to tie emigrant settlers to those they had left behind. Letters were also a means of integrating the Old World and the New, of tying the familiar domestic landscapes, people, and relationships of home into the new and increasingly familiar world of a face-to-face colonial community. On both sides of the Atlantic, receiving or sending even one brief letter reaffirmed who one was and where one fitted into the world.

The transatlantic community sustained by correspondence was for many intensely personal, and despite distance in time and space, remained surprisingly immediate. Letters became an integral part of the ongoing cycle of British emigration and were one of the central pillars of the emigrants' world. Throughout Great Britain and Ireland, they frequently became the centrepiece of discussions in family parlours, churches, and taverns about the viability of "going to America." Letters from Upper Canada that included personal accounts of the journey and life in the New World helped to make the imagined world of emigration more real and tangible; at the same time, letters that arrived in the backwoods of the colony nourished the imagination of emigrant settlers with images of familiar landscapes and faces. The arrival of family members or friends of former neighbours, sometimes years later, reinforced these rather ethereal transatlantic communities. The receipt of letters, parcels, and even newspapers – even the appearance of a complete stranger with an introduction from a former acquaintance – was enough to sustain this world, both in its tangible form and in its participants' imagination.

In 1832, a little more than two months after his arrival at Quebec, one member of the first group of Petworth emigrants, eighteen-year-old Obediah Wilson, penned his first letter home. Compared with many other first letters, this was short almost to the point of curtness. It did, however, include all the information that he thought his parents would need. "I take this opportunity to inform you that I am well," he began, and he hoped "that these few lines" would find them the same. His experience on board ship received two lines: "I was seven weeks coming over; I was three weeks seasick; but I arrived safe."[21] The letter mentioned nothing of the confusion, bewilderment, and excitement that undoubtedly attended his ship's arrival at Quebec or the eager but probably anxious wait while the vessel was towed upriver to Montreal; or what some of his companions described as the "tedious journey" by durham boat and on foot to Prescott and then by steamer to Kingston.[22] Apparently of greater importance to Obediah was that he had "a place" with a couple he liked, fifteen miles from Kingston. Moreover, he liked "the ways" of the area "very well, at present." He then asked, "I want to know whether Edward [one of his brothers] is coming over; if he is put it in your letter." Then, in what other emigrants would have recognized as an almost ritualistic ending, Obediah wrote, "Remember me to my old master and mistress, and all enquiring friends. So no more at present. I remain your dutiful Son until death." One essential element remained.

Obediah concluded, "I want you to write as soon as possible. Direct your letter to H. Hough, at Ernest Town, thirteen miles from Kingston."[23]

Each year, hundreds if not thousands of emigrants of all social classes and occupations wrote home to announce their arrival and to report on the state of their health and that of their companions.[24] Sometimes these first letters were sent almost as soon as the family or the individual landed at Montreal or Quebec (or, in the case of Harriet Pengelly and Anne Langton, New York). A number included a journal or an account of the voyage and a promise to write again when settled.[25] Many emigrants waited and wrote their first letters weeks or even months after they had landed, and they included some "account of Canada" or a commentary about "the state of the country" (as they had apparently promised their readers before they left home), in addition to information about their own circumstances. As William Knox's first letter home to his uncle explained, "I would have written you before this time to have acquainted you of our safe arrival in this country. But knowing that Mr George Gounlock had written to Greenhill shortly after we arrived here I told him to let you know that we were all well and I would write you as soon as we got a settlement."[26]

Not surprisingly, emigrants' first letters home varied widely in tone and content. Some had to report the death of a companion or child on the voyage or how ague, scarlet fever, cholera, or other diseases had devastated family and friends.[27] Others noted that the country was "discouraging at first" or that because of injury or ill health, they had initially had problems finding work.[28] But most letters, particularly those written after emigrants had found work or taken up land, expressed satisfaction with the country and the writer's situation; and implicitly, and often explicitly, they included assurances that they "did not repent [their] journey."[29] George Hill's mother and father must have received some comfort when their son concluded his letter, "We left you almost broken-hearted, but you may be satisfied that we have bettered our condition by coming here."[30] Perhaps most importantly, the arrival of George's letter was concrete proof that he was still alive.

For most newly arrived emigrants, the purpose of their first letter was to make contact and to renew what they obviously hoped would be an ongoing relationship with those at home. Many expected that not only would the initial recipient read their letter but that its contents and often the letter itself would be passed among "Dear Friends And Relations."[31] Mary and Arthur Stokes explicitly asked that their brothers and sisters write and they added, "Please pass this letter to others."[32] William

Upton's letter to his mother asked that she give his love to all his brothers and sisters, and said, "Tell them that can write to write to me soon."[33] In his letter to Ann in March 1822, giving her instructions on her journey to Upper Canada, John Gemmill asked her to give his "best respects to all enquiring friends and well wishers."[34] Others sent salutations to specific neighbours, former employers, or members of the extended family.

Many new arrivals were obviously very conscious that they were unlikely ever to be able to return home. John Stedman (another of the Petworth emigrants) wrote a long first letter home, chronicling his arrival in Quebec, his journey to the interior, and his satisfaction at having been engaged by a farmer to work for the next year. Towards the end, he wrote, "So my dear father and mother, Give my love to uncles and aunts and all enquiring friends and tell them if [they] lived as [I] can in this country it [would be] a comfort to them." And he concluded poignantly, "You are there and I am here; I live in hopes [to] meet again where the Angels do also." In anticipation that his family would write and perhaps some members might actually join him, he then carefully wrote "a Direction for John Stedman," which included his township, county, district, colony, and continent and ended, "Where I am about four thousand miles from home."[35]

Sending news, information, and messages to family and friends was clearly only one purpose of an emigrant's first letter home. Just as important was to urge the readers to reply as soon as possible. Almost without exception, the letters included such statements as, "I long to hear from them all"[36] or pleaded, "Please to let us hear from you as soon as convenient after receiving this; and acquaint us with all particulars, and how you all are."[37] John Luff, an apprentice and one of the Petworth emigrants, wrote to his aunt saying, "Whether we shall have the pleasure of seeing each other in this world again, lord only knows; if we should not, I wish you would join me in writing, it seems to be the only satisfaction we can truly have here."[38]

It was clearly important to those who had newly arrived in Upper Canada to know that they had not been forgotten and, indeed, that they remained part of their communities at home. For the first few weeks or months, many must have felt betwixt and between. They were no longer residents of a particular village or neighbourhood in Great Britain or Ireland; at the same time, they had few connections or commitments to new communities in America. First letters were a way of asserting their continuing relationship with communities at home; and the responses to these letters reassured them that they still had a place in the world, an identity that was firmly rooted in place and time – one which they had taken with them to America and on which they could forge new relationships. Many new arrivals therefore waited anxiously for some acknowledgment from those they had left behind.[39]

Not all (and perhaps not even most) emigrants wrote to reassure the family of their safe arrival. As many of the "information wanted" notices suggest, some men had emigrated to escape family or financial responsibilities. Even those with the best of intentions may have found that once they were in America, it was easy to disappear, leaving wives and children at home unknowingly deserted.[40] Many more new arrivals probably did not have the ability or the means to write. Most were nonetheless determined to let those at home know that they had arrived safely and, later, to tell them how they were settling in.

Those who arrived in Upper Canada as part of a group, like John Gemmill or members of the Petworth expeditions ten years later, or those who joined family or former neighbours already established in the colony, could always find someone to write on their behalf or, at the very least, could send greetings that would be expected to reach those at home. In the 1820s John Gemmill frequently sent messages from former shipmates and current neighbours in Lanark County, through his son Andrew, to friends and relatives in the old neighbourhood. In the summer of 1823, for example, he asked Andrew to "acquaint all Enquiring friends that Dr. Gemell John McFarline Walter Stirline James Cohune's family are all well."[41] Three years later, in a postscript to a letter, he wrote, "James Colquhoun wishes us to mention to you if you could hear anything of his brother Robert to let him know that he is well & is surprised that he has not heard from him for more than two years."[42] Andrew tracked down James Colquhoun's brother and reported back to his father. Unfortunately, the situation in Upper Canada had changed. "In your letter you desired me to let James Colquhoun know that you [had heard] from his brother," John wrote Andrew the following August, 1827. But now John had to ask Andrew to break the news to the brother that James was "no more": "He was killed in April last while at work upon his own land."[43] More often, Andrew was given a happier commission. A year after John reported James's death, he asked his son, "Give James Wrights Compliments to Mr David Strachan and Wife" and "if David Strachan be writing to his sister he may let James Wrights Relations know that he is in good health."[44]

Various members of the Petworth parties also regularly wrote home on behalf of their companions and neighbours. Soon after he arrived in 1832, John Copelain asked his brother to pass on Mrs Kinshott's regards "to all her husband's family." He explained that since her arrival, Mrs Kinshott had "lost her very dear and only friend" and, soon afterwards, her child, and that she would write to her in-laws when she was finally settled.[45] James Rapson, another member of the first Petworth group, not only wrote letters on behalf of other emigrants[46] but also regularly sent his family news about his companions (some of whom were now near neighbours, and others he had heard about second or third hand), knowing that this information would be passed on.[47] For both John Gemmill and James Rapson and their friends, the world of emigration was a small world and continued to be characterized by face-to-face communication even when such conversations spanned the Atlantic. The intimacy of this world was also apparent to other Petworth emigrants who arrived in subsequent years and sought out James Rapson for advice and assistance.

In many ways, emigrant correspondence recreated and was an extension of the familiar relationships of village life. What is striking is that even with only intermittent correspondence, or with news received second or third hand and months if not years out of date, the assumption of a shared community persisted. So, too, did the apparent immediacy of the relationships. This was undoubtedly one of the factors that encouraged some family members or friends who emigrated years later to assume that a face-to-face relationship could be resumed and that they could call on those in the New World for emotional and physical support when they arrived in the colony.

Not all, of course, participated in or maintained their connections with this dynamic transatlantic community. Many new arrivals to British North America were restless and moved frequently to look for work or for better opportunities. Friends and family in Great Britain and Ireland too might move in response to local circumstances. Many on both sides of the Atlantic refused to give up hope that some lost family member or friend could be found, however. In addition to the hundreds of "information wanted" notices placed by emigrants and settlers looking for a particular individual or family, colonial newspapers sometimes printed cards of family members or friends "at home" who were hoping to get in touch with "lost" relatives abroad. In 1835, for example, English friends offered a reward to anyone who had information about Ann

Hall. "A native of London," Ann had come to Canada three years earlier with a Chelsea pensioner and his wife, who had subsequently died. No one had heard from Ann since she had written in July 1832.[48] In 1835 Charles Stephens's family was growing increasingly anxious. He and his brother Alexander had left Dundee in 1832. After they had arrived in Upper Canada, they had stayed together for some time, but then Charles, a blacksmith, had gone to Kingston to find work. His brother had written to him a number of times, but without any response. Alexander's notice to the public stated that he "and his relatives in Scotland are anxious to be informed of said Charles Stephens."[49]

Often the problem for those in the British Isles was finding the beneficiary of an estate. In some instances, executors used a local agent to conduct the search. In 1829, for example, "A.B." began to look for George Long, "a Tailor by trade" who had left England ten years earlier with his wife and four children. It was thought that he now lived "somewhere near Philadelphia" and was a farmer. His wife's family, who lived near Knightsbridge, London, were trying to contact him, for he would "hear something to his advantage."[50] In 1829 Catherine Evans of Colham, Shrewsbury, Shropshire, contacted the *Herald* office in Kingston for help finding her brother Spencer Evans, who had been discharged from the Queen's Rangers some twenty-five years earlier and was, she thought, now living in Upper Canada.[51] At other times, the family or its agent in Great Britain or Ireland made a direct appeal.[52] Infrequently, an anxious parent or sibling would write directly to the postmaster of the relative's last known address in America to try to track the person down.

Many emigrants and their families were determined not to lose touch. A sense of familial obligation, ongoing business affairs, or just the need to maintain the image of familiar faces and places promoted an extensive correspondence which, in a few instances, continued into the second generation. Maintaining such a correspondence had significant difficulties. Paper was often scarce, and postage, which was paid in part by the recipient, was relatively expensive and beyond the means of many.[53] Moreover mail "service" was haphazard at best. Although the larger centres in Upper Canada had postal service that linked Halifax, Quebec, and Montreal to the interior, for much of the period the most economic and quickest route for mail was through New York.[54] As John Scott advised his uncle Andrew Redford in 1835, "I wish they [letters] could be sent by New York. It is cheaper by that way."[55] After the introduction of the penny post in Great Britain, and with the increasing use of steamships to carry the mail, those at home began to direct their letters through Halifax. "Postage is nothing now," John Scott told his cousin in 1840. "I suppose you know that you must send all letters or papers now via Halifax – they come cheaper and just as quick."[56] Even so, to the frustration of correspondents on both sides of the Atlantic, letters were often misdirected or lost in transit.

Almost a year after arriving in Lanark, John Gemmill grew increasingly concerned that he had heard nothing from his wife Ann. He had already written twice and "had got no answer." Ironically, even this third letter, which included detailed instructions about the family's reunion, took almost nine months to reach Glasgow and arrived long after Ann had already left home.[57] The frustration with mail to Scotland persisted. In one of his first letters to son Andrew, John noted, "We are sorry to here that you have only received one letter in the course of two years. We have not been neglectfull of writting to you neither is the Country as poor but it can produce plenty of Paper but it is the post offices that must be neglectfull of not forwarding them."[58] Ten years later, many of the Petworth emigrants were having a similar problem. After almost nine months in the colony, Henry and Charlotte Tribe, in-laws of James Rapson, had sent four letters home and still had received no reply: "We do not know whether the letters passes from England, or not; we think that the letters are stopped, as we can not get no answers, but I hope that you will answer these few lines by return post, for we long to hear from you."[59]

In Upper Canada, some letters from home arrived at their destination only to languish because the intended recipient did not know they were there or, as often seemed to happen, because the emigrant had left the area altogether. Local newspapers regularly published lists of letters waiting to be picked up. Isaac Wilson, the pre-War of 1812 emigrant living just outside York, discovered to his dismay in 1821 that "they now have a regulation at the post office ... to send all letters remaining unclaimed after three months down to the General Post Office at Quebec." He had not been to York for some time, and the new clerk did not know him; as a result, he explained to his brother Jonathan his letter "was sent with a raft."[60] Harriet Pengelly, on the other hand, ever anxious to receive news from home, made a point of checking the post regularly and was always sorely disappointed when there was "none from home."[61] Mary Gapper, after deciding to marry Edward O'Brien and remain in the colony, remarked that mail sent by way of York in 1836 was delivered by "an Indian ... who now calls regularly at very irregular times."[62]

To avoid expensive postage and problems with the mail service, letter writers on both sides of the Atlantic frequently relied on friends, acquaintances, or agents who were travelling overseas to carry their mail. It appears that a few Lanark residents returned home to visit, to fetch their family, or to go to college. Each time they left, they carried letters from John Gemmill to his son.[63] In his fourth letter home to his parents in December 1832, the Petworth emigrant John Worfold said he hoped that they had "receive[d] the letters I sent ... before; I had sent three." His first he had entrusted to "the doctor [who] promised to put them in the Dorking Post or call and deliver them" to a neighbour. The one from York, he said, "I gave to a person who came out in the vessel with us and was going back to fetch his family." This man had promised to put the letter in the London post. "And the one from Quebec I expect will cost you," John explained to his parents, rather apologetically. "I could not afford to pay the post to England for you."[64]

Personally delivered letters were a double benefit to the recipient. When the son of the Reverend William Bell from Lanark went "home" to college and delivered John Gemmill's letter, Andrew also received a first-hand account of his father and the family and could get detailed answers to the myriad questions that could not be answered by post.[65] Isaac Wilson was "pleased to inform" his brother Jonathan in the summer of 1821 "that John Barnes and his wife [had] arrived at York" and he had received Jonathan's note. "I am much obliged to you for your kindness," he wrote, "as they will afford me much information and entertainment." As Barnes had arrived with a letter from Jonathan asking Isaac to assist the bearer in any way he could, Isaac ruefully concluded that they would also afford him "some vexation, no doubt."[66] Seven years later, Isaac received a letter from his brother delivered by a Mr Wilson and Henry Sproat, who were travelling in the colony. Isaac was disappointed that the men had been "in a great haste back again" and he had had "very little talk with them."[67] When Joseph Allanason delivered another letter from his brother in 1832, "he stayed with me a day or two," Wilson recorded, "and gave me much information about my old neighbours."[68]

Entrusting acquaintances, friends, or family members with letters did not guarantee their speedy or safe arrival. Before Allanason delivered the letter, he had already spent some time travelling around America. Even so, for much of the period, "private conveyance" was less expensive and could be more reliable than the "regular" post.[69] However, sometimes the traveller or acquaintance forgot to put the letter in the post on the other side of the Atlantic or found it too much trouble to deliver it. George Pashley was disconcerted to find that his letters had not been delivered as promised. "This week I was informed that our Letters we had sent to Eng were within 2 miles of our own house because the man we expected to take them had fallen sick so they did not set off till the end of Jan."[70] Nonetheless, the imminent departure of a friend, or a visitor returning home, or the sailing of a particular ship presented an opportunity to write and make contact. Mrs Murray of Glasgow timed her letters to her sons in Montreal by the sailing of particular ships from Greenock, and she eagerly looked for letters from America by the returning ship. "How delighted we are," she wrote to her eldest son, James, "[when] we received [in November] by return of Cpt Neill from Canada a packet of letters from Tom & William dated 19 September when were both well."[71]

Whether letters were mailed or sent with a traveller on the day they were written, they usually took months to reach their destinations. Correspondence between family and friends often crossed each other. News and information might be repeated in a subsequent letter when the writer realized, or feared, that the first had not arrived. This may help explain, in part at least, why some correspondents waited weeks if not months to reply to a letter; or if one arrived particularly late, saw no need to reply at all.[72] And there was, of course, the perpetual problem that writing took time and considerable thought and effort, all of which were at a premium in most new settlers' lives. What is so startling, therefore, is the sense of immediacy and often the conversational tone of many letters.

John and Ann Gemmill's lengthy correspondence with their son Andrew undoubtedly served a number of purposes. In many of his early letters, John tried unsuccessfully to convince Andrew – and, through him, John's brother and daughters – to join the family in New Lanark. As John explained, "It is not very pleasant for us to have the family [in] Scotland when we can all live very comfortable here."[73] While Andrew considered his options, John, the "loving father" (as he always signed his letters), also wanted to make sure that Andrew continued to feel part of the family and its world in the colonies. Between May 1823 and August 1830, John and Ann's letters always began with an acknowledgment of Andrew's previous letter or letters. Andrew's letters took at least two months, sometimes up to six, to arrive, and John rarely answered right away. Early in the correspondence he explained, "We would have written you sooner had we thought you were not coming on the testimony of the last letter you received."⁷⁴ Later, when it was evident that Andrew was not going to join his family in Upper Canada, John and Ann had other reasons for the delay. In early December 1826, in a letter that acknowledged two of Andrew's letters dated up to nine months before, John wrote, "My neglect in answering them deserves some apology but I must only make the same claim as you do <u>want of time</u>."⁷⁵ This was in no way an indication of John's lack of interest in events at home or his appreciation of Andrew's letters. In November 1829, John began, "I received your kind leters of 20th May on the 14th August last and have also to acknowledge the receipt of yours of the 22 July and also of the one you wrote prior to that date." John apologized for his "apparent neglect," explaining, "Distance from the post office and the few opportunities that occur in this distant settlement must plead my excuse." He continued, "Do not suppose it was from want of affection or anxiety on your welfare and do not let it prevent you from writing whenever inclination leisure or a favourable opportunity offers." Andrew's letters were "always welcomed with much pleasures."⁷⁶ John penned this letter – and indeed all his letters – as though he was picking up on a conversation with his son.

In May 1823, for example, John and Ann wrote, "We received your letter datted the 26th of March in which we were very Glad to hear of your welfare but very sory to hear of that Melancholy account of the Capt and crew of that Ship that we came out in." A month later, John commiserated with farm neighbours on the loss they must have suffered as a result of a great storm the previous December.⁷⁷ The following year, he was "happy to hear of a fine crop at home and that markets [were] reasonable and that employment in general [was] plentiful and rather better paid at home."⁷⁸ Most letters also included answers to questions Andrew had posed, and reported on local conditions in the colony, circumstances and news of neighbours (many of whom Andrew would have known), and progress made on the farm.

Of prime and increasing importance, however, was news about the health and welfare of various family members, and the primary focus of most of the transatlantic conversations revolved around family affairs. Each letter from Upper Canada began with an almost formulaic greeting. In June 1823, for example, John began, "Dear son, We received your letter datted the 26ᵀᴴ of March on the 26 of May and the other Dated the 29 of March which Gave us Great Pleasure to hear of your Well fare and they find us all in good health at Preasant thank God for it."⁷⁹ Such almost ritualized openings were not empty rote; they were a crucial affirmation of the intimacy that existed between the writer and the recipient and a clear declaration of what was of greatest concern to both. Each of John and Ann Gemmill's letters included references to their and their children's health; they also specifically alluded to the power of the Almighty. In November 1825, Ann and John told Andrew, "This at present leaves us in the full enjoyment of that valuable Blessing for which we have great reason to praise God."[80] The letters also always asked after family members still in Scotland, and they admonished Andrew when he did not include information concerning his sisters' welfare. "We were very much Surprised," the couple wrote in May 1823, "that you never Mention nothing about your two Sisters Margeret and Jane."[81] A month later, they asked Andrew to "be so good as to lett them know of our Welfare."[82] The Gemmills' letters presumed that the ongoing relationship between Lanark, Upper Canada, and Glasgow rested on far more than passive interaction. John expected Andrew to pass on information and to assume some responsibility for the welfare of his sisters.

At the same time, John and Ann were ensuring that Andrew remained part of the family circle in Upper Canada. Their letters reported major family events. Andrew vicariously followed his sisters as they went "out to service" and watched as the little ones, including David, who had been an infant when he left home, go to school. In 1826 Andrew heard of the marriages of sisters Ann and Mary, and in turn he related his own marriage in 1827. To John, this was an opportunity to extend the family network, and thereafter his letters included greetings to "all your [Andrew's] relations in Scotland." Two years later, while rejoicing with Andrew over the birth of his first child, John wrote, "We think that you forgot to mention her name and hope you will have a better memory when you write next."[83]

Especially in the early years, when all the children were living in the parental household, Andrew was drawn farther into life in Lanark when John's letters included notes of specific greetings from other members of the family. Sometimes, it was a brief "Jennet sends her best respects to you"[84] or, somewhat later, "Your Brothers & Sisters all join in love to you & your Family, David [the youngest son] has some recollection of you … but says he would know you better if you would send him the suit of cloaths."[85] Through her father's letters, Jennet, who was two years younger than Andrew, teased him about being a bachelor: "She thinks that if you do not bring a wife with you that you will remain an Old Batchelor that you would not get a Negor or Indian Squaw in the Country they will think so little of you."[86] In one of the few letters from Andrew that have survived, he replied, "Tell Janet to belief herself besides those black Ghosts of Indians."[87]

The occasion of Jennet's engagement to be married about six months later best illustrates the texture of this imagined familiar fireside. At the end of April 1824, a postscript cryptically noted, "Janet will be married before you come here so you put on spurs."[88] There may have been some hope that Andrew would arrive in time to be the best man. But John reported in November, "Since you did not come forward to be the best man, they made as merry as they could without you." And later in the same letter he passed on a message from Jennet: "As soon as you send intimation of your comming they [Jennet and her new husband] will Joyfully saddle the Tea Kettle and have everything ready to make you comfortable but they dare not put it on yet lest the bottom boil out of it before you come."[89] A year later, as John continued to hope that Andrew and his sisters would arrive, he bemoaned, "If you don't come soon, the Bottom <u>will</u> be out of the kettle."[90] One of Andrew's brothers, John, reintroduced the teapot to the transatlantic conversation many years later: "But my Mother says that if you don't come soon she is afraid that you have to take your tea out of the pot for the botem is out of the old tea ketel and she has got A new one and she is afraid that it will go the same way before you reach this place."[91]

The references to the familiar and domestic tea kettle – which in many Scottish homes was the symbol of welcome – helped create the illusion of a continuing and face-to-face relationship within a family divided by the Atlantic. By 1832, it must have been clear to all that Andrew and his new young family were unlikely to emigrate. Three years earlier, John had told Andrew that he "had almost despair[ed] of the realization of your wishes of our meeting again with the rest of my family around my fireside." He turned to his faith to help sustain him. The Gemmills shared an unshakable belief that "Kind Providence … provided all things liberally."[92] All their trials and tribulations, including family separations, were "from the Supreme Disposer of Events," John observed, and were "generally for our good."[93] Thus, he took solace that "though that [the family's reunion] may not take place upon earth, let us with the Divine assistance conduct ourselves in such a manner that we look forward to our meeting together in another and better world."[94]

In the meantime, the Gemmills created their own world – one with a tea kettle on the hob – in which, through their imagination, they shared their concerns, their triumphs, and their sorrows. And the whole family took part in the conversation that lasted for more than ten years. After the birth of the first of Jennet's children, John told Andrew that she was "living in great hopes of her son being heir to your inheritance ... You made this promise & she will make you keep it."[95] At the age of eight, young David was proud of the gold piece that Andrew had sent from home.[96] And when Andrew's brother, young John, wrote his first letter (and apologized for his spelling), it was sent to Andrew with the hope, wrote John, "that you are intending to pay us a visit sure that would be a hapy meting."[97] This was a world that offered all its participants emotional support – and a continuing sense of security. And for John Gemmill and his family, it provided a means of remaining part of the larger community of the extended family and friends at home in Scotland while they helped to create a new community abroad.

Frances Stewart, Mary Gapper O'Brien, and such women as Catharine Parr Traill and Susanna Moodie too maintained a regular transatlantic correspondence with family and friends in Britain. For Mary, like a young Harriet Pengelly, the arrival of letters and packages from home were a delightful treat, particularly after she had decided to marry Edward O'Brien and remain in the colony.[98] As she explained to her sister Lucy in England in 1832, "The real event of importance which glads the day is the arrival of letters."[99] In her letters home, Mary grieved with her sister over the death of her nephew, and she delighted when she received news that all were healthy and well.[100] Sometimes, opening letters and parcels from home took on a ritualistic quality, as Mary described in her journal in May 1831, when she received a number of packages and letters together: "I opened packet after packet with various degrees of interest, fitted on my cloak, admired my carpet, treasured up my books." But the one "desired packet" was not to be found. It arrived that evening: "I was half inclined to run away by myself to open it but this I thought would be churlish." Instead, she sat down "very demurely & leisurely undoing the string so as not to excite attention." Even then, Mary hesitated about where to begin: "The least interesting could not be read first & the most interesting I was half afraid to venture upon." She started with the childrens' dispatches "sure to excite only pleasurable interest." Only then did she venture "on Lucy's & Mr Sharpe's": "Breathing when I reached the last line of these I could then read them again to the party & go on in peace to the rest."[101] Even letters with bad news were welcomed. Mary "fretted" when letters did not arrive, and when they did they were cherished and often reread time and again.[102] In the summer of 1836, just after the birth of her third child, she wrote in her journal, "A letter from Lucy arrived a few hours after my baby & I am not very sure which was the more welcome."[103]

For women and men, both the newly arrived in the colony and those who had become well settled, letters were part of a sustained transatlantic conversation. As the Peterborough area resident Isabelle Brownlie wrote to her brother at home in a lengthy letter, "But I will tire you with my talk for I think I am talking to you but I dought I will never have the pleasure to do but if we never meet in this world I hope we will meet in the happier one."[104] Until that day, the very act of writing allowed one to enter the familiar world of family and friends. Although one might be replying to news that was months old or renewing contact after a lengthy silence, the transatlantic correspondence nearly always had a sense of immediacy. For Isabelle, as for Mary O'Brien and thousands of others, this imaginary world was as real and present as the physical world in which they now lived.

For many, the continuing connection to home was reinforced by unfinished business or family obligations. John Gemmill seems to have expected Andrew, as the eldest son, to assume some responsibilities for the two sisters who were still in Scotland.[105] John also gave Andrew authority to deal with various financial matters on his behalf. In October 1824, for example, he gave his son power of attorney to settle Ann's father's estate on the family's behalf. One of Andrew's uncles was claiming that Ann had signed away her share. "Your Mother signed no receipt or discharge accepting the £40 her father left her," John wrote Andrew. John thought that Andrew would have no problem sorting out the matter with Ann's brother William. But the dispute with her brother John was another matter: "We think Uncle Johns conduct very unproper and the sooner you set about getting the business put to rights the better."[106] Three years later, Andrew was again given authority, this time to settle a debt claimed by a former neighbour.[107] Throughout the years, John offered Andrew advice on how he might proceed, but it is clear that he had confidence in his son. Five years after the affair of the will had begun, he told Andrew, "You have at least got the better of your Uncle," and expressed his satisfaction that the estate was finally settled.[108]

Isaac Wilson, a settler in Upper Canada, too relied on his younger brother Jonathan to represent his interests at home. Isaac and Jonathan maintained a regular correspondence from the time of Isaac's arrival in the colony in 1811 until his death in 1838.[109] Like many other emigrant settlers, Isaac does not seem to have written letters per se, although Jonathan apparently did. Instead, Isaac sent home an annual or semi-annual journal that was filled with details about the landscape and local politics and described his health, his work establishing his farm, and gave news of his neighbours; and, after his sister and family arrived in 1819, their news too. In 1811 Isaac was not sure that he intended to remain in the colony. The coming of war in 1812 "confounded" his plans to travel and see something of America; it also permanently interrupted Jonathan's plan to join him in Upper Canada.[110] Isaac made a brief visit home in 1814 to settle some affairs after his father's death in 1812 and undoubtedly to see his mother. He was restless, however, and he returned to his farm outside York a year later, explaining to his brother, "I have fixed myself here for some time to come if not for life."[111] Even so, for the next twenty years, Isaac still considered himself very much part of the old household and community. He kept up to date with "the state of affairs at home"[112] from Jonathan's letters, from newspapers Jonathan sent him, and from the first-hand reports of newly arrived emigrants or travellers who occasionally appeared with letters or packages. He also periodically offered advice to his brother about how to manage various family affairs.[113]

There is no question that a significant part of the relationship with his brother rested on settling their father's estate and managing the family farm. Isaac was the oldest son, executor of his father's estate and the principal heir. In 1820 he announced, "As it is now my fixed determination to settle for life at the place where I now am," it would be best to sell the farm, Birkbeck.[114] Three years earlier he had told his brother, "If you wish to continue it as a farm, I have no objections to have the value of it estimated by any impartial man." This was so that his brother would not have to pay more than it was worth.[115] We do not know what Jonathan's response was, but he must have been rather startled by Isaac's decision to sell Birkbeck. In the end, the brothers obviously reached an agreement; Jonathan rented out the farm and notified Isaac that he was entitled to receive some of the proceeds. Isaac, who was already financially secure, did not expect "to receive any further benefit from it," he told his brother. After all, Jonathan was looking after their mother. Moreover, Isaac was "much pleased" by his brother's reports of how he was managing the situation.[116] For his part, Isaac gave Jonathan power of attorney to act in his stead, and he began to assume some responsibility for the well-being of their sister Fanny and her family, who had arrived in 1819.[117] Isaac continued to offer his brother advice, however. It was only after the death of Isaac's mother (which he first heard about second hand)[118] and the eventual settlement of their parents' estate that Isaac

Wilson's direct financial interest with home came to an end.[119] Ironically, on his death in 1838, the flow of funds was reversed. Each of Isaac's brothers and sisters inherited a part of his estate, and his nephew Matthew spent considerable time explaining the situation to his aunts and uncles in Great Britain and working out how best to transfer funds.[120]

The tangible bonds of family obligations and entitlements bound many emigrants to Britain long after they had begun to settle into their new homes. Only a relative few, however, would have had an inheritance to collect or were entitled to the proceeds from an ongoing business interest. Yet sons and daughters, sisters and brothers, parents and children often continued to feel a sense of responsibility for kin – especially for their parents – on the other side of the Atlantic. Shortly after Isaac Wilson returned from his visit home, he wrote to his brother saying, "I hope my mother and you are living agreeably together in the way I left you. You must indulge her as much as you can to preserve peace among you."[121] Mother and son obviously did not live together for long. In 1824 Mrs Wilson's house was broken into. After expressing his sorrow at the damage, Isaac wrote, "It is gratifying to me to hear that things are taken care of," and he thanked his brother for his efforts.[122] Three years later, Isaac commented, "I am sorry to hear my Mother has not her health so well as usual. I think it would be better for her to try to live along with Ann or somebody than to live any longer by herself, so that she could be taken care of in case of sickness."[123] Divided by the Atlantic, there was little that Isaac could do directly for his mother, however, except provide advice and encouragement to her and his brother.

When all the children had left home, the situation could become even more complicated and worrying. For some, the problem was resolved when their parents decided to join them in America. A number of letters from Upper Canada urged parents to come, offering to send them "some assistance" for the passage.[124] Others asked friends or relations still in Britain to ensure that Mother or Father was settled and healthy. Two Petworth emigrants, for example, George and Mary Boxall, asked friends to "pray leave" their "poor mother at Henly, a sovereign" before they left.[125]

Emotional and financial support flowed both ways. John Scott's first letter to his uncle Andrew Redford was prompted by the loan of fifty pounds received from Andrew and "other kind friends."[126] Mary O'Brien periodically received monetary gifts from Aunt Sophie, for which she was always most grateful.[127] And for the first few years in the

Belleville area, Fanny and William Hutton relied on funds they received from his parents to offset their growing debts. Although Fanny was a hesitant and apparently infrequent correspondent, she explained in a lengthy letter to "Dear Mrs Hutton" (as the letter began) the specific circumstances that had given rise to one particular request for assistance in this "time of trouble."[128] The details of the problems concluded with a plea for help: "The present exigency of our circumstances had prompted me to through ourselves on your kindness." If the immediate family could not lend them the "sum asked by William," she said, or "if you take a different view of our affairs from us," then she and William "would be glad" of "any suggestions which may at any time strike any of you as useful or necessary to us."[129]

Although most new arrivals could not expect financial assistance, a number did look forward to receiving parcels from family and friends at home. Isaac Wilson was "much obliged" to his brother for sending local newspapers, and he offered, "If you would like to have a newspaper from York, I could send you one."[130] Isaac also often received parcels from his brother that had been brought by recently arrived emigrants. "I believe I received everything safe," he wrote to Jonathan in 1822. "Both newspapers, one pair of good stockings, and the spectacles I find very useful."[131] Fanny Hutton, John and Anne Langton, and Mary O'Brien were delighted when packages arrived containing cloth, books, and clothing that were often difficult to find in Upper Canada. Often as important were small tokens or presents from family and friends at home. David Gemmill's new watch, Anne Langton's pictures drawn by her brother, and other mementos became treasured possessions. They were physical representations that the recipient was not forgotten;[132] they reinforced the emotional ties to home, and they helped keep alive the images of family and friends and the landscape of their youth.

Six years after he left home, John Scott wrote to his cousin, "My heart still warms when I think on many localities in my native land I used to frequent and the friends and acquaintances I have left behind – tho' I have forgotten the names of many persons and many places, with the Poet I can still exclaim – 'yet he behold her with the eyes of spirit – He sees the form which he no more shall meet – She like a passionate thought is come and gone – while at his feet the bright well bubbles on.'"[133] John Scott was certainly not the only emigrant who wrote home with vivid images in his mind. As one of his brothers wrote, "You can scarcely form any idea of a person's feeling and Emotion who has been absent from his native country so long as I have been." He explained,

"Time and distance gives a sort of enchantment, a melancholy pleasure which words are quite unable to express."[134] For the two brothers, even after years away, the landscape of Scotland continued to capture their imagination and give them a connection to home. In his letters, Archibald Scott remembered walking to school with friends past local landmarks and wondered what had happened to his old schoolmaster. This was the place, he wrote, where he was born and spent his childhood: "It seems as I was then completely happy."[135]

Such racking homesickness was not shared by all in the family. John explained to his cousin in 1844 that most of his brothers and sisters, who were all younger than he, did not "care much about seeing Scotland again." Of course, his parents could "never forget old friends, old faces and bygone times in Scotland," but after ten years in the colony he and his siblings were "all naturalized now." John continued, "I am now become part Dutchman, part Canadian and part everything else for I live among all kinds of people and feel at home with them all."[136] A year later, he commented that he understood when many of his acquaintances who had gone home for a visit had thankfully returned "home" to Upper Canada. "They could not remain in the Old Country" he explained, because they were "so accustomed to American habits." John felt the same and declared, "We are now, of course, all Canadians."[137]

At the same time, John and his cousin William Knox still wanted their uncle to send them "a newspaper occasionally," and John particularly wanted him to send "as often as possible the old 'Courant.'" He and William both offered to return the favour by forwarding local colonial newspapers to Scotland. From their letters, it is evident that many members of the family read newspapers from home carefully. In the spring of 1840, for example, Isabell Scott, John's sister, asked her aunt to pass on her compliments to Mrs Riddle. Isabell had seen the announcement of her marriage in the paper and wished her "much joy."[138] In 1843 William Knox thanked his cousin for the hometown *Kelso Chronicle*, with its news of "all" local marriages. Still a bachelor himself, William was both pleased and a little startled to find that so many of his former friends were setting up households of their own. "I hope they will all live Hapy in the Married State," he told his cousin, and at the end of the letter he asked to be "minded ... to all enquiring Friends and be sure and Write me Soon."[139] For the Scott family, newspapers from home were a welcome supplement to letters from family and friends.

Unlike the Gemmills, the Scotts seem to have been indifferent correspondents. In 1840 John Scott started a letter to his cousin, ostensibly in reply to a letter he had received two years before, stating, "I dare say all my friends in Scotland imagine I have quite forgotten them if they judge from the lapse of time that had taken place since I wrote last." But this could not be further from the truth, he said. "Nothing would give me greater pleasure than to revisit them." His only excuse for his "negligence" was that his cousins had written in the interim. His long letter described in some detail the events of the last three years in the colony, including his involvement in helping to put down the civil unrest. His letter ended: "After the lapse of six years my heart still warms when I think on many localities in my native land which I used to frequent and the friends and acquaintances I have left behind."[140]

Even after years away, for the Scott children and cousins living in Upper Canada, letters and newspapers from home were tangible evidence that they had not been forgotten. As William Knox wrote to his cousin in 1843, "I was beginning to think you had forgotten me altogether as it was such a very long time since I had received a Letter from Hermiston [the home farm]. I can assure you nothing for this long time gave me more pleasure than your Letter which I received last Month."[141] Letters and newspapers evoked images of home. Emigrant settlers knew that this was often an imaginary world. But they maintained the sense of a shared landscape and a shared past with those they had left behind. Although relationships were often idealized and landscapes unchanging, this increasingly imaginary world was very real in many emigrant settlers' minds. As they wrote home, they could see the faces and places of those they wrote to; they could smell the teapot brewing on the hearth and could hear the sounds of cattle or sheep, or the marketplace. This provided much of the foundation for the conversational nature of emigrant letters and the immediacy of their tone. Many, like John Scott, "fondly yet wish again to see my old Fetherlaw and my friends there."[142] In the meantime, letters would have to suffice.

Those writing in Britain were often at a disadvantage. They did not see the places where family and friends lived and could not feel the colonial landscape. As Isaac Wilson commented to his brother, "An account of all the changes that take place among my old neighbours is very pleasing for me to read along with various other incidents that may occur." But he recognized that "a relation of such items from here would be quite uninteresting to you."[143] Whereas Isaac could picture his brother and mother and knew intimately the architecture and landscape of home, Jonathan was writing to someone in a foreign and unimaginable landscape. Even with the detailed descriptions of life and the new farm in Upper Canada, Isaac's brother was unable to "see" this new world. Indeed, Isaac's accounts and his frequent reminders about how different America was from home probably only served to reinforce its "foreignness."

For those who remained behind, maintaining the transatlantic community may well have been more difficult, particularly if emigrant settlers did not have the means or desire to return for a visit. But maintain it many did, and in the process they vicariously became part of the emigrants' world. For those waiting for letters from home and then responding often months and sometimes years later, the post was a vital part of their new lives. Maintaining contact over a great distance was not easy. The vagaries of the mail complicated the problems created by mobile populations and accidents, illness, or even death that abruptly ended such connections. Many emigrants, either by choice or by chance, lost touch with family at home. Many others were determined not to. Even those who did not write sent and received "reports" to and from family and friends at home. The arrival of visitors from the other side of the Atlantic certainly strengthened these long-distance relationships; for most, however, their continuing ties to home depended on the vital links of letters.

Transatlantic correspondence was an integral part of the emigrants' world. In the early years, it provided a sense of place and reassurance as they negotiated their way through a strange land. Many wrote home, either regularly or after years of silence, to renew bonds of affection. Sending and receiving letters also affirmed their identity as fathers, mothers, sisters, brothers, and cousins – in short, as part of a familial network that was rooted not in time and place but in relationships of affection and obligation. In many ways, this part of the emigrants' world rested on imagined landscapes, faces, and relationships. For the Gemmills, the Scotts, the Wilson brothers, and the thousands of others both at home and away, this transatlantic web of kin and community was central to their lives.

Conclusion

A year after Harriet Pengelly left Liverpool, her diary continued to offer testimony to the importance of letters from home. Although in the spring of 1836 she no longer despaired when on post day there were no letters, she still sometimes "shed very bitter tears" of disappointment.[1] As Harriet observed, "I must bear it with patience," but her "fears" at receiving no news from home were "maddening."[2] And when the precious letters finally arrived, they often brought both reassurance and unhappiness. For Harriet, the anniversary of the day she and Robert "sailed from England" was worthy of comment. "Fatal day" she cryptically concluded.[3] But she took comfort that next year she would at least have the opportunity to visit "a mother so justly adored" and "a father so truly beloved" who were now divided from her "by the Atlantic."[4]

In the end, Robert made the trip home alone. Shortly after her last diary entry in April 1836, Harriet died. During the passage home that summer, Robert was "very, very unhappy." His shipboard journal recorded a poignant ambivalence that many emigrants undoubtedly shared. He wrote that he wished he "had not left Canada." At the same time, "I regret more & more, every hour having brought my poor dear dear departed wife to this Country."[5] A year later, Robert returned to the colony and made it his home.

For the Scotts, who had arrived in Upper Canada a year earlier, returning home for a visit does not seem to have been an option. Although various Redford cousins joined them over the next ten years, and although both John Scott and his cousin William Knox longed to see friends and family in Scotland, the various branches of the family were never reunited. John Gemmill, on the other hand, did gain one of his fondest wishes. In 1842 his eldest son Andrew came to Lanark for a visit.[6] His life was in Scotland, however, and to his parents' great disappointment, he returned home within a few months.

George Forbes, who had left Scotland for Upper Canada in 1845 to seek his fortune, never seems to have returned home, even for a visit. But over the next fifteen years, he did maintain at least an annual correspondence with his father and his brother Charles, who resisted George's frequent entreaties to join him in the colony. Three years after his arrival, George had accepted this. "I do not expect that any of you will come out here now," he wrote. "I should like to see you all face to face," he added, but returning home for a visit was too expensive to contemplate. Meantime, he told them that he imagined them "all seated round the coutry ingleside of an evening ... altogether there."[7] By mid-century, George had married "the widow Thain," the widow of his former employer, and as his letters home reported, he "had more work than he could do."[8] He nonetheless continued to regard the family at home as a source of emotional and financial security; he requested and received a loan of £38 from his father in 1853–54 (for which he was truly grateful), and in 1858, although firmly settled in the New World with a growing family of his own, he continued to imagine that the family could be reunited: "Sometime we thought some of you were coming out and that you would walk in some fine morning and take us be surprise." But, as he conceded, "by all appearances that is not likely to happen in a hurry."[9]

The Huttons returned for a working holiday in the mid-1850s. By then, they had virtually given up farming, and William had become a very able member of the colonial civil service. Despite Fanny's initial resistance to emigrating to the colonies, she seems to have become reconciled to her new life. Certainly, the first few years were difficult. In an attempt to maintain the family's status as "gentle" emigrant settlers, William was forced to take up teaching to supplement the family's income. His letters home suggest that Fanny assumed much of the responsibility for maintaining the farm, with the assistance of her children and, when possible, hired help. Thomas and Ellen Langton and Aunt Alice never saw England again. But Anne Langton did go home, in 1847, after her brother John married and her mother and aunt had died. She returned to the colony three years later to help raise her nieces and nephews.

We have no real idea how Joseph Wilson and his family – or the Harts or Peters – fared after they arrived in the colonies. And one wonders whether George Pashley and his family stayed in Cobourg or whether, like so many new arrivals, they moved in search of better opportunities or to continue the work of the Lord. The fate of the thousands of emigrants whose names appear briefly in "information wanted" notices in colonial newspapers – or in the extant records of various benevolent societies or the reports of emigrant agents – remain completely in shadows. Some undoubtedly returned home disillusioned with what they saw as the broken promises of the New World. Others, after a time in Upper Canada, continued on their journey and looked for a new home in the United States or in the far west of the continent, or they may have gone to one of the other parts of the British Empire, perhaps Australia or South Africa.

For many, and perhaps most, "home" continued to be the village or town of their youth in Great Britain or Ireland. For most Irish, Scots, and English who made their way to the New World between 1815 and 1845, the process of emigration did not sever ties with families, friends, and the familiar landscapes of home. As they wrote home from Upper Canada, read and reread letters from their own or their neighbours' families and friends, and as they quizzed newly arrived emigrants or eagerly scanned newspapers for news of "home," these emigrant men, women, and children were reaffirming their membership in communities that spanned the Atlantic. For many, although their decision to emigrate had broken up families and divided them from kith and kin, it had also often rested on a determination to reunite families and rebuild familiar communities. As daughters and sons left parents when they boarded ships bound for the New World, they often did so in the company of cousins or in order to join friends or siblings. When wives left home to find and join their husbands, they were obliged to leave friends and neighbours and, most often, their extended kin. In the first half of the nineteenth century, the Atlantic was both a barrier that divided families and friends – a fearful hurdle to be overcome for those thinking of leaving home – and the means by which parents and children, sisters, brothers, and cousins, and friends and neighbours who lived on two different continents maintained vibrant relationships.

Participation in the world of emigration did fundamentally alter the relationships between those at home and those who were away – and this was not just a question of distance. Individuals and families who (usually after considerable thought) had decided to leave home gradually began to enter a world that those who had no interest in emigration could not appreciate or really understand. Despite what were often detailed descriptions in letters from Upper Canada and in the growing number of accounts written by travellers, emigrants, and settlers that were available in Great Britain and Ireland, the New World was still a foreign land. And it must have been increasingly difficult for George Forbes's parents in Scotland or Andrew Gemmill in Glasgow to imagine what life would be like for family members who were now settled in Upper Canada. And for those emigrants who gradually came to identify themselves as settlers, or Canadians, their sense of home became an increasingly imaginary and undoubtedly idealized world whose contours never changed.

The passing of first-generation emigrant settlers invariably changed the dynamics of the transatlantic community. For David and John Gemmill junior, who had been very young when the family left home for Lanark in Upper Canada, Scotland was not even a dream. It was a foreign land. For the Scott children, and particularly John Scott's youngest brothers and sisters, the family farm of Hermiston was at best a hazy memory. But brothers and sisters and then cousins on both sides of the Atlantic were often determined to maintain a familial connection. Andrew Gemmill in Scotland, for example, asked in 1825 that his father send him details of the family history. "Before I say any more," John replied, "I shall first comply with your request with respect to the statement of marriages, births & Deaths of the Family." Then, starting with his own birth, John listed when and where his wife and children had been born, gave the date and place of each of Andrew's sisters' marriages and the birth of their children. "For Margrate & yourself," John wryly concluded, "I daresay you can find the dates of marriage yourself."[10]

Bachelor Isaac Wilson, too, was concerned to maintain the memory of his family intact. His last surviving letter to his brother, in December 1834, included details of his niece's marriage to a Scotsman whom she had met in York and told of the birth of their first child. Isaac also noted that he and his sister expected that his nephew Matthew would soon be married. Jonathan did not know these children; the last time he had seen them was more than fifteen years before. But they had been part of his life, through letters from his brother and infrequently from his sister Fanny. When Matthew wrote to Jonathan in April 1838 to announce Isaac's death, it was evident that Uncle Jonathan had not really been part of his life. "It is with regret that we have to undertake to write to you at this time to inform you of our Uncle Isaac Wilson's death," his letter began. After a brief description of how Isaac's health had deteriorated over the winter, Matthew formally stated that he and his brother had been named executors and they were in large part writing to ask in "what medium you wish to have your money remitted to you." Although the letter was signed "Your affection Nephews," it ended with a postscript: "We understand there is a small sum of money due to Mother from you which had not been received in this country yet, which she wishes us to mention to you."[11]

Uncle Jonathan was clearly offended by this letter, and in his reply to Matthew he obviously asserted his position as uncle, with all the emotional baggage that he anticipated should surround that relationship (and not the impersonal connection of a legatee). Matthew responded, "I received your letter in which you chide me severely and justly if I could not give you good reasons for sending such a short and unsatisfactory letter." Matthew tried to explain: "At the time I wrote I had a very different opinion of you to what I have now. As you had never written to me and as I had never so much as heard my Uncle say anything respecting you, you were an entire stranger to me." He was now, he said, "determined, though contrary to the wishes to the rest of my Family's wishes," to let Jonathan know everything he could about Isaac's last months "in hopes that I shall find you as faithful to me as my Uncle was in his lifetime."[12] Matthew then provided various details of his uncle's life and death and explained the terms of the will. He ended the letter, "Your dutiful and affection nephew, Matthew Waite." Matthew and his uncle continued to correspond for the next two years. Matthew's letters began to include greetings to his aunts and cousins in Britain; and he urged his uncle to visit them. A large part of this burgeoning relationship certainly rested on the need to settle Isaac Wilson's estate. But Matthew's correspondence also reflects a growing personal connection with his uncle in Britain and his desire to embed himself in a web of kin and community that spanned the Atlantic.

The death of John Scott's father was reported home by both John and his cousin William. In November 1845 John passed on "the sorrowful intelligence" that his "dear Father [had] departed this life."[13] After relating, in some detail, his father's growing physical deterioration over the five days before he died, John recounted, "Thus, My dear Uncle and Aunt, passed away from amongst us, the spirit of a loving Husband, an affectionate parent and a sincere and upright Christian." John took some solace that "Providence" had been remarkably kind "in sparing" his father for so long, and that after ten years in the colony, their wilderness farm was now "in a worldly view prosperous."

John appears to have been determined not to lose the vital connection with "home" that had so strongly flowed through his parents' generation. He cherished news from home that he received from "several old acquaintances who [themselves] have been home." He obviously did not expect ever to make the trip himself, but, he asked his uncle and family, "Will we not see some of you here?" In the meantime, he said, "Write me soon," and "Be sure, if you can, to send me particularly about all their [his cousins'] ages, birthdays ... and everything about yourselves & prospects and my old friends."

For John Scott, who spent most of this adult life in the colonies, Scotland and the family and friends of the Old World continued to play an important part in his life and in his understanding of his place in the world. Even though he and his family had undoubtedly recognized as they boarded the ship that took them to America that they would never see home again, Scott (like all those who left Great Britain and Ireland in the first half of the nineteenth century) took with him considerable emotional as well as physical baggage. The latter might be lost or stolen on the voyage; the former could not.

Many carried their faith across the Atlantic, and it was a source of strength and reassurance. It was also one of the central things that continued to unite them with those they had left behind. John Gemmill, George Pashley, and thousands of others knew that even if they were not reunited with kin in this life, they would be in the next. In the meantime, they had to trust in God and be thankful for his blessings. George Pashley's faith also provided him with an entry into a community of believers that offered emotional sustenance and physical assistance, as it did for thousands of others. As they listened to the familiar liturgy in churches and meeting houses throughout Upper Canada, they also maintained an ongoing connection with the community of believers at home.

Emigrants also brought with them identities rooted in place and time and personal circumstances – identities that shaped their experiences both in the world of emigration and after. They were Scots, Irish, English, or Welsh; they were tailors, doctors, labourers, farmers, and gentlemen and women. It is not surprising that George Pashley seems to have been equally perturbed by the companions on board ship who refused to join him in prayer and by the Irish emigrants who accompanied the family up the St Lawrence River. It is also not particularly remarkable that he seems to have sought out settlers from "home" – Yorkshire men and women – who offered a welcome sense of familiarity in a foreign land. John Gemmill was fortunate that he emigrated and settled in the company of Glaswegians and neighbours. For many, the need to find like folk in the New World extended to asserting their identity with a particular region or village at home. Those who placed "information wanted" notices that included details about the individual they were seeking almost always included their ethnicity; and often they noted the specific community they had called home. In part, this was undoubtedly to help the public identify them; it was also an affirmation of the identity of those who were looking.

In the world of emigration, participants were also identified – and identified themselves – by class, gender, and place in the family circle, and each of these had an immediate influence on their experiences in this difficult liminal space. Gentlemen and gentlewomen who travelled first class were usually relatively comfortable and could avoid many of the difficulties encountered by those who, if only briefly, had to live below decks. No one could escape, however, the physical and emotional tumult of Atlantic storms, seasickness, and fears of shipwreck. Those who had little choice whether they would go or stay – such as children and reluctant wives – must have found the experience of the ocean crossing particularly difficult. Whether in a cabin or travelling steerage, emigrants did try to shape their surroundings and activities to reflect the world they had left. Women spent considerable time looking after children, feeding their families, and attending to "housekeeping" chores. While children played, husbands tried to find or maintain their own routines. Without livestock to tend, a craft to pursue, or business to see to, this could often be difficult. Even Joseph Wilson and William Peters, who had regular prayer meetings to lead, found the voyage tedious.

It was perhaps the Atlantic crossing and the subsequent journey into the interior that, for most participants in the emigrants' world, marked the personal transition from the Old World to the New. Spending weeks cut off from the rest of the world, fearful that one might not arrive, and wondering, at least periodically, whether this really had been the right decision, had a profound impact on all involved. Many clung tenaciously to old identities and familiar activities as the only way to cope in this nether world. Those travelling in a neighbourhood party may have found the sense of dislocation somewhat muted. For most, however, the isolation of the Atlantic was accentuated by the foreignness of one's companions. Yet after weeks of being thrown together, a sense of shared purpose gradually developed. Despite differences in rank and occupation, in age and gender, and in expectations and experiences, participants became part of a community of emigration – one they shared with those who had gone before and those who would come after. It was, in many respects, an imaginary world, but one whose membership continued after they had landed in Quebec or Montreal.

In the end, those who became part of the emigrants' world relied on their identities within their families to see them through. From the beginning, emigration was a family affair. Even when individual family members were not present, emigrants carried with them their identity as husbands and wives, parents and children, cousins and even distant kin. Their relationships with kin helped sustain them both on the journey and once they arrived in the colony. This is not to suggest that everyone who left home was eager to participate in the world of emigration. Harriet Pengelly was certainly not the only young woman who was fearful at the prospect of leaving home and was miserable throughout the journey. At the same time, even in her private diary there is a matter-of-fact acceptance that she and Robert would leave home, an attitude that was undoubtedly shared by the hundreds of wives who were seeking their husbands. Even Frances Stewart and her husband Thomas – who were financially secure, could travel in relative comfort, and had an immediate entrée into colonial "society" when they arrived in Upper Canada – were apprehensive about their decision to emigrate and what the future held. Certainly, many emigrants were never reconciled to living in the colonies, and some, at least, returned home disillusioned and disheartened. Most stayed, either secure in the knowledge that they had made the right decision or because they were unable to imagine returning or could not afford to do so. All were touched by their experiences in this liminal world of emigration, however.

The world of emigration that had been and continued to be instrumental in creating communities in the New World must, for many, have begun to fade as they settled into new lives in the colony. Yet it was one of the fundamental spaces which most in the colony had shared. Certainly, few if any had entered the world of emigration as men and women of empire or with the expectation that they were creating a "greater" Britain and were civilizing the world. They had left home for a variety of reasons, and the decision to go had been rooted in personal circumstances. Most had taken a considerable time making up their minds, and even after they had arrived in Upper Canada, they continued to look back across the Atlantic to those they had left behind. The "tide" of emigration of the first half of the nineteenth century flowed both ways. It was its own world with its own networks of peoples and experiences. When one steps back, it may appear like an undifferentiated force of nature. At its heart, however, were individual men and women, who left home and remade home as part of family and kin groups and who were connected to this world by their connections to each other.

A Note on Sources: Reading and Writing about the Emigrants' World

The idea for this project began when, as I was canvassing local Upper Canadian newspapers for my study *Wives and Mothers, School Mistresses and Scullery Maids,* I kept coming across cards from newly arrived emigrants who were looking for a relative or friend. At the time, they were tangential to my study of women and work, but I did wonder what these people, particularly the women who were looking for their husbands, were doing and how they found themselves in this situation. I returned to the subject some time later expecting to write a nice little article about women and migration. I soon discovered, however, that these women and men were part of a complex and interconnected world of emigration and that their stories were intimately tied to their relationships to their families and communities. Trying to capture and understand their experiences led me to the voluminous and often contentious literature on immigration-emigration – what most scholars now simply term migration. Many of the historiographical debates about particular issues dealing with migration from Great Britain and Ireland in the first half of the nineteenth century are included in the notes for each chapter. What follows is a brief overview of some of the scholarship that shaped my own thinking on the subject – and provided much-needed direction on how best to "get at" the emigrants' world and the lives of those who were part of it.

For much of the twentieth century, the classic works on immigration to North America included Marcus Lee Hansen's *The Atlantic Migration, 1607–1860: A History of the Continuing Settlement of the United States* (1940), ed. Arthur M. Schlesinger (Cambridge, Mass.: Harvard University Press, 1951); Oscar Handlin's *The Uprooted*, 2nd edn (Boston: Little Brown, 1973); and, in the Canadian context, Helen Cowan's *British Emigration to British North America, 1783–1837* (Toronto: University of Toronto [1937], 1961). These and other scholars were primarily interested in the "push-pull" dynamics of the process, and they deftly used government records to tell stories of men, women, and children who were "pushed" out of their homes and "pulled" to the land of opportunity. Cowan's *British Emigration*, reprinted in 1961, remains a very useful account of British policy during the period. So does H.J.M. Johnston's *British Emigration Policy, 1815–1830: Shovelling Out the Paupers* (Oxford: Clarenton Press, 1971) and W.S. Shepperson's *British Emigration to North America: Projects and Opinions in the Early Victorian Period* (Oxford: Basil Blackwood, 1957).

In the last forty years or so, however, the grand studies of migration and the accounts of government policy have largely been overtaken by a new generation of scholars who have asked fundamentally different questions about the process of migration. Historians, sociologists, economists and those wanting to trace familial roots have consciously stepped out of a "top down" approach and have increasingly been interested in the complexity and particularity of migrants' experiences. In part this was a consequence of a growing awareness of the ethnic complexity of North American societies and the recognition by some that this was not a particularly new phenomenon. Others wanted to retell the story of the nation state and to bring to light what Canadian historian Franca Iacovetta has called "the clash and accommodations" of various immigrant communities and the way that immigrant communities related to and influenced the shape of the host society.[1] Studies of migration and migrants now reflect a panoply of dynamic images and relationships that were played out in place and time, in which the forces of ethnicity, gender, race, and class interact and intermingle.

For many North American historians, their interest in migration is directly linked to their attempt to understand the project of nation building. There are still heated debates among U.S. colonial historians, for example, about whether a unique "American" identity was rooted in the arrival in the seventeenth century of English Puritan migrants who were drawn to the New World because of their desire for religious freedom. Timothy Breen, in *Puritans and Adventurers: Change and Persistence in Early America* (New York: Oxford University Press, 1980), Virginia DeJohn Anderson, in *New England's Generation: The Great Migration and the Formation of Society and Culture in the Seventeenth Century* (New York: Cambridge University Press, 1991), and Alison Games, in *Migrations and the Origins of the English Atlantic World* (Cambridge: Harvard University Press, 1999) are three among many who have persuasively argued that such simple equations distort the historical record. David Hackett Fischer, for example, contends in *Albion's Seed: Four British Folkways in America* (New York: Oxford University Press, 1989), that migrants from Great Britain to colonial America in the seventeenth and eighteenth centuries transplanted a number of regional cultures, or "folkways," that persisted for some time. Although many are sympathetic to Fischer's interpretation, he has also evoked heated opposition, as is evidenced in a "Forum on Fischer, *Albion's Seed*," in *William and Mary Quarterly*, April 1991. In the Canadian context, a number of historians continue to assume that the more conservative political and social culture of the nation is rooted in the "tory" ideology of the loyalist refugees of the American Revolution. Others, such as Philipp Buckner and his colleagues who explore the "British world" in the nineteenth and twentieth centuries, argue that British North America and then Canada became British in large part because of the arrival of hundreds of thousands of migrants from Great Britain, who brought with them particular social and political sensibilities.[2] Franca Iacovetta, on the other hand, has emphasized the multicultural nature of the nineteenth- and twentieth-century nation state, and this is particularly clear in her edited collection, *A Nation of Immigrants* (Toronto: University of Toronto Press, 1995).

Studies of immigration – coming into the country – and of acculturation take as their vantage point the new host community. They look "out" from North America to try to understand how particular cultural practices and political propensities persisted and shaped New World societies. They are primarily concerned with the relationship between immigration and nation building. These works raised fundamental questions – about who came and why and what assumptions they brought with them – which my study could not ignore. At the same time, the focus here is on leaving home – of looking towards North America – and this raised other questions and concerns.

Charlotte Erickson was one of the first American scholars to emphasize the complexity of European migrations in the nineteenth century, and the questions she raised in her many articles on the subject and in *Leaving England: Essays on British Emigration in the Nineteenth Century* (Ithaca & London: Cornell University Press, 1994) continue to resonate in the literature. (Erickson herself credits the 1960 article by Frank Thistlethwaite, "Migration from Europe Overseas," recently reprinted in *A Century of Euro Migrations, 1830–1930*, ed. Rudolph Vecoli and Suzanne Sinke [Urbana: University of Illinois Press, 1991], for first bringing these issues to the fore.) Among other things, Erickson argued that nineteenth-century migration was not primarily "national in scope" (British, German, or Italian, etc.) but was "constituted by particular streams from one village or region to a particular country or city elsewhere."[3] She also contended that "the movement overseas" in the nineteenth century "needed to be interpreted in conjunction with internal migration"[4] – an observation that Dirk Hoerder has recently embraced in *Cultures in Contact: World Migrations in the Second Millennium* (Durham: Duke University Press, 2002). This was also one of the basic findings of Bernard Bailyn's influential study, *Voyages to the West: A Passage of the Peopling of America on the Eve of the Revolution* (New York: Knopf, 1986). Based on an impressive analysis of all available data, Bailyn concluded that the movement of Europeans, particularly those from Great Britain and Ireland to America in the 1760s and early 1770s, was an extension of movement within Western Europe. Bailyn identified and analysed two streams of migration – the provincial and the metropolitan (from London) – and argued that each was propelled by different economic and social factors. Among other things, *Voyages to the West* suggested that the migrations of the post-1815 period were but an extension of that of the eighteenth century, interrupted by war and revolution. *Voyages* also made it clear that the Atlantic Ocean was not so much a barrier as a conduit and means of communication – an understanding that echoed Ian Steele's *The English Atlantic, 1675–1740* (Oxford: Oxford University Press, 1980). Such grand narratives do not really consider, however, how or even whether such factors as ethnicity, specific regional circumstances, or even particular individual situations may have influenced the decision to leave home. What is often termed human agency, and the role that family and community had in the process, is too easily lost amid the "streams" of Britons.

One of the central issues that both *Voyages* and the "information wanted" notices in colonial newspapers raise is how those who arrived in Upper Canada in the first half of the nineteenth century identified themselves and understood their world. There is considerable debate among scholars about whether "Great Britain" and even the "British Empire" are useful categories of analysis. British scholars now generally agree that in the eighteenth century, "the notion of a British state is misleading."[5] Despite the conclusions of Linda Colley, in *Britons: Forging the Nation, 1707–1837* (New Haven: Yale University Press, 1992), Jane Ohmmeter persuasively argues that until well into the nineteenth century, the category "British History" remains but "a synonym for the collective political histories of England, Scotland, Wales," and perhaps Ireland. Only the elites embraced any sense of "Britishness." Most who lived in Great Britain and Ireland and those who emigrated to the New World identified themselves not as British or Britons but as English, Irish, Scots, and Welsh, and this study uses this terminology.

Such a basic assumption about the importance of ethnicity is evident in the way most scholars now frame their studies of migration from Great Britain and Ireland. American and Irish historians have been fascinated by the large number of Irish who left home for the New World in the eighteenth and nineteenth centuries, and particularly by the famine migrations of the late 1840s. Within the community of Irish studies, debates about who migrated and why are protracted and heated. For Kirby Miller, nineteenth-century Irish migrants were "exiles" who were forced to flee their home as a result of economic, social, and political pressure. In *Emigrants and Exiles: Ireland and the Irish Exodus to North America* (Oxford & New York: Oxford University Press, 1985), most of his subjects are Catholic labourers who took their particular world view, and the bitterness bred of prejudice and poverty, to America. In *Irish Immigrants in the Land of Canaan* (Oxford: Oxford University Press, 2003), Miller acknowledged that in the early part of the century, a significant number of Irish migrants were Protestants who had some means. He continues to view the Irish migration as unique, however, when compared with that of other Europeans. Donald Akenson disagrees. In *If the Irish Ran the World* (Kingston & Montreal: McGill-Queen's University Press, 1997), Akenson persuasively argues that Irish migrations in the eighteenth and nineteenth centuries (if not before) were not "an exception to the patterns that … dominated Western Europe."[6] More importantly, Akenson illustrates in *The Irish in Ontario* (Montreal & Kingston: McGill-Queen's University Press, 1984) that most Irish emigrants to British North America in the first half of the nineteenth century were not Catholic; they did not congregate in colonial cities; and they did not, as many have argued, become part of a new working class that fuelled the emergence of the new industrial state. Those who arrived in Upper Canada in significant numbers were Protestant farmers who soon became successful and were assimilated into colonial society. Cecil J. Houston and William J. Smyth's study, *Irish Emigration and Canadian Settlement: Patterns, Links, and Letters* (Toronto: University of Toronto Press, 1990), shares this understanding.

The question "What about the Irish?" has led other historians to undertake local detailed studies of migration in the nineteenth century.

In *Irish Migrants in the Canadas* (Montreal & Kingston: McGill-Queen's University Press, 1988), Bruce Elliott followed Protestant farmers from Tipperary to their new homes in Leeds and Landsdowne, Upper Canada, and concluded that far from being pushed out of Ireland, they were "rational men and women who crossed the Atlantic after weighing carefully the advantages and disadvantages of remaining where they were."[7] Ties of kinship and community shaped both their leaving and their patterns of settlement and encouraged others to follow. In *A New Lease on Life: Landlords, Tenants, and Immigrants in Ireland and Canada* (Montreal & Kingston: McGill-Queen's University Press, 1994), Catharine Anne Wilson explored the situation of a group of Irish tenants who left Lord Cashel's estates and settled on Amherst Island, Upper Canada. She persuasively illustrates that the tenants' personal circumstances and community networks were of greater significance in their decision to leave home than their ethnic identity. The debate about who these Irish migrants were and why they left home continues. What is clear is that ethnicity alone does not explain the motivation to migrate or the nature of the experience itself.

There is somewhat less debate, though no less interest, about emigration from Scotland to North America in the nineteenth century. As Marjory Harper has recently noted, much of the focus continues to be on Highland migration and the clearances.[8] But as she and others have cogently argued, the "Scottish story" is no less complex than any other. As Marianne McLean, *The People of Glengarry: Highlands in Transition, 1745–1820* (Montreal & Kingston: McGill-Queen's University Press, 1991), and J.I. Little, *Crofters and Habitants: Settler Society, Economy and Culture in a Quebec Township, 1848–1871* (Montreal & Kingston: McGill-Queen's University Press, 1991), illustrate, Scots migrants, like the Irish, not only left their "nation" but also left particular communities; they were propelled by specific circumstances which they confronted at home, and they were encouraged by ongoing networks of kin and community abroad. The work of Scottish historian T.M. Devine – *Scottish Emigration and Scottish Society* (Edinburgh: John Donald Publishers, 1992), *The Scottish Nation* (London: Penguin, 1999), and *Scotland's Empire, 1600–1815* (London: Penguin, 2003) – has been particularly useful for this study. But it is primarily the continuing scholarship of Marjory Harper, including her *Emigration from North-East Scotland*, vol, 1: *Willing Exiles* (Aberdeen: Aberdeen University Press, 1988), "British Migration and the Peopling of the Empire," in Andrew Porter, ed., *The Oxford History of the British Empire: The Nine-*

teenth Century (Oxford: Oxford University Press, 1999), and with Michael E. Vance, *Myth Migration and the Making of Memory: Scotia and Nova Scotia 1800–1990* (Halifax & Edinburgh: John Donald Publishers, 1999), that has been particularly illuminating.

As Bruce Elliott notes in "Regional Patterns of English Immigration,"[9] although the English have usually be seen, erroneously, as the numerical majority of migrants, they remain largely invisible in the literature on nineteenth-century migration to North America. Indeed, the ubiquitousness of "Englishness" seems to have blinded scholars to considering migrants from England as a distinct group. Charlotte Erickson's classic works, *Leaving England* and *Invisible Immigrants* began to resurrect the history of English immigrants to the United States, based on ships' records and correspondence. Wendy Cameron and Mary McDougall Maude's *Assisting Emigration to Upper Canada: The Petworth Project 1832–1837* and *English Immigrant Voices* (both published by McGill-Queen's University Press in 2000) have been invaluable additions to the literature. But as Elliott notes, what is needed are studies similar to his *Irish Migrants* that trace the regional and familial origins of English migrants, in order to begin to appreciate both who they were and why they may have left home. This is painstaking work, and until very recently it has been done only by genealogists interested in family roots.

These and other studies make it abundantly evident that a migrant's ethnicity cannot be discounted; it is also clear, however, that ethnicity was not a driving factor in the decision to leave home. One also has to consider issues of class, gender, place in the family, and the emigrants' personal situations at a particular time, in their own immediate community or region, and the information they received from friends and family who had gone before. I assume, as Dirk Hoerder has recently declared in his very fine study, *Cultures in Contact: World Migrations in the Second Millennium*, that one must have an appreciation of both the circumstances in the leaving society and "the human agency of particular men and women."[10] As David Fitzpatrick eloquently stated in *Oceans of Consolation* (Ithaca and London: Cornell University Press, 1994), this study wants to get at the experiences and understandings of the migrants themselves. To do this, it relies heavily on their own understandings of their circumstances – understandings seen through the "information wanted" notices they placed in local newspapers, the journals and diaries they kept, and the letters they sent home. Within this framework, the fundamental dynamics were not, as many earlier historians of migration have assumed, individual men and women who struck out on their own for the New World or streams of undifferentiated migrants; rather, it was husbands and wives, parents and children. Based on the record, and echoing the conclusions of others – notably David Fitzpatrick's study of Irish migrants to Australia and David Gerber's recent *Authors of Their Lives: The Personal Correspondence of British Immigrants to North America in the Nineteenth Century* (New York: New York University Press, 2006) – this study argues that emigration was a decidedly family affair. It also assumes that it is in the everyday experiences of emigrants – as they made their decisions, prepared to leave home, and coped with the journey itself – that one can begin to appreciate what David Cressy has called "the emigrants' world." I am particularly indebted to Cressy's *Coming Over: Migration and Communication between England and New England in the Seventeenth Century* (Cambridge: Cambridge University Press, 1987). His emphasis on the importance of the continuing lines of communication across the Atlantic and his assumption that the experience of the crossing had a profound impact on emigrants' lives and expectations have certainly shaped this study.

This study rests on two very different kinds of primary sources. Few historians have mined the "information wanted" notices that regularly appeared in colonial newspapers. The one exception is Ruth-Ann Harris. In her introduction to *The Search for Missing Friends,* she notes that "the advertisements in this volume ... provide valuable social and demographic information on Irish immigrants in North America,"[11] and her introduction offers an analysis of where Irish emigrants came from, who they were, and their patterns of mobility in North America. "Information wanted" notices also offer historians an insight into how their authors' presented themselves and their situation to the general public.

A more traditional source are migrants' letters, journals, and diaries. There is considerable debate among historians about whether personal correspondence really brings us any closer to understanding why people left home and what their experiences were on the journey. I share Charlotte Erickson's view that letters are a "unique historical source."[12] In *Invisible Immigrant: The Adaption of English and Scottish Immigrants in the Nineteenth century* (Ithaca & New York: Cornell University Press, 1972), she cautioned, however, that letters that were published at the time have to be viewed with rather more skepticism than manuscript collections, for they were published to promote a particular political purpose – either to encourage or to discourage emigration. Terry McDonald's recent article, "Come to Canada While You Have a Chance," in *Ontario*

History (Autumn 1999), shares this concern. My study rests on a reading of both published and unpublished letters and journals. Initially, I had intended to rely primarily on unpublished manuscript sources, because too often published collections, even those that have appeared recently, are heavily edited, and one is never sure what has been left out. As others have found, a surprising number of letters and journals have survived. Much of what is used here is from collections in the Archives of Ontario, Trent and Queen's universities, the National Library of Scotland, the Scottish Record Office, and the British National Library. Particular collections were selected based on when the letters were written or at least when the correspondence was begun (between 1815 and 1845), and on the requirement that one of the correspondents was in Upper Canada. I was particularly fortunate that many surviving letters of the Petworth emigrants, brought together by Wendy Cameron, Mary McDougall Maude, and Sheila Haines, appeared during the preparation of this study. With their detailed explanations of the provenance of the letters and as complete a transcription as possible, both *English Immigrant Voices*, and the companion volume, *Assisting Emigration to Upper Canada*, have been mined extensively.

How one "uses" emigrants' letters as a source is a matter of some debate. Certainly, they are no more "objective" or reliable than other sources. As many others have found, reading migrants' correspondence requires one often to "read between the lines." David Fitzpatrick's *Oceans of Consolation* was particularly influential in my own reading of emigrant correspondence. Fitzpatrick also highlighted the need to appreciate how distance and time shaped the tone and subject of letters. In our world of instant communication, one is immediately struck by how long letters could take to cross the Atlantic. Jane Harrison's *Until Next Year* (Ottawa: Canadian Postal Museum, 1997), and Judith Hudson Beattie and Helen M. Buss's edited collection, *Undelivered Letters to Hudson's Bay Men on the Northwest Coast of America, 1830–57* (Vancouver: University of British Columbia Press, 2003) both explain the mechanics of "the mails" and the difficulties that many encountered. As David Gerber has very recently discussed in *Authors of Their Lives*, sending and receiving mail took time, knowledge, and often scarce funds. Letters, journals, and diaries were also a form of what is now called "life writing." Royden K. Loewen, in *Hidden Worlds: Revisiting the Mennonite Migrants of the 1870s* (Winnipeg: University of Manitoba Press, 2001), and a number of others, including David Gerber, have discussed how letters, journals, and diaries were a way for their writers both to make sense of the new worlds they were encountering and to "form" themselves in their new lives without losing connections to the old. The published and unpublished letters used here are certainly evidence of this, and, where possible, I have tried to tickle out the worlds, assumptions, and sensibilities behind the written words.

It must be stressed that the subjects of this emigrants' world are not intended to be representative of any particular national or ethnic grouping or of any particular age, gender, or class. Although all these factors certainly influenced emigrants' decisions to leave home, their experiences of the journey, and what they found in the New World, at heart this is a social history of migrating families. It assumes that family networks were the basis of those streams of migrants that so influenced the development of Upper Canada in the first half of the nineteenth century. At the same time, families were rooted in face-to-face communities – both physical and imagined – and the very experience of migration continued to shape those communities for some considerable time. Without the work of so many other scholars, the stories here could not have been told.

Notes

INTRODUCTION

1 *Niagara Herald*, 21 June 1830.
2 *Canadian Freeman*, 25 August 1831.
3 *Chronicle and Gazette*, 1 October 1831.
4 Ibid., 22 March 1834.
5 Ibid., 23 September 1835.
6 *Colonial Advocate*, 4 February 1830.
7 *Toronto Patriot*, 18 October 1833. "Information wanted" notices appeared in most newspapers throughout North America in the nineteenth century, and the same notice was often reprinted in various newspapers. Many of them included a brief note on the bottom: "Editors of papers" in other jurisdictions "will be doing the cause of humanity a service by giving the above an insertion." See Ruth-Ann M. Harris and Donald M. Jacobs, eds., *The Search for Missing Friends: Irish Immigrant Advertisements Placed in the Boston Pilot* (Boston: New England Historic Genealogical Society, 1989), for an example of how two scholars have used these notices.
8 Charlotte Erickson, *Leaving England: Essays on British Emigration in the Nineteenth Century* (Ithaca & London: Cornell University Press, 1994), 2. See also Dudley Baines, *Emigration from Europe 1815–1930* (London: Macmillan, 1991), 7. The economic and social dislocations in Great Britain and Ireland after the end of the Napoleonic Wars have been examined in considerable detail by a number of scholars. In addition to references noted below and in "A Note on Sources: Reading and Writing about the Emigrants' World," see Linda Colley, *Britons: Forging a Nation, 1707–1837* (New Haven & London: Yale University Press, 1992); the classic, E.P. Thompson, *The Making of the English Working Class* (Middlesex: Penguin, 1970); Andrew Porter, "Intro-

duction: Britain and the Empire in the Nineteenth Century," and P.J. Cain, "Economics and Empire: The Metropolitan Context," both in *The Oxford History of the British Empire: The Nineteenth Century*, ed. Andrew Porter (Oxford: Oxford University Press, 1999).

9 Our ability to determine, with any level of accuracy, how many English, Irish, Scots, and Welsh emigrated to North America in the post-1815 period is very limited. The colonial records for the period are not complete. The statistics provided in N.H. Carrier and J.R. Jeffery, *External Migration: A Study of the Available Statistics, 1815–1950*, General Register Office, Studies in Medical and Population subjects, no.6 (London: HMSO, 1953), are based on port of departure and entry, not ethnicity, and they made no distinction between passengers and emigrants. Local port authorities and shipmasters also frequently failed to keep any records, and those that were maintained were often incomplete and inaccurate. In *The Irish in Ontario: A Study in Rural History* (Kingston & Montreal: McGill-Queen's University Press, 1984), 14–15, Donald Harman Akenson highlighted the difficulties of even "guestimating" emigration to Upper Canada during this period. For further discussion, see Marjory Harper, *Willing Exiles*, vol. 1 of *Emigration from North-East Scotland* (Aberdeen: Aberdeen University Press, 1988), ch. 1, "The Emigration Business," especially the tables with the notes (35–44).

10 There is considerable debate among scholars of the "new" British and Atlantic histories about whether "Great Britain" and "British Empire" are appropriate or even useful categories of analysis. Some of these debates are considered in "A Note on Sources." For the purposes of this study, references will either be made to "Great Britain and Ireland" or to the "British Isles." An individual's "nationality" will be his or her association with one of the three kingdoms: England (and this will often include Wales), Scotland, and Ireland.

11 Bruce Elliott has cogently argued that "factors such as trade cycles, the impact of war, industrialization and the agricultural revolution affected different localities and regions ... in different ways and to different extents and with varying chronologies and impacted upon social classes differently"; see his "Regional Patterns of English Immigration and Settlement in Upper Canada," in *Canadian Migration Patterns: From Britain and North America*, ed. Barbara J. Messamore (Ottawa: University of Ottawa Press, 2004), 53.

12 There are a number of studies of migration from Great Britain and Ireland in the seventeenth and eighteenth centuries that indicate that the migrations of the nineteenth century were not a new development. Some of these are discussed in "A Note on Sources." See, among others, Bernard Bailyn *Voyages to the West: A Passage of the Peopling of America on the Eve of the Revolution* (New

York: Knopf, 1986); David Cressy, *Coming Over: Migration and Communication between England and New England in the Seventeenth Century* (Cambridge: Cambridge University Press, 1987); Nicholas Canny, ed., *Europeans on the Move: Studies in European Migration 1500–1800* (Oxford: Clarendon Press, 1994); Alison Games, *Migrations and the Origins of the English Atlantic World* (Cambridge, Mass.: Harvard University Press, 1999). T.H. Breen, *Puritans and Adventurers: Change and Persistence in Early America* (Oxford: Oxford University Press, 1980); Virginia DeJohn Anderson, *New England's Generation: The Great Migration and the Formation of Society and Culture in the Seventeenth Century* (New York: Cambridge University Press, 1991).

13 Cain, "Economics and Empire," 37, estimates that between 1815 and 1900 "only one-fifth of emigrants went to the Imperial frontier and four-fifths to the United States." See discussion in Elizabeth Jane Errington's "British Migration and British North America, 1783–1860," in *Oxford History of the British Empire: Canada*, ed. Phillip Buckner (Oxford: Oxford University Press, 2007).

14 This is based on a reading of more than 350 notices from new arrivals. Approximately 70 percent were Irish, 25 percent were Scottish, and the rest were English or Welsh. It would appear that this roughly corresponds to the proportions of those who actually arrived in the colony during this period. Based on Canadian census data, Bruce Elliott notes that the Irish outnumbered the English almost three to one (Elliott, "Regional Patterns of English Immigration," 53). It should be noted, however, that the Scots' preferred destination was British America, and a significant portion of them went to Upper Canada; see Harper, *Willing Exiles*; also her "Crossing the Atlantic: Snapshots from the Migration Album," in *Canadian Migration Patterns*, ed. Messamore; and T.M. Devine, *The Scottish Nation* (London: Penguin, 1999), 470–1. Until the end of the nineteenth century, the English preferred the United States, while the Irish tended to arrive (although not necessarily settle) in British America, particularly in the 1830s and 1840s. But as Donald Akenson (and now others) has clearly shown, the Irish were by far the largest ethnic group in Upper Canada in the nineteenth century (Akenson, *The Irish in Ontario*). See also the discussion in "A Note on Sources."

15 As with numbers and "nationality," it is impossible to determine, with any certainty, the occupational and economic profiles of British and Irish migrants during this period. Charlotte Erickson (*Leaving England*) and Marjory Harper (*Willing Exiles*) argue persuasively that farmers and rural people were particularly attracted to the opportunity of gaining land in the New World. Certainly, Bruce Elliott's migrants were farmers and their families, who were drawn to Upper Canada by the availability of land; see his *Irish*

Migrants in the Canadas: A New Approach (Kingston & Montreal: McGill-Queen's University Press, 1988). As others have noted, however, labourers and gentlemen also were attracted to British America. For further discussion of this see, Marjory Harper, "British Migration and the Peopling of the Empire," in *The Oxford History of the British Empire: The Nineteenth Century*, 76–8.

16 Elliott, "Regional Patterns of English Immigration," 53.
17 For further discussion on the use of emigrant correspondence, see "A Note on Sources."
18 David Gerber, *Authors of Their Lives: The Personal Correspondence of British Immigrants to North America in the Nineteenth Century* (New York: New York University Press, 2006). See also discussion in "A Note on Sources."
19 See discussion in Akenson, *The Irish in Ontario*; and in Cecil J. Houston and William J. Smyth, *Irish Emigration and Canadian Settlement: Patterns, Links, and Letters* (Toronto: University of Toronto Press, 1990). Both make this point abundantly clear.
20 For a discussion of some of these debates, see "A Note on Sources."
21 David Fitzpatrick, *Oceans of Consolation: Personal Accounts of Irish Migration to Australia* (Ithaca & London: Cornell University Press, 1994), 3.
22 Ibid.
23 Ibid., 5.
24 Cressy uses this phrase very effectively in *Coming Over*, ch. 7, and it brings to mind the *Imagined Communities* (London: Verso, 1983) discussed by Benedict Anderson, which rested on images and assumptions that were created and sustained not just by personal experience and face-to-face communities but were extended to the world that was created by print media.

CHAPTER ONE

1 Redford Papers, Scottish Records Office (SRO), GD1/813/1, 29 August 1835.
2 *Scots Times*, 26 June 1832; *Chronicle and Gazette*, 3 June 1840, from *Herald* (London); *Canadian Emigrant*, 6 July 1833; *Christian Guardian*, 3 July 1830; *Kingston Chronicle*, 26 June 1830.
3 This characterization was used frequently in both the British and colonial press. See for example, *Manchester Guardian*, 17 April 1830; *Kingston Chronicle*, 3 November 1818 and 26 May 1832; *Cobourg Star*, 17 May 1832, from *Fife Herald* and *Bell's Messenger*.
4 Marjory Harper, *Willing Exiles*, vol. 1 of *Emigration from North-East Scotland* (Aberdeen: Aberdeen University Press, 1988), 7.
5 David Fitzpatrick, *Oceans of Consolation: Personal Accounts of Irish Migration to Australia* (Ithaca & London: Cornell University Press, 1994), 35. For fur-

ther discussion of emigrants' motives, see Dirk Hoerder and Horst Rossler, eds., *Distant Magnets: Expectations and Realities in the Immigrant Experience, 1840–1930* (New York & London: Homes & Meier, 1993); Dirk Hoerder, *Cultures in Contact: World Migration in the Second Millennium* (Durham & London: Duke University Press, 2002), 16–18; and David A. Gerber, *Authors of Their Lives: The Personal Correspondence of British Immigrants to North America in the Nineteenth Century* (New York & London: New York University Press, 2006).

6 *Edinburgh Saturday Post*, 8 March 1828. See also article from *Bell's Weekly Messenger*, reprinted in *Kingston Chronicle*, 24 May 1822; *Christian Guardian*, 21 May 1834, from *Cork Chronicle*; *British Whig*, 8 July 1834, from *Glasgow Chronicle*.

7 From Edinburgh *Scotsman*, quoted in *Kingston Gazette*, 8 September 1818.

8 *Kingston Gazette*, 17 December 1819; from *Greenock Advertiser* reprinted in *Kingston Chronicle*, 11 August 1820. Such rhetoric persisted throughout the period. See, for example, a report in a London paper that commented wryly, "The bee is on the wing, but the drone is left behind" (report from London paper in *Christian Guardian*, 2 June 1832). See also reports in *British Whig*, from *Glasgow Chronicle*, 8 July 1834; "Howison," *Blackwood's Edinburgh Magazine*, 1824, 536; *Christian Guardian*, from an Enniskillen report, 11 June 1830; *Kingston Chronicle*, taken from *Greenock Advertiser*, 11 August 1820; *Kingston Gazette*, taken from the Edinburgh *Scotsman*, 8 September 1818.

9 "Bandana on Emigration," *Blackwood's*, September 1826, 474. See also *Kingston Chronicle*, 24 May 1822. As Marjory Harper notes in "British Migration and the Peopling of the Empire," these debates were not new and they continued throughout the nineteenth century. With few exceptions, the government "avoided positive intervention"; see *The Oxford History of the British Empire: The Nineteenth Century*, ed. Andrew Porter (Oxford: Oxford University Press, 1999), 77. For details of earlier British policies, see Bernard Bailyn, *Voyages to the West* (New York: Knopf, 1986), ch. 2. For discussions of the few government programs to assist emigrants to relocate in Upper Canada, see, Bruce S. Elliott, *Irish Migrants in the Canadas* (Kingston & Montreal: McGill-Queen's University Press, 1988); Harper, *Willing Exiles*; and Elizabeth Jane Errington, "British Migration and British America, 1783–1867," in *Oxford History of the British Empire: Canada*, ed. Phillip Buckner (Oxford: Oxford University Press, 2007). Older accounts that detail various projects of assisted emigration to Upper Canada include Helen Cowan's *British Emigration to British North America, 1783–1837* (Toronto: University of Toronto, 1928); H.J.M. Johnston's *British Emigration Policy, 1815–1830: Shovelling*

Out the Paupers (Oxford: Clarendon Press, 1971); and S. Shepperson's *British Emigration to North America: Projects and Opinions in the Early Victorian Period* (Oxford: Blackwell, 1957).

10 "America" was a continental vision and one that included the British colonies. Thomas Haliburton, for example, who wrote *An Historical and Statistical Account of Nova Scotia in Two Volumes*, (Halifax, 1829), characterized "the history of America," which included all the former and current British possessions, as the "story of the progress of man from a state of nature towards civilization"; quoted in Daniel John Keon, "The 'New World' Idea in British North America: An Analysis of Some British Promotional, Trade, and Settler Writings, 1784 to 1860" (Kingston: PHD thesis, Queen's University, 1984), 243–4. British newspapers, reporting ships sailing for "America," regularly included those bound for Quebec and Halifax, as well as for New York, Philadelphia, and New Orleans. And many travellers referred to their trips to and travels in "America" (Keon, "The 'New World' Idea," 241). See also John MacGregor, *British America* (Edinburgh and London, 1832), 439, who explicitly stated: "In America, as well as in the United States as in the British possessions ... since the 'first planting of North America until the present time' those with the necessary attributes would succeed in the wilderness" (Keon, "The 'New World' Idea," 242, and bibliography, 268ff). See also Martin Doyle, *Hints on Emigration to Upper Canada* (Dublin: Curry, 1831); John MacGregor, *Observations on Emigration to British America* (London: Longman, Rees, Orme, Brown, and Green, 1829). This was also evident in the letters that emigrants sent home. See, for example, many of the letters in *Emigration: Letters of Sussex Emigrants* (London, 1832).

11 Keon, "The 'New World' Idea," 76. Keon notes: "It is impossible to determine exactly how popular the traveler and settler books were." The British magazine *Monthly Review* noted in 1822 that "every month brings forth books of travels through Canada or the Western State of America" (quoted in Gerald Craig, ed., *Early Travelers in the Canadas, 1791–1867* [Toronto: Macmillan, 1955], xviii). Keon himself looked at 450 such accounts that were published between 1784 and 1860 (75–6). The "new" imperial history has given rise to a number of studies of how travellers' accounts were read and understood. See, among others, Robert H. MacDonald, *The Language of Empire: Myths and Metaphors of Popular Imperialism, 1880–1918* (Manchester: Manchester University Press, 1994); William W. Stowe, *Going Abroad: European Travel in Nineteenth-Century American Literature* (Princeton: Princeton University Press, 1994); Sara Mills, *Discourses of Difference: An Analysis of Women's Travel, Travel Writing, and Colonialism* (London: Routledge, 1991); Mary Pratt, *Imperial Eyes: Travel Writing and*

Transculturation (New York: Routledge, 1992); Patricia Jasen, *Wild Things: Nature, Culture, and Tourism in Ontario 1790–1914* (Toronto: University of Toronto Press, 1995).

12 A brief review of the *Manchester Guardian* (1821–40), the London *Observer* (1821–40), *Scots Times, True Scotsman,* (1838–41), *Edinburgh Saturday Post* (1827–28), and *Blackwood's Edinburgh Magazine* for the period indicates that each included quite a wide range of information about British North America. In addition to reports of emigration and settlements, the press paid considerable attention to the nature of the land, the flora and fauna, local colonial politics, and the colonies' history. By the 1830s, reports from or about the colonies were commonplace. Marjory Harper notes a similar phenomenon for an earlier period. She concludes that "letters from early settlers, together with the reports of early travelers, the glowing accounts of soldiers who returned from the war, and the increasing attention paid to America in the Scottish Press ... all helped to spread information about the New World" (*Willing Exiles*, 2).

13 Kathleen Wilson, *The Island Race: Englishness, Empire, and Gender in the Eighteenth Century* (New York: Routledge, 2003), 32. As Wilson notes, this idea of an imagined community created by the press was first raised by Benedict Anderson in *Imagined Communities: Reflections on the Origins and Spread of Nationalism* (London: Verso, 1983). In many ways, the world of emigration was as much an imagined community as it was a physical one.

14 *Counsel for Emigrants and Interesting Information from Numerous Sources* (Aberdeen: John Mathison, 1834); *Sequel to the Counsel for Emigrants* (Aberdeen: John Mathison, 1834); William Catermole, *Emigration: The Advantages of Emigration to Canada* (London, 1831). Harper notes the popularity of *Counsel* in her study *Willing Exiles*, 54–8. Throughout the first half of the century, there appears to have been considerable appetite for emigrants' guides. Some, like *Counsel, Sequel,* and *Chamber's Information*, often refused to give specific advice; rather, they were concerned to present all sorts of information and expected readers to choose what they needed. Others were clearly promotional, like Catermole's *Emigration*.

15 William Blane, *An Excursion through the United States and Canada during the Years 1822–1823*, reprint (New York: Negro Universities Press, 1969), 163. See also comments in Martin Doyle, *Hints on Emigration to Upper Canada* (Dublin, 1831); MacGregor, *Observations on Emigration*; Edward Talbot, *Five Years' Residence in the Canadas* (London, 1824), 220; and *Six Years in the Bush in Upper Canada, 1832–1838* (London, 1838), 86.

16 "Upper Canada," *Blackwood's*, August 1832, 244. See also James Inches, *Letters on Emigration to Canada* (Perth, 1836), 204.

17 *Views of Canada and the Colonies by a Four Years Resident* (Edinburgh, 1844), 247. See also *Hamilton Spectator*, 16 August 1838, quoting from the London *Times*. This became a particular concern after the famine migrations began in 1847. One commentator declared, "To make Canada the sink of Ireland – one Ireland in the world is enough" (*St Catharines Journal*, 29 July 1847, quoting from the London *Times*). A number of commentators recognized the dilemma much earlier. See "Upper Canada," *Blackwood's*, August 1832, 238.

18 *Bell's Weekly Messenger* (London), quoted in *Kingston Chronicle*, 24 May 1822. See also James Taylor, *Narrative of a Voyage to, and Travels in Upper Canada* (Hull: John Nicholson, 1846), 86. Although Taylor thought there were advantages to emigration if an individual was prepared, he also advised that before the prospective emigrant leave home, he "picture himself in a hut in a foreign land." In an image bleaker than most drew, Taylor wrote that, the new settler "will wildly look about the place he has chosen for his habitation for his wife and family, whom he had perhaps dragged from home almost against their will" and will see their "returning looks of despair" 89.

19 William Hutton to landlord, 19 April 1833, quoted in Gerald E. Boyce ed. *Hutton of Hastings: The Life and Letters of William Hutton, 1801–1861*, (Belleville: Hastings County Council, 1972), 5. All future references from the Hutton correspondence are from this collection and will be referred to by date and page.

20 For more details on this, see Elliott, *Irish Migrants*; Donald Harman Akenson, *The Irish in Ontario* (Kingston & Montreal: McGill-Queen's University Press, 1984); Wilson, *A New Lease on Life: Landlords, Tenants, and Immigrants in Ireland and Canada* (Kingston & Montreal: McGill-Queen's University Press, 1994); Harper, *Willing Exiles*; Eric Richard, "Leaving the Highlands: Colonial Destinations in Canada and Australia," in *Myth, Migration and the Making of Memory: Scotia and Nova Scotia 1700–1990*, ed. Marjory Harper and Michael E. Vance (Halifax & Edinburgh: Grosebrook Research Institute for Atlantic Canada Studies, Fernwood and Donald Publishers, 1999); T.M. Devine, *Scotland's Empire* (London: Allen Lane, 2003), *The Great Highland Famine* (Edinburgh: John Donald, 1988), and *The Scottish Nation* (London: Penguin, 1999); Kirby Miller, *Emigrants and Exiles* (Oxford & New York: Oxford University Press, 1985); Cecil J. Houston and William J. Smyth, *Irish Emigration and Canadian Settlement: Patterns, Links, and Letters* (Toronto: University of Toronto Press, 1990); Barbara Messamore, ed., *Canadian Migration Patterns from Britain and North America* (Ottawa: University of Ottawa Press, 2004), Hoerder, *Cultures in Contact*; Gerber, *Authors of Their Lives*.

21 Studies of English migration to America based on limited shipping records suggest that farmers and farm labourers made up about one-quarter of the

adult males who arrived in the United States in 1831. "The agricultural sector as a whole was not over represented among English emigrants" that year, Charlotte Erickson concludes, but those who had either owned or managed farms emigrated in much higher proportions relative to their numbers than in the general population. She suggests that the proportion of "agriculturalist" emigrants who landed in Quebec that year was probably even higher; see Charlotte Erickson, *Leaving England* (Ithaca & London: Cornell University Press, 1994), 126–66, 148–9. See also Harper, *Willing Exiles*, for discussion of Scottish farmers' attraction to emigration, and Elliott, *Irish Migrants*, for a case study of the migration of Irish farm folk to Upper Canada.

22 See Elliott, *Irish Migrants*.
23 Noted in letter to mother, 19 April 1833, *Hutton of Hastings*, 5–6.
24 Ibid.
25 Ibid.
26 Blane, *An Excursion*, 167. See also *Counsel for Emigrants*, 36, 37.
27 Extracts of Diary of George Leith, 21 August 1834, MS69, Archives of Ontario (AO), Leith, who lived outside Hamilton, had visited the colony, returned home to marry, and then brought out his new bride. Isaac Wilson, who arrived in Upper Canada before the War of 1812 and settled near York, frequently told his brother Jonathan about meeting men "prospecting the land." See, for example, a comment on 20 August 1825 that John Barnes's father and family had at last joined him. They "all came safe and live in a house near to him," (Isaac Wilson Diary, AO, MS199). See also diary of John Thompson, vol. 2, 12 August 1834, which noted that he had met a Mr Sheppard who was thinking of settling (AO, MU846, 1-T-2).
28 John Howison was one of many who stated at the beginning of their accounts of life in America that they intended to give accurate information. Without this, John Howison noted, Britons were "the slaves of vague reports" (*Sketches of Upper Canada* (1821; reprint, Toronto: S.R. Publishers, 1965), 61).
29 John Gemmill Family Papers, reply to James Hendry, March 1826, AO, MU7424. These questions were specifically referred to in John Gemmill's reply. As with so many emigrants' letters, only one side of the conversation is extant. Although it is likely that this is the same John Gemmill who left Glasgow in 1821, to establish a home for his family, and whose story is first mentioned in the introduction and picked up again later in this and subsequent chapters, it is impossible to confirm. This collection of letters ended up in the Archives of Ontario; other Gemmill family letters are in the Scottish Record Office.
30 Hendry was referring to the company formed in 1824 that purchased crown land in Upper Canada and resold it to settlers for a profit. Agents in Upper Canada encouraged settlers to buy plots, and those in Great Britain encour-

31 John Gemmill Family Papers, 7 April 1832, AO.
32 Ibid., 21 March 1833, AO.
33 Ibid., 31 March 1834, AO.
34 Mary and Edward O'Brien and others also responded to questions from those at home who were thinking of emigrating. On 28 January 1831, Mary recorded "a request to write a letter for the information of some Monmouthshire folks who are wishing to come." Mary was a firm advocate of emigration, and she frequently urged other family members to join her and her mother in the colony (Journals of Mary O'Brien, AO, MS199).
35 This type of information was quite common in the letters used for this study. For example, Fanny Hutton's cousin told the family that "the climate was not so severe as he had expected to find it" (noted in letter to mother, April 1833, in *Hutton of Hastings*, 5–6). See also letters of Mary and Arthur Stoakes to Mary's brother, John Colquohoum, Scottish Record Office (SRO), GD1/814/5. See also John Macintosh to James McNicol, 8 May 1833, "Emigrants Letters," in National Library of Scotland (NLS), ACC7020. In *Authors of Their Lives*, David Gerber notes that the content of letters was often circumscribed by what the writer assumed was of interest to the intended reader. See, in particular, his discussion in the chapter "Writing with a Purpose."
36 See, for example, *Emigration: Letters from Sussex Emigrants who Sailed from Portsmouth in April 1832* (Petworth, 1833); *Letters from the Dorking Emigrants ...* (London, 1833); *Letters from Sussex Emigrants...* (Chichester, 1837). *Letters and Extracts of Letters from Settlers in Upper Canada* (London, 1834); *Authentic Letters from Upper Canada*, edited by Rev. Thomas Radcliffe (Dublin, 1833; reprint, Toronto: Macmillan, 1953).
37 See discussion in Wendy Cameron et al., *English Immigrant Voices* (Montreal & Kingston: McGill-Queen's University Press, 2000), xxxi. As is discussed in "A Note on Sources," there is considerable debate among scholars today about the "authenticity" of such letters and their value for current studies of migration.
38 Redford Papers, 29 August 1835; see also letter of William Knox to Andrew Redford, 14 February 1842.
39 In the 1830s, British commentary and propaganda began to present pastoral images of Upper Canada. For example, a passage in *Sequel to Counsel for Emigrants* noted that amidst "the tall dark forest ... rise the settlers' farm-houses with their huge wooden barns," carefully tended gardens, and just down the road "a neat white painted cottage with its shrubbery and flowers" (59). Ear-

lier, *Counsel for Emigrants* had observed that improvements in roads, canals, and other modes of conveyance were already "transforming little villages in the wilderness into great and populous towns," and settlers were "busy as the Hives of wild bees so common in forest, and clearing The Bush away to give place to fields of wheat, Indian corn and potatoes" (10).

40 John Scott to Andrew Redford, Redford Papers, October 1834.
41 Ibid., August 1835.
42 William Hendry to Mrs Charles Henry, 15 August 1834, "Emigrant Letters," NLS, ACC9479. See also letters in Cameron et al., *English Immigrant Voices*.
43 Hendry to Hendry, 15 August 1834.
44 Forbes Letters, 18 January 1846, SRO, RH4/80.
45 Reprinted in *Counsel for Emigrants*, 33, 34. Erickson notes in her classic study, *Invisible Immigrants: The Adaption of English and Scottish immigrants in Nineteenth-century America* (Ithaca & London: Cornell University Press, 1972), that most immigrant letters were not meant for publication, and many new arrivals refused to recommend that others join them as they feared being held responsible if the decision did not work out (36 passim). Letters sent from Upper Canada did not seem loath to encourage family members and friends to follow.
46 John Scott explained to his uncle, "Being a farmer here is like laying out Compound Interest, whereas at home, you lay out your money, and have enough ado to get back the principal" (SRO, GD1/813/1, 29 August 1835).
47 "Emigrant Letters," SNL, ACC9479, 15 September 1834. Nonetheless, he concluded, "I don't know any of my friends who have not with help do very well here once they are over." Mary O'Brien, too, would have been happier if her sister Lucy and family had emigrated. After many years of sending information, Mary wrote a long letter on 26 September 1836, apparently prompted by a request from Lucy "on the subject of your emigration.": "I cannot know how to begin or what to say, My dear Lucy, on a subject that interests us to such a degree that my judgement and opinion are, I have no doubt, biased a good deal" (Journals of Mary O'Brien).
48 Mary McNicol to James McNicol, McNicol Letters, 2 August 1831, NLS, ACC7020. John Scott described how at least some "poor people" could "elbow their way along to independence." They took wild land, paid the first or second instalments, improved it as much as they could and then sold it for "twice or thrice what they paid for it" and then took up "another piece of land with a fairer prospect of paying for it" (Redford Papers, 29 August 1835).
49 McNicol Letters, 2 August 1831.
50 Redford Papers, letter from William Knox to Andrew Redford, 14 February 1842, SRO, GD1/813/6.

51 Medd Papers, 23 January 1820, Trent University Archives (TUA), 81–001/12. Similar sentiments were reflected by many of the Petworth emigrants in their letters home.
52 Harper, "British Migration", 83. See also her lengthy discussion in *Willing Exiles*, 210–36.
53 Elliott, *Irish Migrants*, 6.
54 See discussion in Elliott, "Regional Patterns," and Peter N. Moogk, "Reluctant Exiles: Emigrants from France in Canada before 1760," in *Immigration in Canada: Historical Perspectives* ed. Gerald Tulchinsky (Mississauga: Copp Clark Longman, 1994) for the role such factors could play in the decision to emigrate.
55 Cowan, *British Emigration*, 178–80, estimates that, over the entire period, about 10 percent of emigrants were assisted. The proportion varied considerably, however, and may have been as much as 25 percent in 1831–32 when local conditions were particularly dire. See also Johnston, *British Emigration Policy*, 84–5, and Harper, "British Migration", 83. It must be stressed that most emigrants paid for their own passage, or were assisted by family members and friends. Starting in the 1820s, some parishes, such as a few in Kent, did send out paupers to North America. Within a few years, parishes in Sussex, East Anglia, and on the Wiltshire-Somerset border were sending parties of emigrants to America. A number of the early groups were landed in the United States. After American authorities objected and introduced various regulations to deter shipmasters from unloading paupers on their shores, Quebec became the preferred destination; and after the passage of the new Poor Law in 1834, parish assistance was officially sanctioned and regulated. See discussion in the following chapter. Considerable aid was privately organized. The Petworth Committee, for example, sponsored about 1,800 men, women and children over its five-year history. See Wendy Cameron and Mary McDougall Maude, *Assisting Emigration to Upper Canada: The Petworth Project, 1832–1837* (Kingston & Montreal: McGill-Queen's University Press, 2000); and Cameron "English Immigrants in 1830s Upper Canada: The Petworth Emigration Scheme," in *Canadian Migration Patterns*, ed. Messamore.
56 John Gemmill may have been on the *David of London*; this voyage is described in John McDonald, *Emigration to Canada: Narrative of a Voyage to Quebec and Journey from There to New Lanark in Upper Canada* (Edinburgh, 1823). It is likely that the Gemmills took advantage of subsidized emigration that was organized by a number of Scottish MPs and local landed elite in 1821. The purpose of the Glasgow Committee on Emigration, first formed in 1819, was twofold: "to coordinate and supervise

the activities of the various emigration societies" that had been organized in the region over the previous year; and to pressure Parliament to provide prospective emigrants with direct financial assistance. See Michael E. Vance, "The Politics of Emigration: Scotland and Assisted Emigration to Upper Canada," in *Scottish Emigration and Scottish Society*, ed. T.M. Devine (Edinburgh: John Donald, 1992), 37–61, 41.

57 John Gemmill Family Papers, SRO, TD293/1/5, 2 March 1822.
58 On the back of the letter was a handwritten receipt dated "November 2, 1822," a full six months after Ann had left.
59 John Gemmill Family Papers, 21 June 1823, SRO.
60 Ibid., 8 November 1824. See also letter to father from George Forbes, 21 January 1846, in which he wrote that he could make a "comfortable living" (SRO, RH4/80).
61 John Gemmill Family Papers, 30 April 1824, SRO.
62 Ibid., 17 September, 30 April 1824, SRO.
63 Ibid., 21 November 1825. It is suggested by C. Bennett, *The Lanark Society Settlers* (Renfrew: Ont.: Juniper Books, 1991), 121, that Andrew was not permitted by either the port authorities or the emigration society that sponsored the rest of family, to leave home because he had a club foot. This may have been the case, though there is no mention of this in the letters. What is evident is that Andrew did consider emigrating a few years later, but it was not until the early 1840s that he saw the rest of the family when he came for a visit.
64 John Gemmill Family Papers, John to Andrew, 30 April 1824, SRO.
65 Ibid., 6 December 1826.
66 Ibid., 2 May 1828.
67 Ibid., 24 November 1829.
68 Charlotte Erickson argues that the prospect of owning land was key for many emigrants. In this way, they could gain "a livelihood without having to work for or take orders from anyone be he employer or landlord" (*Invisible Immigrants*, 27). See also Cameron and Maude, *Assisting Emigration to Upper Canada*, chaps. 3 and 4.
69 Elliott, *Irish Migrants*, 6. Elliott argues throughout his study that this assumption – the need to provide for children and the family's future – was the primary driving force for emigration.
70 William Hutton to mother, 22 April 1834, *Hutton of Hastings*, 10.
71 Ibid., 30 May 1834, 14.
72 Ibid., 20 June 1834, 18.
73 Ibid., letter to John, 26 June 1834, 28. See also lengthy letter to mother.
74 Ibid., William Hutton to Fanny Hutton, 8 June 1834, 32–3.

75 Ibid., quoted in William Hutton to Mother, 23 September 1834, 35.
76 See Leonore Davidoff and Catherine Hall, *Family Fortunes: Men and Women of the English Middle Class* (Chicago: University of Chicago Press, 1987); Amanda Vickery, *The Gentleman's Daughter: Women's Lives in Georgian England* (New Haven: Yale University Press, 1998). For a discussion of this in the Upper Canadian context, see Elizabeth Jane Errington, *Wives and Mothers, School Mistresses and Scullery Maids* (Montreal & Kingston: McGill-Queen's University Press, 1995).
77 There are some fascinating studies within the "new" imperial history that explore this and how women, both by their actions and by their presence in the colonies, influenced assumptions about settler societies. For a brief discussion of this, see R. Kranidis, *Imperial Objects: Essays on Victorian Women's Emigration and the Unauthorized Imperial Experience* (New York: Twayne Macmillan, 1998), and *The Victorian Spinster and Colonial Emigration: Contested Subjects* (New York: St Martin's Press, 1999); Catharine Hall, ed., *Cultures of Empire: Colonizers in Britain and the Empire in the Nineteenth and Twentieth Centuries: A Reader* (New York and Manchester: Manchester University Press, 2000); Lisa Chilton, "A New Class of Women for the Colonies," in *The British World: Diaspora, Culture, and Identity*, ed. Carl Bridge and Kent Fedorowich (London: Cass, 2003); Adele Perry, *On the Edge of Empire: Gender, Race and the Making of British Columbia, 1840–1871* (Toronto: University of Toronto Press, 2001).
78 See, for example, Andrew Picken, *The Canadas* (London, 1832), appendix, who recounted the story of a labourer who had returned home for his wife but she would not accompany him back to the colonies for fear of the voyage. In *Chambers*, it was recommended that husbands had to "pay the greatest attention to females, who are apt to be flustered when they hear the noise of the waves or high winds or the sailors tramping about in a bustle on the deck above" (quoted in *Counsel for Emigrants*, 105). For those consulting guides, such advice could not have been particularly reassuring. For further discussion of attitudes to and expectations of women emigrants, see Elizabeth Jane Errington, "Information Wanted: Women Emigrants in a Transatlantic World," in *Canada and the British World*, ed. Phillip Buckner (Vancouver: University of British Columbia Press, 2006), and "'Where Is Patrick Dundon?' Emigration and Re-creating Communities in Ontario" in *Celebrating One Thousand Years of Ontario's History* (Toronto: OHS, 2001).
79 Henry Kerr to brothers John and Robert, 8 July 1842, Kerr Letters, NLS, ACC1416/2. It would seem that Mary O'Brien's sister Lucy was also very reluctant even to consider emigrating, despite Mary's frequent entreaties. From some of the references, it does seem that Lucy could have been per-

suaded if her husband had wanted to go. See Journals of Mary O'Brien, 27 November 1828, 23 August and 26 December 1829.

80 As an interesting aside, it was not always men who went ahead. "Report of Lieutenant Rubidge," in *The Canadian, British American, and West Indian Magazine*, 377–8, noted that his party included a woman and two children. The husband was going to emigrate later.

81 See Howison, *Sketches of Upper Canada*. Isaac Wilson recounted on 24 June 1817, "Since I began this letter about 27 families has arrived at York who left England last spring" (AO, MS1999.) Patrick Shirreff noted in *A Tour Through North America* (Edinburgh, 1835) that whole families emigrated to join relatives "who had settled some years before." He met a party of emigrants that included persons of all ages, from infants to women over seventy (181). See also *Journal of an Excursion to the United States by a Citizen of Edinburgh* (1835). Existing passenger lists of those arriving in U.S. ports in 1831 include a high proportion of married couples, many with young children; see Erickson, *Leaving England*.

82 E.S. Dunlop, ed., *Our Forest Home* (Toronto, 1902). For biographical material on Frances Stewart, see Joyce C. Lewis, *From Douro to Dublin: The Letters of Frances Stewart* (Peterborough: Trent Valley Archives, 1994).

83 See, for example, *Letters from Dorking Emigrants* (London, 1833), which included letters from a number of men who had "gone ahead" and intended to send for their families.

84 MacGregor, *British America*, vol 1, noted that the Irish emigrants were particularly known for sending back remittances to assist family members. But this was a practice that many followed, and by the early 1830s the Canada Land Company, like other companies and private individuals, was offering to arrange the transfer of funds to Britain. Advertisements offering this service appeared in the newspapers on both sides of the Atlantic in the 1830s and 1840s. See, among others, notice in the *True Scotsman*, 2 April 1833, from the British Linen Company and its links to the Bank of Montreal; notice of Messrs Buchanan & Co., Montreal, Kingston *Chronicle and Gazette*, 14 January 1830, directed particularly at Irish emigrants; and 14 January 1835, John H. Green of Kingston, who offered to send money "to the old country," *Chronicle and Gazette*. Notices from the Canada Company in the 1840s warned settlers about "unscrupulous individuals" who offered such services but had no intention of carrying them out; see *Bytown Gazette*, 29 November 1842 and 25 April 1844. For further discussion of the importance of remittances, see Harper, "British Migration and the Peopling of the Empire"; Houston and Smyth, *Irish Emigration*; and many of the studies considered in "A Note on Sources."

85 This was also true of other family members. See, for example, Ann Thomas's letter to her father, 15 October 1832, in Cameron et al., *English Immigrant Voices*, 68–9; and John Gemmill Family Papers, SRO, John Gemmill to Andrew, 21 November 1825, "Write when you get to Quebec."
86 *Colonial Advocate*, 9 July 1829.
87 *Christian Guardian*, 11 September 1839.
88 *Kingston Chronicle*, 14 January 1832. The following discussion is based on a reading of over thirty notices from women looking for their husbands. Not all are specifically included in the subsequent discussion but will be included in chapter 4, which looks at emigrants' experiences in that liminal period between the time of their arrival at Quebec or Montreal and their settlement in the colony.
89 *Niagara Herald*, 21 January 1830.
90 *Kingston Chronicle*, 21 September 1821.
91 This speculation is based on a number of notices that clearly indicate that wives had not heard from their husbands at all and that marriage breakdown was not infrequent in Upper Canada. See Errington, *Wives and Mothers, School Mistresses and Scullery Maids*.
92 The mobility of migrants to America is taken for granted by most scholars. And there is certainly ample evidence of this. In addition to discussion here concerning "lost" relatives or friends, and many of the works cited in "A Note on Sources," a number of classic studies explore patterns of mobility and persistence in colonial settlements. See, for example, David Gagan, *Hopeful Travellers: Families, Land, and Social Change in Mid-Victorian Pell County, Canada West* (Toronto: University of Toronto Press, 1981); Michael Katz, *The People of Hamilton, Canada West: Family and Class in a Mid-Nineteenth Century City* (Cambridge, Mass.: Harvard University Press, 1975). For an evocative study of one family's experience trying to find a place in the colony, see C.J. Houston and W.J. Smyth, "Geographical Transiency and Social Mobility: The Illustrative Odyssey of Irish Immigrant Wilson Benson, A Well-Known Canadian Unknown," *British Journal of Canadian Studies* 7, no. 2 (1992): 345–55.
93 *British Whig*, 15 December 1837. The same was true of Mrs William Banks and her four children (*Kingston Chronicle*, 21 September 1821); Mrs John Kenelly, looking for husband whom she had not heard from in three years (*Bytown Gazette*, 7 October 1841). See also notice for Simon Cullerton (*Bytown Gazette*, 26 September 1839), who had left home in 1836 and was last heard of in New York State in 1837; and Julia Kain, looking for Thomas, who had left County Galway three years before (*Niagara Herald*, 21 January 1830).
94 *Farmer's Journal*, 4 March 1829.
95 This was a theme that a number of travellers and colonial promoters stressed, partly, in their attempt to convince prospective emigrants to settle in British

America instead of the United States. See, for example, "MacGregor's British America," *Blackwood's*, June 1832; "Hochelaga," *Blackwood's*, October 1844; and *Counsel for Emigrants*, viii, which noted that British American "society was more agreeable and in a great measure more like what we have been accustomed to." James Pickering, *Emigration or No Emigration: Being the Narrative of the Author's ... from the Years 1824–1830* (London, 1830), 36, observed that he felt immediately at home in Upper Canada. One British commentator noted in 1844 that residents there were "nearer to us now than Edinburgh was to London eighty years ago." As a result, settlers in the New World "feel now less as colonists than fellow inhabitants" (*Views of Canada*, 1–2).

96 Most who emigrated from Lord Cashel's estate in the mid-1820s and 1830s, for example, were "overwhelmingly of marriageable age or recently married." As Wilson notes in *A New Lease on Life*, 176, emigration offered a "viable alternative for non-inheriting sons," and their marriage was one of the "precipitating events," as discussed by Elliott, in "Regional Patterns of English Immigration."

97 This was a constant theme in much of the discourse on emigration. Upper Canada was presented as a good poor man's country: "A man with large capital is not so likely to live in clover as the man of small," many judged. Too often, gentlemen were not willing to do the physical work required in the colony. Certainly, "those who can afford to purchase farms with houses, and the land partly clear, will be in a very superior situation to those who must be content with wild land in the bush." But even then, a man had to be "willing and able to undertake the necessary labour of cultivating the soil and to brave some difficulty at the outset" ("Upper Canada," *Blackwood's*, August 1832, 243). See also MacGregor, *British America*, 454; *Views of Canada*, 38 and 112; Taylor, *Narrative of a Voyage*, 86; Talbot, *Five Years' Residence*, 225; Blane, *An Excursion*, 106; *Canada as It Is*, 69–71; Doyle, *Hints on Emigration*, quoted in *Brockville Gazette*, 29 November 1832; "Letters on Emigration," *Canadian, British American, and West Indian Magazine*, May 1839, 155; and *Counsel for Emigrants*, xiii. Howison, *Sketches*, 259, noted that these men had to be "practically" engaged in farming. And gentlemen were warned, "Nobody should emigrate with a view to farming, but persons who can and will work their own lands and will not hesitate to ... set their hearts to all kind of labour" (*Sequel to Counsel*, 59). For a discussion of "gentlemen" pioneers, see Patrick A. Dunae, *Gentlemen Emigrants: From the British Public Schools to the Canadian Frontier* (Vancouver & Toronto: Douglas & McIntyre, 1981).

98 Letter of 13 May 1832, in *I Bless You My Heart: Selected Correspondence of Catharine Parr Traill*, ed. Carl Ballstadt et al. (Toronto: University of Toronto Press,

1996), 39. For biographical details concerning the Traills and Moodies, see Charlotte Gray, *Sisters in the Wilderness: The Lives of Susanna Moodie and Catharine Parr Traill* (Toronto: Viking, 1999) and references therein.

99 Harriet Pengelly Diary, Pengelly Papers, TUA, 70-001. See further discussion in chapters 2 and 5.
100 "Letters" July 1833, SRO, GD1/814/6.
101 Ibid., 16 June 1835.
102 Mrs Murray to James, 4 December 1833 and 22 January 1834, Murray Family Papers, NLS, MS162.92.
103 Ibid., 29 March 1834.
104 George Forbes to his parents, 30 October 1848, SRO, TD73/124/1/8.
105 But like the Gemmills, the family remained divided, and after he realized that Charles and his sister Jean would soon marry, he acknowledged. "I do not expect any of you will come here" (Forbes Letters, 15 July 1848, SRO, RH4/80). Some young men, such as Isaac Wilson, originally did not intend to stay in the colony, but as sojourners they planned to return home in a year or two; see Isaac Wilson Diaries, AO, MS199, and discussion in chapter 5 following. See also *Letters from Dorking Emigrants*, 22–4.
106 *London Morning Post*, reprinted in *Chronicle and Gazette*, 29 March 1843. See also "The Canada's," *Manchester Guardian*, 31 August 1832; and *Views of Canada*, 434.
107 Picken, *The Canadas*, 36, 126. Talbot, in *Five Years' Residence*, 127, noted that "women were scarce" in Upper Canada. One settler rather derisively commented that he could readily find husbands for single or young widowed women emigrants who had "a snug jointure or disposable fortune" (Radcliffe, *Authentic Letters*, 26). See also Catermole, *Emigration*, 95; Robert MacDougall, *The Emigrant's Guide to North America* (1841), ed. Elizabeth Thompson (Toronto: Natural History, 1998), 5. As Hasia R. Diner has concluded in one of the few studies specifically of women and emigration in the first half of the nineteenth century (*Erin's Daughters in America: Irish Immigrant Women in the Nineteenth Century* [Baltimore: John Hopkins University Press, 1983]), single Irish women often migrated without men, and, indeed, by mid-century the number of single women emigrants equalled if not surpassed the number of single men. For non-North American destinations, see C. MacDonald, *A Woman of Good Character: Single Women as Immigrant Settlers in Nineteenth-Century New Zealand* (Wellington: Bridget Williams Books, 1990); Jan Gothard, *Blue China: Single Female Migration to Colonial Australia* (Melbourne: Melbourne University Publishing, 2001).
108 George Forbes to parents and brother, 18 July 1845, SRO, RH4/80.
109 John Scott to Andrew Redford, 29 August 1835, SRO, GD1/813/1.

110 John Holden to his family, 6 November 1832, in Cameron et al., *English Immigrant Voices*, 157–8.
111 *Christian Guardian*, 15 November 1837.
112 *Colonial Advocate*, 8 October 1835.
113 *Kingston Gazette*, 31 May 1817. See also "Distressed Brother Looking for Thomas Greig," *Kingston Chronicle*, 22 March 1822; "Thomas Looking for John Mullet," *Farmer's Journal*, 5 September 1827; "Campbell Brothers Looking for Each Other," *Christian Guardian*, 18 September 1841.
114 *Chronicle and Gazette*, 28 June 1834.
115 Ibid., 12 October 1844. Such examples add a twist to the importance of chain migration as a motivation for leaving home. Studies by Elliott, *Irish Migrants*, Wilson, *A New Lease on Life*, Harper *Willing Exiles*, and others all suggest that the chain was much more direct. And certainly most notices and letters indicate that most new arrivals who were joining relatives in the colony did so after only a few years. But it is surprising how many arrived many years later.
116 *Chronicle and Gazette*, 24 October 1835. There was some problem when someone was looking for a sister who may have married and changed her name. See, for example, *Christian Guardian*, 8 June 1836, where Leticia Ingham thought her sister might have married; and 8 March 1837, where Louise was looking for her sister who had married; see also *Hallowell Free Press*, 24 July 1832, notice of Ann Bleakney.
117 SRO, GD263/68/1/2, 20 August 1839. Catharine also wrote to Barbara (see 20 August 1839, in *I Bless You in My Heart*, 42–4). Michael Scott of Quebec sent a letter to his sister Janet in Glasgow shortly after receiving word of the death of their invalid sister whom Janet had been attending. "The separation from our friends and relations by death is at all times a painful event but it is the more so when those are taken among who were the nearest and most dear to us," he wrote. Now that Janet no longer had to look after Isabella, he urged her to join him in Canada. "I can make you comfortable," he wrote, and "at our time of life – 62 and 66, we can not expect now to be long in this world we are now the only two of our family left." Janet died before she even received this invitation. In a letter two days later to his nephew Alex Fraser, Michael noted that he had just received this news – which was very unexpected. He then thanked the family "for the very great attention you paid to my sister at all times" (SRO, TD217/1412, February 1849).
118 *Kingston Chronicle*, 19 November 1824; *Upper Canada Gazette*, 14 October 1824; *Niagara Gleaner*, 6 November 1824; *Upper Canada Herald*, 22 February 1825. A similar notice appeared two years earlier in the *Kingston Chronicle*, 4 January 1822.

119 Martha Vicinus, *Independent Women: Work and Community for Single Women, 1850–1920* (Chicago: University of Chicago Press, 1985). James Hammerton, *Emigrant Gentlewomen: Genteel Poverty and Female Emigration 1830–1914* (Canberra: Australian National University Press, 1979). In *Wives and Mothers, School Mistresses and Scullery Maids*, I discuss waged work available for single women in Upper Canada.

120 See W.A. Langton, ed., *Early Days in Upper Canada: Letters of John Langton* (Toronto: Macmillan, 1926); H.H. Langton, ed., *A Gentlewoman in Upper Canada* (Toronto: Clarke, Irwin, 1950).

121 John to father, 28 July 1834, in Langton, ed., *Gentlewoman*, 4.

122 *Manchester Guardian*, 17 April 1830.

123 *Scots Times*, 26 June 1832. There was considerable emphasis in the discourse on the need for emigrants to be young and healthy. For example, one traveller explicitly stated, "None but the young should venture" to Upper Canada. "Man ... must be transplanted early, or the experiment will not thrive" (Bond Head, *Forest Scenes and Incidents* [London, 1838], 356, quoted in Keon, "The 'New World' Idea," 107). See also "The Canadas," *Manchester Guardian*, 31 August 1832; *Views of Canada*, 434; Doyle, *Hints*, 66. In a "Letter from the Ettrick Shepherd," *Blackwood's*, March 1820, the narrator advised that Upper Canada "is not a place for old men like me."

124 *Counsel for Emigrants*, 123.

125 William Phillips to his father, 28 July 1832, in Cameron, et al., eds., *English Immigrant Voices*, 23.

126 *Counsel for Emigrants*, 123. Anne Langton recorded that her brother John had given money to a neighbour "to enable him to procure some comforts for his old father and mother who had come out to end their days with him" (Langton, ed., *Gentlewoman in Upper Canada*, 52). They had been accompanied by a sister, with the permission of her husband, and "if she gave her encouragement after seeing the country, he would follow."

127 Charles Moore to his father, c. June 1833, in Cameron et al., eds., *English Immigrant Voices*, 119.

128 *Kingston Chronicle*, 13 September 1822. See also "Parents Looking for Nancy and Becky Fox," *Christian Guardian*, 13 October 1847; *Toronto Patriot*, 25 September 1840; *Chronicle and Gazette*, 20 February 1841; "From Thomas Wright," *Niagara Gleaner*, 14 August 1830; and Mrs Dolan looking for son-in-law, *Colonial Advocate*, 1 May 1834. Many arrived in the colony in "distressed" circumstances. For example, "Looking for Michael Kerry," *Chronicle and Gazette*, 20 February 1841; "Looking for John Ford," *Chronicle and Gazette*, 2 February 1842; "Looking for William Hocker," *Chronicle and Gazette*, 18 January 1834.

129 *Upper Canada Gazette*, 8 July 1840. See also notice of Ann Dundoon and her daughter, who were looking for son, Patrick. *Niagara Herald*, 21 January 1830.
130 *Christian Guardian*, 31 July 1833.
131 *Colonial Advocate*, 28 February 1833. This seems to have been the situation of Ann Dunlop, a widow who decided to leave Aughnacky, Ireland, in 1830 to join her son Thomas (*Niagara Gleaner*, 14 August 1830).
132 *Chronicle and Gazette*, 27 November 1844. See also *Colonial Advocate*, 8 October 1829; "Looking for James Muller," *Upper Canada Gazette*, 16 January 1838.
133 There was an intriguing story in the *Observer*, 9 March 1834, of a meeting in Aberdeen to try to prevent "clandestine emigration." It was decided to send a petition to Parliament to try to stop these emigrants before they left home, or to recover the property of those already in America.
134 For further discussion of the complexity of these transatlantic connections, see Dirk Hoerder, *Creating Societies: Immigrant Lives in Canada* (Montreal & Kingston: McGill-Queen's University Press, 1999), chap. 3; Gerber, *Authors of Their Lives*; and Fitzpatrick, *Oceans of Consolation*.
135 Forbes Letters, 20 April 1849, SRO, TD73/124/1.
136 John Langton to Father, 12 August 1835, in W.A. Langton, ed., *Early Days in Upper Canada*, 145.
137 It is difficult if not impossible to trace reverse migration. But many diaries, both published and unpublished, make references to individuals who "regretted leaving home" and had decided to return. John Reilly commented, in *Journal of an Excursion to the United States and Canada* (Edinburgh, 1835) that a group he met "felt ashamed to go home immediately" and were going to wait for at least a year. See also Traill, *The Backwoods of Canada*, 27, 45.
138 Taylor, *Narrative of a Voyage*, 79. See also Bell, *Hints to Emigrants*, 164. This was a term used to illustrate to prospective emigrants the need to make a considered decision. See also *Sequel to Counsel*, 47. Howison noted in *Sketches*, 62, that he had met emigrants who had arrived ill prepared, had become depressed, and planned to return home.

CHAPTER TWO

1 Stewart Family Papers, Trent University Archives (TUA), 70–008/1/6, Frances Stewart to Honoria, 26 April 1822.
2 Ibid., Stewart to Harriet, 11 March 1823, from Douro.
3 John Gemmill to wife and family, 2 March 1822, John Gemmill Family Papers, Scottish Record Office (SRO), TD293/1/5.
4 Ibid. The letter was received on 22 November; the family left on 22 May.

5 Travellers' accounts usually discussed the climate of Upper Canada at some length. Particularly in the early years, there was some concern about whether emigrants from the British Isles were "suited" for the northern regions of the continent. For many, Canada was "synonymous with ice, snow and winter" – "a frozen desert," a "Canadian Siberia"; see William Catermole, *Emigration* (London, 1831), 118; James Pickering, *Emigration or No Emigration* (London, 1830); and James Inches, *Letters on Emigration to Canada* (Perth, 1836). Others suggested that although it was cold in winter, the Canadian climate was, on the whole, "good." See, for example, "Review of Upper Canada" *Blackwood's*, August 1832, 257; *Sequel to the Counsel for Emigrants* (Aberdeen: John Mathison, 1834), 12; *Counsel for Emigrants and Interesting Information from Numerous Sources* (Aberdeen: John Mathison, 1834), quoting James Strachan, *A Visit to the Province of Upper Canada in 1918* (reprint, 1968); and *Six Years in the Bush in Upper Canada* (London, 1838), 83. For a discussion of how Europeans viewed the climate of North America in an earlier period, see Joyce Chaplin, "Natural Philosophy and Early Racial Idiom in North America: Comparing English and Indian Bodies" *William and Mary Quarterly*, June 1997.
6 Gerald E. Boyce, ed., *Hutton of Hastings* (Belleville: Hastings County Council, 1972), Hutton to Fanny, 8 June 1834, 33.
7 Ibid., Hutton to his mother, 23 September 1834, 40.
8 George Forbes to family, 18 January 1846, Forbes Letters, Scottish Record Office (SRO) RH4/80.
9 From a London paper, reprinted in the *Brockville Gazette*, 17 May 1832.
10 *Emigration: Letters from Sussex* (London, 1833) v, vi. Those chosen for assistance were also given a quite generous luggage allowance. Those who were part of the Dorking party were also provided with food and clothing. The luggage allowance for each member over the age of fourteen was five hundredweight of goods. See also discussion in Wendy Cameron and Mary McDougall Maude, *Assisting Emigration to Upper Canada: The Petworth Project, 1832–1837* (Montreal & Kingston: McGill-Queen's University Press, 2000), chap. 2.
11 See notices in British papers, particularly reports from Scotland in the *Cobourg Star*, 2 May 1832, about disposing of house and stock; John MacGregor, *Observations on Emigration to British America* (London, 1829), 34; John MacGregor, *British America* (London, 1832), 1:456–7.
12 *Chamber's Information*, 1835, 2.
13 *True Scotsman* (Glasgow), 23 May 1840.
14 MacGregor, *Observations*, 34. He particularly noted spades, shovels, scythes, sickles, hoes, ploughs, traces, ironwork for a plough, and a harrow.

15 Catermole, *Advantages of Emigration*, reprinted in *Counsel for Emigrants*, 107. "Extract of a Letter from a Settler in Upper Canada," reprinted in the *Cobourg Star,* 30 January 1833.
16 *Sequel to Counsel for Emigrants*, 51; *Counsel for Emigrants*, 107.
17 "Extract of a Letter from a Settler in Upper Canada," reprinted in the *Cobourg Star*, 30 January 1833. See also William Bell, *Hints to Emigrants* (Edinburgh, 1824), 211, who recommended that emigrants should take "nothing but what is absolutely necessary." See also Andrew Picken, *The Canadas* (London, 1832), 24; Joseph Bouchette, *The British Dominion in North America* (London, 1831), 1:286 and 424; "To Emigrants" from *Canadian Magazine* in *Cobourg Star*, 22 May 1833.
18 Ann Mann to children, 2 January 1837, in Wendy Cameron, Mary McDougall Maude, and Sheila Haines, eds., *English Immigrant Voices* (Montreal & Kingston: McGill-Queen's University Press, 2000), 252. See also William Cooper to brother, 5 February 1833, ibid., 98; and unknown to Uncle and Aunt, 17 January 1839, ibid., 285.
19 William Courtnage to siblings, 10 January 1837, in Cameron et al., eds., *Voices*, 256; William Baker to Father, Mother and siblings, 13 March 1833, ibid., 110.
20 "Letter to Mother," 22 October 1833, *Counsel for Emigrants*, 123. See also Mary and George Boxall to his father, 25 September 1836, in Cameron et al., *Voices*, 230.
21 William Baker to father and mother, 13 March 1833, in Cameron et al., eds., *Voices*, 111. See also Stephen Goutcher to wife, 17 January 1833, ibid., 97; William Phillips to father and mother, 28 July 1832, ibid., 23.
22 Charlotte Evans to brother, 18 August 1832, in Cameron et al., *Voices*, 37. See also James Parker to friend, 1 September 1833, ibid., 150; and discussion in Marjory Harper, *Willing Exiles* (Aberdeen: Aberdeen University Press, 1988), 109–11.
23 See John Langton to his father, 11 July 1837, in *Early Days in Upper Canada*, ed. W.A. Langton, (Toronto: Macmillan, 1926), 183–9. This seems also to have been the case for the Stewart family.
24 From a London paper, reprinted in *Kingston Chronicle*, 25 August 1818; "The Emigrants Voyage to Canada," *Blackwood's*, November 1821; *Manchester Guardian*, 17 April 1830.
25 See advice from Catermole quoted in *Counsel for Emigrants*, 107; *Counsel*, 79; Robert MacDougall, *The Emigrant's Guide to North America* (1841), ed. Elizabeth Thompson (Toronto: Natural History, 1998), 14.
26 "Letter from Zorra," 19 September 1833, *Counsel for Emigrants*, 55. See also Catermole, *Emigration*, part 4: "General Advice to Emigrants"; MacGregor, *British America*, 1:457–8.

27 Hon. E. Stanley, *Journal of a Tour in North America* (London, 1830), 9.
28 Colonial newspapers frequently included brief snippets from British papers about "the rage for emigrating." For example, the *Brockville Gazette*, 10 May 1832, noted that "nearly 100 ships of the first class" were fitting out at London. The *Christian Chronicle* noted emigration on a "grand scale," reporting on 13 May 1840 that "twenty vessels of large burden" were preparing to leave Limerick. A year later, it reported that thirty vessels were loading emigrants at Liverpool (12 May 1841).
29 Bruce Elliott stresses that the availability of transport to America, and indeed "the physical means of ... even reaching a port of embarkation," were important factors; see his "Regional Patterns of English Immigration," in *Canadian Migration Patterns*, ed. Barbara J. Messamore (Ottawa: University of Ottawa Press, 2004), 53. Marjory Harper (in *Willing Exiles* and "Crossing the Atlantic") noted that one must appreciate the "mechanisms of transportation" from a particular region to have some understanding of who went and when. A classic study of the Atlantic networks in the eighteenth century and their impact on communities on both sides of the ocean is Ian H. Steele's, *The English Atlantic 1675–1740: An Exploration of Communication and Community* (New York: Oxford University Press, 1986).
30 Catermole, *Emigration*, 80. See also *Chamber's Information*, 2. Indeed, almost without exception, the emigrant guides in the 1830s and 1840s, as well as government pamphlets, advised leaving in the spring.
31 See John Howison, *Sketches of Upper Canada* (1821; reprint Toronto; S.R. Publishers, 1965), 247, need to arrive by July; Bell, *Hints*, 210; Picken, *The Canadas*, 299; *Views of Canada*, 253; *Chamber's Information* (1835), 2.
32 Stanley, *Journal of a Tour*, 9.
33 These tidbits from shipping advertisements are drawn from the hundreds that appeared in the *Manchester Guardian*, the *Scots Times*, and the *Observer*.
34 See Harper, *Willing Exiles*, 210–36, for a discussion of the formation and work of the Glasgow Committee. Others in Scotland "assisted" parties of residents to emigrate to the colonies. See Michael E. Vance, "The Politics of Emigration: Scotland and Assisted Emigration to Upper Canada," in T.M. Devine., ed. *Scottish Emigration and Scottish Society* (Edinburgh: John Donald Publishers, 1992), 37–61, 41. As Harper notes, landlord-assisted migration became the most common – "and notorious – feature of the nineteenth-century transatlantic movement" ("British Migration," in *Oxford History: The Nineteenth Century*, 80). See also Harper, *Willing Exiles*, 128–30; Cameron and Maude, *Assisting Emigration to Upper Canada*; T.M. Devine, *The Scottish Nation, 1700–2000* (London: Penguin, 1999).

35 Diary of a Voyage of John Hart, National Library of Scotland (NLS), TD1082.
36 See also reports in the Kingston *Chronicle and Gazette*, 10 August 1833 of chartered vessels from the Highlands; various comments in the Sutherland Papers, NLS, Dep 313/468; "Bicester Committee," *Observer*, 25 May and 29 March 1830; *Canadian Emigrant*, 12 July 1834 which included a notice of the Children Friends Society in London; Kingston *Chronicle and Gazette*, 14 June 1834. See Harper, *Willing Exiles*, 88–91, for a discussion of how smaller groups of emigrants from a particular community arranged passage together.
37 Most county record offices in England contain often detailed records of correspondence between the Colonial Office and local authorities regarding parish emigration. The Bedfordshire Record Office (BRO), for example, contains correspondence, detailed lists of who was sent, the provisions provided, contracts with local transporters and shipmasters, and considerable discussion of how best to assist in relocation. Various parishes in Bedfordshire sent out paupers in 1831. Families cost £22.15.0 and individuals £6.10.0. Oakley Parish records indicate an account for the cost of luggage to Liverpool, expenses for the emigrants while waiting for the ship to leave, and "hospital fees." See Oakley Parish Records, Miscellaneous, 4 May 1831, BRO, P40/18/65–73; and Hockliffe Parish Register, BRO. See also discussion in Cameron and Maude, *Assisting Emigration to Upper Canada*.
38 Circulars were regularly distributed to parishes informing them of conditions in Upper Canada. The Emigration Commission also established basic standards for victualling and provided parishes and local unions with a list of approved ships. See correspondence and forms in BRO Paupers Union Bedfordshire County (PUBC), 2/1 and 2/2.
39 See correspondence and accounts from Carter and Brown, April and June 1837, BRO, PUBC2/3. By the mid-1840s, these arrangements had been extended to include emigrants bound for Australia. See Harper, *Willing Exiles*.
40 See Emigration Department Circular, February 1836, BRO, PUBC2/1.
41 Journals of George Pashley, Archives of Ontario (AO), MU843, 1-P-1. The family received £2.6s in assistance from George's father.
42 Catermole, *Emigration*, 46–7.
43 *Cork Chronicle*, reprinted in *Christian Guardian*, 21 May 1834. See also reports from London in *Cobourg Star*, 28 May 1834. A report from *Newry Telegraph*, reprinted in *Christian Guardian*, 11 June 1831, noted, "Our quays have lately been exhibiting an unusually crowded and bustling appearance." Kirby Miller notes, in *Emigrants and Exiles* (New York: Oxford University Press, 253), that as a result of the "steady decline of direct Irish trade with North America," Irish emigrants made their way to Liverpool or Greenock to find passage to America.

Charlotte Erickson notes in her "Emigration in 1831," in *Leaving England* (Ithaca & London: Cornell University Press, 1994), that English emigrants usually departed from Liverpool, Hull, Bristol, or London.

44 Catermole, *Emigration*, 47.
45 Harper, *Willing Exiles*, 84.
46 Cecil J. Houston and William J. Smyth, *Irish Emigration and Canadian Settlement: Patterns, Links and Letters* (Toronto: University of Toronto Press, 1990), 80.
47 Report from Liverpool in *Kingston Chronicle*, 22 October 1831.
48 Letter to J.C. Gotch, Northampton Record Office (NRO), 7 July 1823. The letter recounted at some length this emigrant's travails. In the end, his passage was much delayed and much more expensive than originally contracted for.
49 *Chronicle and Gazette*, 14 February 1835; see also "Report from the House of Commons," *Cobourg Star*, 1 June 1834. See discussion in Harper, *Willing Exiles*, 105–11. Miller, *Emigrants and Exiles*, 253–5, noted that "the Liverpool harpies of embarkation" were legendary.
50 MacGregor, *Observations*, 35.
51 Ibid. See also *Chronicle and Gazette*, 30 August 1834, quoting an article from London; Edinburgh *Saturday Post*, 22 September 1827, report of trip to New Brunswick; Picken, *The Canadas*, 32.
52 Oliver MacDonagh, *A Pattern of Government Growth, 1800–1860* (London: MacGibbon & Kee, 1961), 18. As MacDonagh notes, the new regulations and growing bureaucracies related to emigration and colonization inadvertently laid the groundwork of a modern British state. One of the agents appointed "to oversee the trade" was A.C. Buchanan, a Lower Canadian shipping merchant who had considerable knowledge of and interest in emigration. Among other things, he was to enforce the new regulations, prosecute masters for breach of the Passenger Act, and assist new arrivals to find work or to make their way to settlements in the interior. Subsequent Passenger Acts in 1835, 1842, and 1847 further strengthened regulations intended to ensure the welfare and safety of emigrants. By 1845, emigrants could require shipowners to provide them with supplies and lodging if their departure was delayed, and a ship's captain was required to ensure that steerage quarters were kept clean. (For details of these and other acts see MacDonagh, ibid., chap. 4). It is interesting that the act of 1847, reflecting Britain's middle-class concern to maintain propriety between the sexes, required masters to have separate quarters for single women and men.
53 See advertisement in *Scots Times*, 21 May 1833, for example.
54 "Report of House of Commons," *Cobourg Star*, 11 June 1834. See also *Sequel to Counsel for Emigrants*, 51, which reported about Bickett's gang in Liver-

pool; "Dispatch from Sydenham to Lord Russell," *Cobourg Star*, 5 May 1841; Harper, *Willing Exiles*, 106; Miller, *Emigrants and Exiles*, 254.
55 "Extract of a Letter from a Settler ..." *Cobourg Star*, 20 January 1833.
56 Journal of George Pashley. See also "Report from the *Aberdeen Herald*," *Sequel to Counsel for Emigrants*, 10. MacGregor's *Observations on Emigration*, published in 1831, and its subsequent *British America* (1832), for example, included excerpts from the regulations under the Passenger Acts pertaining to what passengers could, by law, require of the captain. MacGregor recommended that emigrants inspect the ship and the accommodation provided, investigate the captain's reputation, and have a clear understanding in writing with him concerning what the price included, the date of sailing, and the destination before paying any fare (MacGregor, *Observations*, 36–8). A pamphlet issued by His Majesty's Commissioners for Emigration in 1832 emphatically stated that to avoid "being exposed to all kinds of imposition," travellers should consult the local government agent for emigration before making any arrangements (*Information Issued by His Majesty's Commission for Emigration* (London, 1832), NLS, GD46/13/184).
57 And in his letter to his uncle, Andrew Redford recommended that others do the same (28 October 1838, Redford Papers, Scottish Record Office [SRO], GD/813/15).
58 Harper, *Willing Exiles*, 100–2.
59 Thomas Radcliffe, ed., *Authentic Letters from Upper Canada* (Dublin, 1833), 10.
60 Ibid.
61 Pengelly Family Papers, Trent University Archives (TUA), 70-001/1/4, Harriet Pengelly Diary. Both Harriet and Robert kept diaries. Robert's tended to be more prosaic than Harriet's and for the voyage itself, chronicled little of his day-to-day affairs or feelings. As will be evident from the following, Harriet's was much more personal, and she partly used it as a confidant.
62 Pengelly Family Papers, Robert Pengelly Diary.
63 Ibid., 2 April 1834, Harriet Pengelly Diary.
64 *Sequel to Counsel for Emigrants*, letters of 11 February 1834 from St Claire River, Upper Canada, 38. See also *Sequel*, 41. See also letter to McNicol from Mary McNicol, 2 August 1832, NLS, ACC7020. Even some of the Petworth emigrants recommended that relatives travel by way of New York. See, for example, William Cooper to his parents and brothers and sisters, 28 July 1832 (Cameron et al., *English Immigrant Voices*, 21).
65 *Counsel for Emigrants*, 120. Earlier, Bell (in *Hints*, 166) had recommended leaving from the west coast of Britain and proceeding directly to Quebec. Andrew Picken (*The Canadas*, 29) also recommended that emigrants leave from the nearest port.

66 Many, including A.C. Buchanan, the emigrant agent in Quebec, believed that many emigrants who landed in British America intended to move on immediately to the United States. There were others of some means who, wanting a shorter and more comfortable voyage, landed in New York and then immediately made their way north to British America. See, for example, *Chronicle and Gazette*, 2 December 1840, which reported that about 12,000 emigrants had arrived in Quebec, 1,200 of whom had gone on to the United States, and that 1,300 had arrived from the United States and come on to Canada. *Chronicle and Gazette*, 26 October 1823, Buchanan's report noted that a lot of British and German emigrants from Philadelphia, about 12,000, had come from the United States; and on 10 May 1834 the paper reported a lot of emigrants arriving from New York by way of the Erie Canal. The *Canadian Emigrant*, 1 December 1831, reported that fewer than usual emigrants had made their way to the United States and many had arrived from New York; and on 26 October 1833 a report estimated that about a quarter of those who arrived in New York had made their way into Upper Canada. See brief discussion in Elizabeth Jane Errington, "British Migration and British North America, 1783–1860," in *Oxford History of the British Empire: Canada*, ed. Phillip Buckner (Oxford University Press, 2007).

67 MacGregor, *Observations*, 38, which, for his intended audience, would have been Quebec.

68 *Counsel for Emigrants*, 120.

69 *Chamber's Information*, 2. Harper argues in *Willing Exiles*, 192–3, that many emigrants were not particularly concerned about the specific destination. Bruce Elliott notes in "Regional Patterns of English Immigration and Settlement in Upper Canada" that many English migrants preferred the New York route (60–1).

70 Redford Papers, William Knox to Andrew Redford, 28 October 1838, SRO, GD1/813/15.

71 Catermole, *Emigration*, 82; *Counsel for Emigrants*, 107. See also *Sequel to the Counsel for Emigrants*, 41. Harper (*Willing Exiles*, 139–40) notes that many Scots at least took this advice. Travelling in steerage was one way to conserve precious resources that would be needed in the colonies. Even some who received aid were not impoverished.

72 *Sequel to Counsel for Emigrants*, 41, 51.

73 *Counsel for Emigrants*, 54.

74 James Parker to friend, 1 September 1833, in Cameron et al., *English Immigrant Voices*, 150.

75 Catermole, *Emigration*, 82. Bell (*Hints*, 165) also recommended that emigrants make sure the ship would not be too crowded. Picken (*The Canadas*, 37) offered similar advice.

76 Radcliffe, ed., *Authentic Letters*, 32. See also Catermole, *Emigration*, 81–2, for discussion.
77 Catermole, *Emigration*, 82. See also Radcliffe, ed., *Authentic Letters*, 9; *Counsel*, 106; James Parker to friend, 1 September 1833, in Cameron et al., *English Immigrant Voices*, 150.
78 *Chamber's Information*, 1835, 2.
79 *Sequel to Counsel for Emigrants*, 51. See also *Counsel for Emigrants*, 54–5; Catermole, *Emigration*, 82; "Information ... by the High Commissioners for Emigration" (London, 1832), 5, noted between 50 and 75 days. Picken (*The Canadas*, 32) recommended provisioning for 50 days. Bell (in *Hints*, 165–6), based on his own experience, advised that emigrants provision themselves, and he provided a detailed list of what would be necessary. Miller (in *Emigrants and Exiles*, 253) notes that most Irish emigrants brought their own provisions.
80 *Sequel to Counsel for Emigrants*, 34.
81 See, for example, *Counsel for Emigrants*, 54–5; "Letter from Zorra," in *Counsel*, 78–9; excerpt from *Chamber's*, 105; Reilly, *Journal of an Excursion to the United States and Canada in the Year 1834: With Hints to Emigrants* ... (Edinburgh: John Anderson, Jr, 1835), 5; Pickering, *Emigration or No Emigration*, 131.
82 Quoted in *Counsel for Emigrants*, 106.
83 *Chamber's Information*, 2. The editors also commented that "some ship owners, sensible of the dangerous mistakes which may be made ... through ignorance" by those who were determined to provision themselves, were "very averse to receive passengers who will not agree to be victualled by the ship."
84 George and Lydia Huton to mother, 10 September 1836, in Cameron et al., *English Immigrant Voices*, 225. John and Ruth Waldon wrote to friends, 9 January 1836 (ibid., 115–16) that although they had had plenty on the voyage, provided by the captain, the friends should still bring oatmeal (to make gruel), onions, lemons, pickles, and a ham or bacon. Not all the Petworth emigrants advised bringing extra provisions. See, for example, John Deaman to William Bookier, 4 September 1836, in ibid., 222; and Unknown to Aunt and Uncle, 17 January 1839, ibid., 286.
85 John Gemmill Family Papers, John Gemmill to wife, 2 March 1822, SRO, TD293/1.
86 *Counsel for Emigrants*, 103.
87 See for example, *Counsel for Emigrants*, 55, 103.
88 See William Baker to father and family, in Cameron et al., *English Immigrant Voices*, 13 March 1833, 111.
89 See, for example, report in *Manchester Guardian*, 1 October 1831; report from *Inverness Herald*, reprinted in *Chronicle and Gazette*, 13 October 1838. See also Miller, *Emigrants and Exiles*, 253–4, and discussion in the following chapter.

90 Isaac Wilson Diaries, 1811–41, AO, MS199, reel 5. See discussion in chapter 5, following.
91 Stewart Family Papers, Frances Stewart Journal, 11 March 1823, TUA, 70-008/1.
92 This is very like the wedding trip that many middle-class Britons took – visiting family – immediately after their marriage.
93 Pengelly Family Papers, Harriet Pengelly Diary, March 1835.
94 John Colquhoun to his mother, 12 November 1841, "Letters," SRO, GD1/814/9.
95 Accounts of shipwrecks were sometimes quite sensational, particularly if the papers could find a "first-hand" account of the tragedy. See, for example, Edinburgh *Saturday Post*, 22 September 1827; *Scots Times*, 17 July 1832; *Canadian Freeman* (York), 26 September 1833; *Canadian Emigrant*, 28 September 1833. The colonial press frequently picked up reports from the British press. The *Christian Guardian*, the *Chronicle and Gazette*, and the *Canadian Emigrant* gave considerable attention to the foundering of the *James* of Limerick (with fatalities of 250); the brig *Fidelity*, the barque *Astrea* (loss of 208 persons), and others. The *Chronicle and Gazette*, 11 June 1834, concluded, "Never, within our recollection, have we had to record such a list of disasters."
96 Harriet Pengelly Diary, April 1835. Miller (*Emigrants and Exiles*, 252–3) notes that this fear of the voyage was particularly acute for Irish emigrants. See also "Report of Lieutenant Rubidge," in *The Canadian, British American, and West Indian Magazine*, October 1839, 375, about three families who changed their minds "and were clamorous to be put ashore."
97 "The Emigrant Ship," *Taits Magazine of October*, reprinted in *Manchester Guardian*, 17 October 1838. See also "The Emigrant," *Canadian Magazine* 1, no. 1 (1833), 12–15.
98 Originally in *Blackwood's*, July 1827, 32. This was then picked up in *Brockville Gazette*, 23 July 1830; *Farmer's Journal*, 26 September 1827.
99 Walter Riddell, in his *Diary of a Voyage from Scotland to Canada, 1833*, ed. William Riddell (Toronto: Associated Printers, 1932), 4,
100 Frances Stewart letter, 1 June 1822, in *Our Forest Home*, ed. E.S. Dunlop (Toronto, 1902), 2.
101 *Manchester Guardian*, 7 May 1842. See also reports from London papers in *Chronicle and Gazette*, 31 May 1837, and *Kingston Gazette*, 25 August 1818; from *Newry Telegraph*, in *Christian Guardian*, 11 June 1830; C.D. Arfwedson, *The United States and Canada in 1832, 1833 and 1834* (London, 1834), 2; Harper, *Willing Exiles*, 90.
102 Medd Papers, John Thompson to friend, 23 June 1819, TUA, 81-001/2.

CHAPTER THREE

1 Pengelly Family Papers, Harriet Pengelly Diary, 20 April 1835, Trent University Archives (TUA), 70–001/1/4.
2 Thomas Radcliffe, ed., *Authentic Letters from Upper Canada* (Dublin, 1833) 110. In *Six Years in the Bush* (London, 1838), 65, the settler commented, in a hopeful message to discouraged emigrants: "Canada is a land of dreams, and what seems a 'baseless' vision one day is a reality the next."
3 *Scots Times*, 17 July 1832.
4 Reported in *Canadian Emigrant*, 20 July 1833, and *Canadian Freeman*, 26 September 1833.
5 See Royden Loewen, ed., *From the Inside Out* (Winnipeg: University of Manitoba Press, 1999), 3–5, for further discussion of the role that keeping a journal and diary had for the author.
6 Journals of George Pashley, Archives of Ontario (AO), MU843, 1–P–1.
7 Elizabeth Peters Diary, Diaries of William and Elizabeth Peters, AO, MS199, 1–5. Not all entries in either diary are dated precisely. References will usually be to original pagination. This pair of diaries reflects some of the different concerns that wives and husbands had during the Atlantic crossing.
8 Diary of a Voyage of John Hart, Scottish Record Office (SRO), TD1082. See also Thomas Yoseloff, ed. *Voyage to America: The Journal of Thomas Cather* (Westpoint, Conn: Greenwood Press, 1973), 11, who noted passengers' frustration at having to go back to the dock after their ship ran afoul of another in harbour.
9 Edward Talbot, *Five Years' Residence in the Canadas* (London, 1824; reprint 1968), 2.
10 Reilly, *Journal of an Excursion to the United States and Canada* (Edinburgh, 1835), 8. See also William Bell, *Hints to Emigrants* (Edinburgh, 1824), 2, who recounted how he and his family went on board just before sailing. Talbot (*Five Years' Residence*) noted that steerage passengers embarked first and then cabin passengers boarded just before sailing.
11 William Peters Diary, 3 May 1830.
12 Diary of a Voyage of John Hart, 22 April 1842.
13 Mrs Langton to William, in H.H. Langton, ed., *A Gentlewoman in Upper Canada* (Toronto: Clarke, Irwin, 1950), 11.
14 Diary of Joseph Wilson, 21 April 1831, AO, ACC10971, MU847.
15 Reilly, *Journal of an Excursion*, 11. This impression was echoed by others. See Yoseloff, ed., *Voyage to America*, 15; William Blane, *An Excursion through the United States and Canada during the Years 1822–23* (1823; reprint, New

York: Negro University Press, 1969), 1, who commented, "Nothing can well be more disagreeable to landsmen than the beginning of a sea voyage. Want of room, of exercise and of occupation added to the sickness that Neptune imposes on them ... all combined to depress their spirits."

16 "Journal of a Voyage to New York," National Library of Scotland (NLS), ACC8813, February 1834.
17 Frances Stewart, 1 July 1822, in *Our Forest Home*, ed. E.S. Dunlop (Toronto, 1902), 5. Such attention in journals to the captain were quite common, particularly by cabin passengers. A cabin passenger aboard the barque *Resolution*, which sailed from Liverpool to Quebec in 1834 judged that Captain Murray was a shrewd, capable, and intelligent man, who went to considerable lengths to make sure that all aboard were as comfortable and healthy as possible; see "Journal of a Voyage from Liverpool to Quebec, 1834," Scottish Record Office (SRO), GD372/327. The author, who was one of four cabin passengers sailing with thirty-four steerage passengers, included numerous references to conversations with the captain. Similarly, Patrick Shirreff noted that the captain of his ship was attentive to passengers; see his *Tour through North America* (Edinburgh, 1835), 6.
18 William Knox to Andrew Redford, 28 October 1838, Redford Papers, SRO, GD1/813/15.
19 Elizabeth Peters Diary, 7.
20 See Journals of George Pashley; John Mann, *Travels in North America, Particularly in the Provinces of Upper and Lower Canada and New Brunswick and in the States of Maine, Massachusetts, and New York* (Glasgow: Andrew Young, 1824). William Peters also often led prayer services (noted in diaries of both William and Elizabeth Peters). See also Reilly, *Journal of an Excursion*, 10, who noted that the captain encouraged attendance at Sunday service; and Diary of Joseph Wilson, 17 April 1831.
21 Bell, *Hints*, 3, described the captain of his ship as a stubborn man, given to drink, who often seemed to go out of his way to make life difficult for the passengers.
22 Reilly, *Journal of an Excursion*, 8.
23 Ibid., 41.
24 Mary O'Brien noted that only the stewards and the ladies' husbands could enter the "inner" cabin; see *Journals of Mary O'Brien*, ed., Audrey Saunders Miller, (Toronto, 1968), 4–5. Talbot, travelling on the *Brunswick*, noted that cabin passengers had a large dining room, two staterooms, each with berths for four, and two bedchambers. There were forty berths in steerage, each to sleep six or more if they were women and children (Talbot, *Five Years' Residence*, 17).
25 Stewart, 1 July 1822, *Our Forest Home*, ed. Dunlop, 4.

26 Reilly, *Journal of an Excursion*, 7–8. Mrs Radcliffe (Radcliffe, ed., *Authentic Letters*, 30) found the second cabin very crowded.
27 Bell (*Hints*, 3) noted that there was no cabin on the *Rothiemuirchus*. He and another family had arranged to have part of the stern partitioned off. This meant that they at least had two windows and were not so crowded. "The Emigrant's Voyage to Canada," *Blackwood's*, November 1821, 455, stated that families travelling in steerage each had their own small compartment.
28 Reilly, *Journal of an Excursion*, 13.
29 See, for example, "Journal of a Voyage from Liverpool," SRO, GD372/327.
30 Shirreff, *A Tour through North America*, 5.
31 "Journal of a Voyage from Liverpool." Even two weeks into the voyage they ate well, being served eggs, coffee, and toasted ham for breakfast.
32 Radcliffe, ed., *Authentic Letters*, 32.
33 Anne to William Langton, 7 June 1837, Langton, ed., *A Gentlewoman in Upper Canada*, 10. George Leith, in his brief account of his voyage, noted that "all the ladies were sick" for much of the time. He watched "some of the gentlemen making great fools of themselves, only it amuses one and spends an hour or two" (16 April 1835). He "sat on deck all day, have bread and milk for breakfast and a bit of turkey or fowl for dinner. Read and work" (23 April 1835); see Diary of George Leith, AO, MS69. William Cather (*Voyage to America*, ed. Yoseloff, 15) reported that he had "breakfast at 9:00; read and then on deck; dinner at 3; played cards, read on deck."
34 The cabin passengers on Pengelly's ship included "3 married ladies, two unmarried, twenty males." Robert noted that the steerage was very crowded and that there were a "great many children" (Pengelly Papers, Robert Pengelly Diary, 6 April 1835).
35 Anne to William, 31 May 1837, Langton, ed., *A Gentlewoman in Upper Canada*, 9.
36 "Journal of a Voyage from Liverpool."
37 Pengelly Papers, Robert Pengelly Diary, 10 April 1835. Apart from one reference to steerage passengers, neither Robert nor Harriet ever mentioned them in their diaries.
38 See, for example, "Journal of a Voyage from Liverpool," which describes how the writer, when on the *Resolution*, was called to attend a sick child. The child recovered.
39 Reilly, *Journal of an Excursion*, 13.
40 "Journal of a Voyage to New York," AO, ACC8813(1). Here, the passenger clearly distanced himself from "the emigrants."
41 Diary of a Voyage of John Hart, 29 April 1842, SRO, TD1082.
42 Journals of George Pashley. This was also the case on the *British Tar*, which carried the Sussex emigrants out in 1834; see *Narrative of a Voyage ... by the*

Petworth Committee (London, 1834), 3. The steerage was divided into three, with one part for single men and boys over fourteen. Each part had its own water closet.

43 Redford Papers, William Knox to Andrew Redford, 28 October 1838.
44 Elizabeth Peters Diary, 7.
45 Redford Papers, William Knox to Andrew Redford, 28 October 1838.
46 Elizabeth Peters Diary, 7.
47 Reilly, *Journal of an Excursion*, 13.
48 See report from London paper reprinted in *Chronicle and Gazette*, 30 August 1834.
49 Reilly, *Journal of an Excursion*, 13.
50 Diary of Joseph Wilson, 17 April 1831.
51 "A Report of the Special Sanitary Committee of Montreal upon Cholera and Emigration for 1834," parts of which were published in colonial newspapers, described the "poor" suffering horrific conditions. These included delayed departures, emigrants running out of food and water, whole families sleeping eight or ten to a berth, etc. (*Chronicle and Gazette*, 14 February 1835). See also ibid., 30 August and 13 September 1834; *Scots Times*, 2 October 1832.
52 "The Emigrant's Voyage to Canada," *Blackwood's*, November 1821, 466.
53 Steele Journal, 26 May 1828, NLS, ACC5814.
54 Ibid., 28 May 1828. For other accounts of shipboard committees, see below; also letter from John Connel (12 July 1845, "My dear," NLS, ACC7021), who noted that a committee of nine gave out bread and water and saw that "good order and cleanliness was kept on the ship." See also Mann, *Travels in North America*. Also *Narrative of a Voyage ... Petworth Committee*, 4, 8, which describes the appointment of a committee of local men and the specific rules set out, which included no swearing. Members of the committee were each paid a bottle of brandy weekly.
55 Steele Journal, 27 May and 16 June 1828.
56 Ibid., 16 June 1828.
57 Ibid., 10 June 1828.
58 Ibid., 17 June 1828. Some passengers publicly thanked the captain. A number of passengers of "the American ship Camillus" placed a notice in the *Scots Times*, 3 July 1832, thanking master John Niven "for his kind attention to us during the voyage." Bell (*Hints*, 21) noted that the captain of his ship oversaw the cleaning of berths and bedding. "Report of Lieutenant Rubidge" (*Canadian, British American, and West Indian Magazine*, October 1839, 376) recounted that he was sailing with a party of Irish emigrant labourers and regularly required the women and children to get on deck, weather permitting, and that bedding be aired.

59 Diary of a Voyage of John Hart, 27, 28 April 1842.
60 Robert Sellar, *A Scotsman in Upper Canada: The Narrative of Gordon Sellar* (Toronto: Clarke, Irwin, 1696), 21. See also Hart, Diary of a Voyage.
61 Diary of Joseph Wilson. See also Steele Journal, which noted, "Cook a madman when drunk," 4 July 1828.
62 Sellar, *A Scotsman in Upper Canada*, 21.
63 See Mann, *Travels in North America*, 2; *Narrative of a Voyage ... Petworth Committee*, 4. Bell noted in *Hints*, 9, that provisions were "bad" on his voyage.
64 Journal of George Forbes, 19 April 1845, SRO, RH4/80.
65 Elizabeth Peters Diary, 13.
66 Ibid., 10.
67 Ibid., 12.
68 Ibid., 9. Joseph Wilson commented that he wished he had brought more wine or ale. The family nonetheless appears to have eaten quite well and particularly enjoyed Jenney's biscuits (1, 5 May 1831).
69 Elizabeth Peters Diary, 10.
70 Diary of a Voyage of John Hart, 27 April 1842.
71 See also Journals of George Pashley, 3, and Diary of Joseph Wilson.
72 Diary of Joseph Wilson, 23 April 1831.
73 Ibid., 3 May 1831.
74 Ibid., 21 May 1831.
75 Elizabeth Peters Diary, 4.
76 Ibid., 6.
77 See comments of Charlotte Willard to Mrs Wolger, 26 August 1832, in *Letters from Dorking Emigrants* (London, 1833), 2. See also comments of Elizabeth Peters and Joseph Wilson. Elizabeth Peters recounted how, early in the voyage, a boy had been severely injured by falling when climbing the rigging (Elizabeth Peters Diary, 4).
78 Diary of a Voyage of John Hart, beginning 30 April. See also an account of measles in John Steele's diary, 1 June.
79 Journals of George Pashley, 4.
80 British newpapers gave considerable attention to the spread of cholera in North America. See, for example, the *Observer*, 2 September 1832; *Manchester Guardian*, 30 April 1832.
81 Diary of a Voyage of John Hart, 16 April 1842.
82 Reilly, *Journal of an Excursion*, 21.
83 Bell, *Hints*, 7.
84 See account (in Steele Journal, 28 June) of Mrs Muirhead delivering a daughter on McNaughtie's berth (so he stood as godfather). See also Shirreff (*A Tour through North America*, 6), who tells of a cabin passenger giving birth to

85 Elizabeth Peters Diary, 21.
86 Ibid., 15.
87 Steele Journal, 10 July, 16. See also Cather, *Voyage to America*, ed. Yoseloff, 19.
88 Elizabeth Peters Diary, 10.
89 Steele Journal, 11 July 1828.
90 Reilly, *Journal of an Excursion*, 11.
91 See Diary of Joseph Wilson, 22 April 1831; Reilly, *Journal of an Excursion*, 22, concerning pigs on board; and "Journal of a Voyage from Liverpool," 11, about chickens on board.
92 Diary of Joseph Wilson, 28 April 1831.
93 Ibid., 18 April 1831; Steele Journal, 12 July 1828, 18. See earlier discussion of how cabin passengers spent their time on board.
94 Steele Journal, 3 June 1828.
95 Diary of a Voyage of John Hart, 2 May 1842. A day after his daughter died, George Pashley recorded, "The forenoon we met a vessel from Quebec which has been 22 days on the voyage & we have been 11. Her name is Royal Adelaide of Portsmouth. She was Bound for Liverpool" (Journals of George Pashley, 13 August 1833).
96 Elizabeth Peters Diary, 8. Sellar (*A Scotsman in Upper Canada*, 24) also frequently recounted seeing sails in the distance, but he also noted the monotony of the voyage. Walter Riddell appears to have recorded each ship sighted; see his *Diary of a Voyage from Scotland to Canada, 1833* (Toronto: Associated Printers, 1932). See also Diary of Joseph Wilson, 22 April 1830, 6–7.
97 Elizabeth Peters Diary, 8–9.
98 C.D. Arfwedson, *The United States and Canada* (London, 1834), 2.
99 Diary of a Voyage of John Hart, 4 May 1842.
100 Diary of Joseph Wilson, 23 April 1831. See also Arfwedson, *The United States and Canada*, who noted celebrating the 4th of July.
101 Diary of a Voyage of John Hart, 14 May 1842.
102 Ibid., 24 May 1842. On the *Resolution*, "as is always the case when the weather is all fine, the sailors and Emigrants are full of fun and amusement. They held an auction today of various things" "Journal of a Voyage from Liverpool," 2 June 1834, SRO, GD372/327.
103 Pengelly Papers, Robert Pengelly Dairy, 7 April 1835.
104 Reilly, *Journal of an Excursion*, 41. Bell (*Hints*, 9) noted that there was frequent grumbling and "at times near mutiny over the lack of provisions." Earlier he had noted that as soon as emigrants came on board, there were disputes

about the berths, and the captain had had to intervene. The passage of the Dorking emigrants appears to have been quite difficult, and Charlotte Willard reported, "There was not a day went over our heads but when there was quarrelling or a fighting" (letter to Mrs Wolger, 26 August 1832, *Letters from Dorking Emigrants*, 18).

105 Elizabeth Peters Diary, 19. Journals of voyages frequently recounted the theft of provisions, bedding, and other goods. See Riddell, *Diary of a Voyage*, 3 May, which included an account of a "jury" that "convicted" an emigrant of "stealing."

106 Steele Journal, 14 July 1828.

107 "The Emigrant's Voyage to Canada," *Blackwood's*, November 1821, 466. Arfwedson (*The United States and Canada*, 2) noted, "The uniformity of a sea-life generally engenders melancholy; the monotony is unsupportable."

108 Diary of a Voyage of John Hart, 22 April 1842. John Howison, *Sketches of Upper Canada* (London 1821; reprint S.R. Publishers, 1965), 5, recounted that on his voyage there were two stowaways "who had been men of deceit and guile and had corrupted the cabin boy." See also account in "The Emigrant's Voyage", *Blackwood's*, November 1821, 463.

109 Diary of a Voyage of John Hart, 23 April 1842.

110 Diary of Joseph Wilson, 23 April 1830.

111 William Peters Diary, 30 April 1830. Later in the voyage (6 May 1830), he noted, "We are sowers in hope that it may be bread cast on the waters to be found after many days ... Although some are very sinful in their words and ways, they appeared to feel the force of truth while I exhorted on the necessity of preparing for Eternity." Elizabeth Peters recorded, "The Cabin passengers & Captain, the sailors and steerage passengers ... have all been very attentive, moreso than some English congregations" (Elizabeth Peters Diary, 7–8).

112 Elizabeth Peters noted that there were two services each Sunday, except for one Sunday when it was too wet, and on another when "the people were all too unwell to hold the services" (Diary, 7–8). See also Diary of Joseph Wilson, who commented with approval on the sermons. Bell (*Hints*, 4) noted that the captain agreed to services twice a day, with a sermon on Sunday, but the pattern was often disrupted by bad weather and work and by some sailors' derision. John Connel wrote to his wife that the captain on their ship addressed the 250 passengers about the need for good order during services ("Emigrant Letters, NLS, ACC7021). Thomas Ross reported home on 7 July 1832 that although he conducted two services a day, he found many of the steerage passengers "immoral & wicked persons" (SRO, MS3439/195).

113 Reilly, *Journal of an Excursion*, 19.

114 Journal of a Voyage, 16 February 1834, AO, ACC8813(1).

115 Journals of George Pashley, 12 August 1833. On the *Resolution*, there was "no respect whatever paid to Sunday" ("Journal of a Voyage from Liverpool").
116 This was particularly apparent in the Diary of William Peters which, in contrast to his wife's, was a chronicle of his faith as well as the voyage.
117 William Catermole, *Emigration: The Advantages of Emigration to Canada* (London, 1831), 83.
118 "Journal of a Voyage from Liverpool."
119 Reilly, *Journal of an Excursion*, 9, 49.
120 Elizabeth Peters Diary, 25. There appears to have been considerable antagonism between those in steerage and in cabins on the trip of the Dorking emigrants; see Cornelius Cousins to Mr John Bartlett, 7 October 1832, who also noted that "the captain & steward ... use us very badly" (*Letters from Dorking Emigrants*, 14–15). The Petworth emigrants Charlotte and William Willard complained to their sister that "they have plenty of every thing in the cabin, we had nothing but musty biscuit and salt beef" (26 August 1832), see Wendy Cameron, Mary McDougall Maude, and Sheila Haines, eds., *English Immigrant Voices* (Montreal & Kingston: McGill-Queen's University Press, 2000), 20.
121 Elizabeth Peters Diary, 15–16.
122 Radcliffe, ed., *Authentic Letters*, 33.
123 Reilly, *Journal of an Excursion*, 48–9. See also Diary of Joseph Wilson, 24 May 1831; and Bell, *Hints*, 4.
124 Radcliffe, ed., *Authentic Letters*, 31.
125 Diary of Joseph Wilson, 21 April 1831.
126 Elizabeth Peters Diary, 2.
127 Diary of Joseph Wilson, 21 April 1831.
128 Radcliffe, ed., *Authentic Letters*, 33.
129 Letter of Dorking residents, 2 March 1822, in *Letters from Dorking Emigrants*, 25. See also letter of William Wright to his father, ibid., 23.
130 Journals of George Pashley, 3.
131 John Connel to family, 12 July 1845, NLS, ACC7021.
132 See, for example, Redford Papers, William Knox to his uncle, 28 October 1838, who noted that the children were never sick but that his wife was sick for weeks. See also *Letters from Canada*, 16; William Peters Diary (which noted the children were best of all); and Steele Journal.
133 Joseph concluded, "It was punishment in the extreme," and it illustrated "the folly of setting out on such a voyage without a proper medical man" (Diary of Joseph Wilson, 22 April 1831). Mary O'Brien (in *Journals of Mary O'Brien*, ed. Miller, 5) noted on 6 September 1828 her relief at getting her sea legs. The passenger on the *Resolution* noted that in his experience, "most passengers

who were very ill at the commencement have been ill every time there was anything like a sea – to such persons, a sea voyage must be a most miserable adventure" ("Journal of a Voyage from Liverpool").

134 Diary of Joseph Wilson, 25 and 26 April 1831. In *Emigration: Letters from Suffolk Emigrants* (Chichester, 1837), many noted the roughness and their seasickness during the seven-week voyage.
135 "Journal of a Voyage from Liverpool," 28 February 1834. Arfwedson (*The United States and Canada*, 4) described the effects of high winds at sea: the women "were silent in a corner, with palpitating hearts ... Children seized with fear, clung to their parents and screamed piteously."
136 "Journal of a Voyage from Liverpool," 4 March 1834.
137 Ibid., 16 March 1834. Similar sentiments were expressed by William Peters, who took solace that all was "the Lord's doing" (William Peters Diary, 7).
138 Diary of Joseph Wilson, 24 April 1831.
139 Diary of a Voyage of John Hart, 27 April 1831. See also Arfwedson, *The United States and Canada*, 5.
140 Diary of a Voyage of John Hart, 29 April 1842.
141 Ibid., 3 May 1842.
142 Ibid., 4 May 1842.
143 "The Emigrant's Voyage to Canada," *Blackwood's*, November 1821, 457.
144 Reilly, *Journal of an Excursion*, 15.
145 Diary of Joseph Wilson, 22 April 1831. See also "Journal of a Voyage from Liverpool," which noted, "The calm is a great relief to such passengers who have been ill ... Now all on deck enjoying themselves."
146 Pengelly Papers, Robert Pengelly Diary, 19 April 1835.
147 Diary of Joseph Wilson, 17 April 1831.
148 Ibid., 1 May 1831.
149 "Journal of a Voyage from Liverpool," 16 June 1834, 19. See also *Journals of Mary O'Brien*, ed. Miller, 16 September 1828, 6, which noted Mary's disappointment at "no progress." Arfwedson (*The United States and Canada*, 3) commented, "How often, whilst meditating on the beauty of the immeasurable heavenly arch, have I not favored I saw a distant shore rising from the deeps; the joy, alas! was short lived: twas only a cloud."
150 Steele Journal, 5 July 1828.
151 Ibid., 12 July 1828.
152 Diary of a Voyage of John Hart, 14 May 1842.
153 Ibid., 17 May 1842. See also comments in Diary of Joseph Wilson, 4 and 5 May, 1830.
154 "Journal of a Voyage from Liverpool"; Blane, *An Excursion*, 5.

155 Diary of a Voyage of John Hart, 16 May 1842. See also Diary of Joseph Wilson, 4 May 1831; and Bell, *Hints*, 28: "The sighting of a large iceberg brought everyone on deck."
156 William Peters Diary, 1 June 1831.
157 Diary of a Voyage of John Hart, 22 May 1842.
158 Diary of Joseph Wilson, 13 May 1831.
159 Elizabeth Peters Diary, 10–11. Arfwedson, *The United States and Canada*, 11: "I heard the magic sounds 'Land!' pronounced from the top of the masthead ... The joyful intelligence passed from mouth to mouth, with the rapidity of light ray ... All were in a most happy state of mind."
160 Journals of George Pashley, 29 August 1833. The passenger on the *Resolution* commented, "Land, once in sight did more to motivate the steerage passengers than any other case that I can bestow upon them" ("Journal of a Voyage from Liverpool," 18 June 1834).
161 Reported by John Hart, of those aboard a brig next to which the *Carlton* anchored the day they rounded the Cape. The passengers had spent thirty-nine days at sea, and their behaviour, Hart commented cryptically, was "truly characteristic of the English" (Diary of a Voyage of John Hart, 23 May 1842). Shirreff, when close to New York, recorded, "My situation was like that of a famishing person with food in view; intense desire without gratification" (*Tour through North America*, 7). Mary O'Brien (*Journals of Mary O'Brien*, ed. Miller, 7) noted that even though it was only "smelly land," it was cause for "general congratulations and excitement" (30 September 1828). Joseph Wilson and his companions were issued some rum by the captain to mark the occasion (Diary, 18 May 1831).
162 William Peters Diary, 2 or 3 June 1830.
163 Diary of a Voyage of John Hart, 27 May 1842.
164 Elizabeth Peters Diary, 26.
165 Diary of a Voyage of John Hart, 27 May 1842.
166 For examples, see Diary of a Voyage of John Hart; Steele Journal; Radcliffe, ed., *Authentic Letters*; and "Journal of a Voyage from Liverpool."
167 Elizabeth Peters Diary, 23.
168 Diary of Joseph Wilson, 19 May 1831.
169 Diary of a Voyage of John Hart, 2 June 1842; 27 and 28 May 1842.
170 Ibid., 30 May 1842.
171 "Journal of a Voyage from Liverpool," 38. By 1834, regulations were more strictly enforced. When three cabin passengers from the *Resolution* launched a small vessel to fish, the captain was very upset, for he feared that all might be seized and fined or imprisoned for breaking quarantine ("Journal of a Voyage from Liverpool").

172 Susanna Moodie, *Roughing It in the Bush* (London, 1852; reprint, Toronto: McClelland & Stewart, 1962), 24–6.
173 Catharine Parr Traill, *The Backwoods of Canada* (London, 1836; reprint, Toronto: McClelland & Stewart, 1966), 19.
174 Steele Journal, 18 July 1828.
175 William Hutton to mother, 23 September 1834, in *Hutton of Hastings*, ed. Gerald E. Boyce (Belleville: Hastings County Council, 1972), 39–40.
176 Diary of a Voyage of John Hart, 31 May 1842.
177 Sellar, *A Scotsman in Upper Canada*, 29–30, noted that once in the St Lawrence, his ship was no longer alone. See also "The Emigrant," *Canadian Magazine*, March 1833, 194–5; and Diary of Joseph Wilson, 21, 22 May 1831.
178 Diary of a Voyage of John Hart, 2 June 1842.
179 Diary of Joseph Wilson, 22 May 1831.
180 Diary of a Voyage of John Hart, 3 June 1842.
181 "Journal of a Voyage from Liverpool," 14 July; Arfwedson (*The United States and Canada*, 12) noted they were "all dressed in their very best" for their arrival.
182 Diary of Joseph Wilson, 23 May 1831. Many of the *Suffolk Emigrants*, 6, spent their two days in Quebec celebrating, and one was drowned. McDougall (*Emigrant's Guide*, 26) warned new arrivals to be careful and guard their luggage. John Howison (*Sketches*) remarked on the "interesting spectacle of emigrants landing." See also Sellar, *A Scotsman in Upper Canada*, 30–1; and "The Emigrant," *Canadian Magazine*, February 1833, 97–9.
183 Steele Journal, 18 July 1828.
184 Elizabeth Peters Diary, 25.
185 Journals of George Pashley, 3 September 1833.

CHAPTER FOUR

1 Journals of George Pashley, Archives of Ontario (AO), MU843, 1-P-1, 8. This portion of the diary was written approximately six months after arrival.
2 William Hutton to his mother, 23 September 1834, in *Hutton of Hastings*, ed. Gerald E. Boyce (Belleville: Hastings County Council, 1972), 39.
3 Ibid., 40.
4 Pengelly Family Papers, Harriet Pengelly Diary, 7 May 1835, Trent University Archives (TUA), 70-001/1/4.
5 Ibid., 8 May 1835.
6 Ibid., 9 and 12 May 1835.
7 Ibid., 17 May 1835.
8 4 October 1828, *The Journals of Mary O'Brien*, ed., Audrey Saunders Miller (Toronto, 1968), 9.

9 Ibid.
10 Ibid., 7 October 1828, 11.
11 Ibid., 16 October 1828, 16.
12 See letter of Thomas Langton to son William, 20 July 1837, in H.H. Langton, ed., *A Gentlewoman in Upper Canada* (Toronto: Clarke Irwin, 1950), 28–9; Mrs Langton's journal, ibid., 15 July 1837, 20.
13 Ibid., Mrs Langton's journal, 4 August 1837, 22.
14 Ibid., 15 August 1837, 28.
15 Catharine Parr Traill, *The Backwoods of Canada* (London, 1836; reprint, Toronto: McClelland & Stewart, 1966), 20.
16 Ibid., 29.
17 Ibid., 31, 39.
18 Ibid., 35, 36. The work of Catharine Parr Traill and other "Canadian" women writers of the nineteenth century has received considerable attention from historians and literary folk. Some, like Patricia Jasen, *Wild Things: Nature, Culture, and Tourism in Ontario, 1790–1914* (Toronto: University of Toronto Press, 1995) have read Susanna Moodie, for example, as both a settler and a tourist who was "free to possess the landscape imaginatively," 25. See also Sara Mills, *Discourses of Difference: An Analysis of Women's Travel Writings and Colonialism* (New York: Routledge, 1991). As Mary Louise Pratt has illustrated in *Imperials Eyes: Travel Writing and Transculturation* (New York: Routledge, 1992), such accounts both chronicle and illustrate the "contact zone" of British North America.
19 Traill, *Backwoods of Canada*, 39.
20 E.S. Dunlop, ed., *Our Forest Home* (Toronto, 1902), 13.
21 Ibid., 11.
22 Diary of Joseph Wilson, 23 May 1831, AO, ACC10971, MU847.
23 Ibid., 24 March 1831. See also Robert Sellar, *A Scotsman in Upper Canada: The Narrative of Gordon Sellar* (Toronto: Clarke, Irwin, 1969), 34–5, who noted the attempt of a thief to carry off luggage.
24 Diary of Joseph Wilson, 26–7 May 1831.
25 Ibid., 1 June 1831.
26 Ibid., 4 June 1831.
27 Ibid., 7 June 1831.
28 Ibid., 7 June 1831. In his introduction to *Emigration: Letters from Suffolk Emigrants* (Petworth, 1833), T. Socknat noted that the journey from Montreal to the interior could be "irksome and tiring." Patrick Shirreff reported seeing emigrants on a bateau "huddled together as close as captives in a slave-raider and very hot and dejected"; see his *A Tour through North America* (Edinburgh, 1835), 143. In *Assisting Emigration to Upper Canada* (Montreal

& Kingston: McGill-Queen's University Press, 2000), Wendy Cameron and Mary McDougall Maude have chronicled the journey upriver of the Petworth immigrants and some of the troubles they had proceeding to York.
29 Journals of George Pashley, 10.
30 Ibid., 12.
31 Ibid., 13.
32 Ibid., 16–17.
33 These reports were ubiquitous in such papers as the *Christian Guardian*, the *Canadian Emigrant*, and the Kingston *Chronicle and Gazette* in the early 1830s and early 1840s. See, for example, *Christian Guardian*, 2 October 1830, 2 July 1831; *Canadian Emigrant*, 27 July and 24 August 1833, 28 June 1834; *Chronicle and Gazette*, 5 August 1840; *British Whig*, 24 June 1834; *Farmer's Journal*, 10 October 1827; *Cobourg Star*, 11 June 1840, 13 July 1842.
34 See, for example, reports in the *Kingston Chronicle*, 21 July 1820 and 23 July 1831; article in the *Scots Times*, 2 October 1832, about the dangers of the trip to the interior.
35 *Farmer's Journal*, 14 August 1828, taken from *Kingston Gazette and Religious Advocate*, 29 July 1828.
36 *Hallowell Free Press*, 19 June 1832. The notice was repeated on 24 July and also appeared in the Kingston *Chronicle and Gazette*, 16 June 1832. See also notice of a father looking for his son, John Mason, aged thirteen, who had been separated from his mother on the trip from Montreal to Kingston (*British Whig*, 29 December 1847).
37 *Kingston Chronicle*, 24 September 1819.
38 *Christian Guardian*, 18 July 1832. See also Thomas Dinnell looking for his daughter Anne, whom he had left in Montreal in the care of James Connor, a blacksmith. All Thomas knew was that Connor had left Montreal and Anne was not to be found (*British Whig*, 22 November 1844). Parents were looking for Michael Cary who had left him in Montreal (*Chronicle and Advocate*, 4 March 1842); sisters Margaret, Jane, and Elizabeth McComb were looking for their brother, who had left them in Montreal (*Colonial Advocate*, 1 November 1827). "The friends" of Catharine Burnes were looking for her; she had been left at Mr Fraser's, a blacksmith, three months earlier, and they now did not know where she was (*Bytown Gazette*, 1 September 1842). Robert Laird had left his daughter with an aunt in Quebec and had not heard from her since (*Christian Guardian*, 19 September 1832).
39 *Christian Guardian*, 20 August 1834.
40 *Bytown Gazette*, 20 September 1837. See also similar notices: looking for Thomas Mollay, who had left his wife and children at Yamaska five months

before (*Kingston Chronicle*, 1 February 1834); "looking for John McGlowin," who had left his wife and child in Montreal two years before and was now supposed to be in the United States (*British Whig*, 11 July 1834); wanting to find Biddy Gilrow, who had parted from her sister "on the wharf at Kingston last July" (*Chronicle and Gazette*, 6 May 1843); Miss Sarah McBride, who had arrived with her mother, two brothers, and two sisters, had gone on her own to Montreal and Kingston and was last heard from in May 1838 (*Upper Canada Herald*, 26 March 1839); brother looking for sisters Margaret, Jane, and Elizabeth McComb, whom he had left in Montreal (*Colonial Advocate*, 1 November 1827).

41 The impact of cholera on the colonies is due for a new study. For now, see Geoffrey Bilson, *A Darkened House: Cholera in Nineteenth-Century Canada* (Toronto: University of Toronto Press, 1980) and C.M. Godfrey, *The Cholera Epidemics in Upper Canada, 1832–1866* (Kingston & Montreal: McGill-Queen's University Press, 1968.)

42 *Bytown Gazette*, 1 June 1843. See also the following notices: Henry O'Grady, who had been left in Quebec by his sister who was now looking for him (*Christian Guardian*, 30 October 1833); brothers divided on journey (*Kingston Chronicle*, 27 July 1821); the sister of James Fitzgerald, who had been left in Montreal and was now looking for him (*Chronicle and Gazette*, 2 November 1833).

43 *St Catharines Journal*, 3 August 1837.

44 *Canadian Correspondent and Advocate*, 30 March 1833.

45 *Cobourg Star*, 8 August 1832.

46 Ibid., 27 July 1836.

47 For example, this was part of the terms of reference for the Kingston Compassionate Society (*Kingston Gazette*, 9 December 1817). It was but one of many such organizations. See also "Terms of the Emigrant Society of Quebec" (*Kingston Chronicle*, 13 August 1819); establishment of hospital "for Sick and Destitute emigrants" (ibid., 29 October 1819); Society for the Relief of Strangers in Distress (*Upper Canada Gazette*, 3 December 1818); Montreal Emigrant Society (ibid., 25 September 1820). Various "ethnic" societies also provided aid to emigrants, including the St Andrews Society. For further information about aid offered to emigrants (and others), see Patricia Malcolmson, "The Poor in Kingston," in Gerald Tulchinsky, ed., *To Preserve and Defend: Essays on Kingston in the Nineteenth Century* (Montreal: McGill University Press, 1976); Rainer Baehre, "Paupers and Poor Relief in Upper Canada," Canadian Historical Association *Papers* (1981); Elizabeth Jane Errington, *Wives and Mothers, School Mistresses and Scullery Maids* (Montreal

& Kingston: McGill-Queen's University Press, 1995); Cameron and Maude, *Assisting Emigration to Upper Canada*, chap. 4.

48 Upper Canadians wanted to encourage emigration from Great Britain and Ireland. At the same time, many expressed concern that the mother country was trying to "shovel out" its paupers and this created considerable resentment. For further discussion of this, see Elizabeth Jane Errington, "Migration and British America 1783–1867," *Oxford History of the British Empire: Canada* (Oxford: Oxford University Press, 2007).

49 The mandate of the agents included "to give information as to the routes, distances and rates of conveyance" to where emigrants wanted to go "and direct those most in want of work to places where they can obtain it" (*Cobourg Star*, 24 May 1836).

50 *Cobourg Star*, 18 July 1832.

51 *Chronicle and Gazette*, 17 May 1840.

52 Ibid., 12 August 1840.

53 Ibid., 18 July 1837. It ran until 8 November 1837.

54 Notice to "The Editors of Newspapers in Upper Canada Lower Canada …" from the Secretary to the Emigrants' Society, Quebec, in *Farmer's Journal* 27 February 1828.

55 Ibid. The report from the Quebec Emigrants' Society tried to embarrass men who had abandoned their families by publishing their names and circumstances and asking that local employers garnishee their wages.

56 Forbes Letters, 18 July 1845, Scottish Record Office (SRO), RH4, 80.

57 Journals of George Pashley, 8.

58 John Counel to mother, 12 July 1845, National Library of Scotland (NLS), ACC7021. Also letter of George and Lydia Halton, who recounted the story of two brothers not recognizing each other, 10 September 1836, in Wendy Cameron, Mary McDougall Maude, and Sheila Haines, eds., *English Immigrant Voices* (Montreal & Kingston: McGill-Queen's University Press, 2000), 244.

59 Shirreff, *A Tour*, 147. Edward Longley asked William Mitchell of West Sussex to tell Mr and Mrs Haylor that if they came to Upper Canada, Edward would assist them. He then gave directions to his residence: "He should make direct for Guelph and enquire for me at Mr McCrea's and he will find me out" (28 September 1835, in Cameron et al., eds., *English Immigrant Voices*, 202). Another of the Petworth emigrants, John Barnes, urged his family to join him and assured them he would meet them at the wharf in Toronto (John Barnes to Father et al., 1 January 1837, ibid., 248).

60 James Rapson to father, 9 July 1833, ibid., 129.

61 *Bytown Gazette*, 14 December 1843.
62 *Colonial Advocate*, 23 August 1832.
63 *Cobourg Star*, 2 August 1831.
64 *Chronicle and Gazette*, 29 May 1839, running to 12 June; also in *Cobourg Star*, 29 May 1839. See also the following: friends looking for a young man, John Clifton of Bucks, who had arrived in Montreal in July 1831 and "since when his friends having no tidings of him are anxious" (ibid., 9 October 1832); sister-in-law looking for Nepthune Rudd who had left England and "has not been heard of since he landed," and she was "anxious" (*Christian Guardian*, 26 April 1837); Michael Toman of Hallowell, looking for his brother, Robert Nixon, who had arrived from Ireland "and proceeded on his way to Hallowell in Upper Canada, since which time no intelligence has been received of him" (*Chronicle and Gazette*, 27 December 1834).
65 *Chronicle and Gazette*, 13 July 1842.
66 Ibid., 1 September 1841.
67 *Patriot*, 28 November 1837; this also appeared in the *Christian Guardian*, 22 November 1837. See also the following notices: looking for Michael Brown Kirwin, "he is requested to make known where he is residing" (*Christian Guardian*, 11 September 1839); James Campbell was "very anxious to discover his [brother's] residence" (ibid., 18 September 1841); father of William Hocker looking for his "present abode" (*Chronicle and Gazette*, 13 January 1834); Ann Happer told her husband to "take note" that she had arrived (*Upper Canada Gazette*, 30 December 1819); father asking his sons to write as "it will be answered immediately and the route taken to join them" (*Chronicle and Gazette*, 7 June 1834); James Garratt looking for his brother William, as he had "just arrived from Ireland" (ibid., 13 July 1842); Mary Crosier wanted to know "the place of residence of her husband" (*Christian Guardian*, 15 April 1844); Michael McGrath looking for his brother Peter, who had "just arrived" (*British Whig*, 22 June 1847); notice of Ann Dunlop looking for her son, Thomas Wright, who had left Niagara "about a fortnight" before she arrived" (*Niagara Gleaner*, 14 August 1830).
68 *Upper Canada Gazette*, 30 December 1819.
69 First notice in *Bytown Gazette*, 14 December 1843. Another, slightly different, version appeared 14 and 21 February 1844. See also situation of Margaret Edwards (*Cobourg Star*, 30 October 1833); situation of wife of Michael Brown Kirwin (*Christian Guardian*, 11 September 1839).
70 *Christian Guardian*, 14 February 1844.
71 *Colonial Advocate*, 19 July 1832.
72 *Cobourg Star*, 28 August 1833. See also notice about Thomas Mullet looking for brother John, who had left Wexford, Ireland, "about the years 1823 or

1824" (*Farmer's Journal*, 5 September 1827). George Pashley noted that on the steamboat taking them to Cobourg there was a young woman who had emigrated to join her brother "who was living in Baltimore, 4ms from Cobourg" (Journals, 12).

73 *Chronicle and Gazette*, 20 September 1843. See also Margaret Edwards staying at the Steam Boat Hotel waiting for husband Thomas (*Cobourg Star*, 30 October 1833).
74 *Christian Guardian*, 23 October 1839
75 Ibid., 23 August 1837.
76 *Chronicle and Gazette*, 13 June 1840.
77 Ibid., 13 June 1840.
78 Letter of A.B. Hawke to W.J. Scott, 24 May 1837. See also Hawke letter, 20 June 1838; Hawke to S.B. Harrison, 2 September 1839, concerning the number of women and children in the sheds in Toronto, Emigration Office Records, Hawke Papers, AO, RG11–1.
79 *Hallowell Free Press*, 12 July 1831. See also "distressed brother looking for Thomas Grieg" (*Kingston Chronicle*, 22 March 1822); Thomas looking for John Mullet (*Farmer's Journal*, 5 September 1827); "Campbell Brothers looking for each other" (*Christian Guardian*, 18 September, 1841).
80 *Hallowell Free Press*, 24 July 1832. See also notice of mother of Alan Elvin, who followed her son to North America four years after he left home; her notice was from Quebec, where she was "in distress and anxious to hear from him" (ibid., 27 November 1844). Margaret Smith was looking for her brother Thomas who was "supposed to be in Kingston or Toronto" (*Chronicle and Gazette*, 3 September 1844).
81 *Cobourg Star*, 8 June 1842. See also notice of brother looking for John, Nathaniel, William, and Robert Clark, who had sailed from Belfast in 1815 (*Chronicle and Gazette*, 4 October 1837); brother looking for David Anderson and Ellenor his wife, "who are supposed to have been in this country for about three years" (ibid., 12 July 1834); brother looking for Margaret Lang, who had sailed from Dublin fourteen years before (*Bytown Gazette*, 6 October 1836).
82 *Christian Guardian*, 5 October 1836.
83 *Farmer's Journal*, 4 March 1829.
84 *Chronicle and Gazette*, 25 October 1835.
85 *Canadian Freeman*, 25 August 1831. See also notice of James Campbell, "anxious" to find his brother George, who had left home four years earlier (*Christian Guardian*, 1 September 1841); Mary Dwyer "anxious" to find her brother who had left home five years ago (ibid., 5 October 1836); sister looking for Michael Shelby (*Brockville Recorder*, 31 August 1843); brother "anxiously" looking for Mary Jennet (*United Empire Loyalist*, 19 April 1828).

86 Ibid., 1 October 1831.
87 *Colonial Advocate*, 31 May 1834.
88 Ibid., 2 September 1843. See also notice of Mrs McQueen, who arrived in Upper Canada in 1831. She was dismayed when she could not find her husband, and by January she and the family were "in distressed circumstances" and obliged to ask the public for help in finding him (*Kingston Chronicle*, 14 January 1832); also, the wife and two children of James McDonagh (in very indigent circumstances) who were anxious to find him (ibid., 23 December 1843).
89 *Kingston Chronicle*, 20 October 1820.
90 *Chronicle and Gazette*, 20 February 1841. See also notice of Thomas Sibbert looking for daughter and son-in-law (*Christian Guardian*, 5 October 1836); and father looking for William Hocker (*Chronicle and Gazette*, 18 January 1834).
91 *Chronicle and Gazette*, 31 July 1833. See also notice of mother looking for daughters Nancy and Betty Fox (*Christian Guardian*, 13 October 1847).

CHAPTER FIVE

1 Pengelly Family Papers, Harriet Pengelly Diary, 27 May 1835, Trent University Archives (TUA), 70–001/1/4.
2 Ibid., 26 May 1835.
3 Ibid., 29 May 1835.
4 Ibid., 5 June 1835.
5 Ibid., 8 June 1835.
6 Ibid., 10 June 1835.
7 Ibid., 14 July 1835. See also 26 August 1835, when Harriet wrote: "Received a nice long letter from Sophy ... very, very happy."
8 Ibid., 14 March, 12 April 1835.
9 Ibid., 6 April, 8 May 1835.
10 Ibid., 26 March, 28 May 1835; also 3 March 1836, when she noted "a very disagreeable day" and that she had written three letters.
11 Harriet Pengelly Diary, 20 August 1835; also 14 August; 5, 10, 12 and 22 September, 1 October 1835.
12 Ibid., 21 August 1835. See also 27 February, 5 March 1836.
13 Ibid., 4 October 1835. See also reference to returning home, 21 July 1835.
14 Ibid., 3 January 1836. See also 16 December and 29 November 1835.
15 Ibid., 4 November 1835.
16 Ibid., 24 January 1836. See also 29 March 1836.
17 Ibid., 1 January 1836.

18 Charlotte Erickson, *Invisible Immigrants* (Ithaca & London: Cornell University Press, 1972) was one of the first historians to gather and analyse nineteenth-century immigrant letters. Not surprisingly, she discovered that most surviving letters were from immigrants of the literate, "middling" ranks of British society. David Fitzpatrick's ground-breaking study, *Oceans of Consolation: Personal Accounts of Irish Migration to Australia* (Ithaca & London: Cornell University Press, 1994), gathers and rests on letters from those who travelled steerage.
19 Harriet Pengelly Diary, 3 August 1835.
20 Journals of George Pashley, 2 or 3 December, Archives of Ontario (AO) MU843.
21 Obediah Wilson to parents, 5 August 1832, in Wendy Cameron, Mary McDougall Maude, and Sheila Haines, eds., *English Immigrant Voices* (Montreal & Kingston: McGill-Queen's University Press, 2000), letter no. 15, 32. Hereinafter, letters from *Voices* will be referred to by date, letter number, and page.
22 George Hills, 5 August 1832, no. 16, *Voices*, 33.
23 Obediah Wilson to parents, 5 August 1832, no. 15, *Voices* 32.
24 Jane Harrison, *Until Next Year: Letter Writing and the Mails in the Canadas, 1640–1830* (Ottawa: Canadian Postal Museum and the Canadian Museum of Civilization, 1997), 2, notes that in a somewhat earlier period, literacy, at least in Lower Canada, was relatively high. The collection of letters in *Voices* attests to this in the Upper Canadian situation; Cameron notes that among the Petworth emigrants, about one-third were literate (ibid., xxvii–ix).
25 In addition to those in *Voices*, see letter of John Connel, 12 July 1845, National Library of Scotland (NLS), ACC7021. See also journal of George Forbes from Canada to Aberdeenshire, included in letter of 18 July 1845; Forbes's first letter was sent to "Dear Parents" on 23 May 1845 (Forbes Letters, Scottish Record Office [SRO], RH4/80).
26 William Knox to Andrew Redford, 28 October 1838, Redford Papers, SRO, GD1/815/15.
27 See, for example, the letter of Rebecca Longhurst to Mrs Weller (mother), 4 October 1832, no. 31, *Voices*, 61.
28 See letter of Simeon Titmouse to — Jackson, 11 September 1832, no. 23, *Voices*, 47.
29 William Hewitt to father and mother, William and Elizabeth Hewitt, 6 July 1836, no. 108, *Voices*, 206. See also Henry Smart to James Napper, 5 November 1832, no. 44, *Voices*, 77.
30 5 August 1832, no. 16, *Voices*, 33.
31 This is the salutation for the letter of Richard Neal, 20 July 1832, no. 5, *Voices*, 16.

32 Letter to John Colquhoun, 10 December 1823, "Emigrant Letters," SRO, GD1/814/5. See also John Barnes to his father, 1 January 1837, no. 126, *Voices*, 246–50, which included specific directions on how and to whom it was to be distributed; also letter of Jesse Penfeld to Mr and Mrs Hill, 1 January 1833, no. 50, *Voices*, 94.
33 Upton to mother, 19 September 1832, no. 27, *Voices*, 52–3.
34 John to Ann, 22 March 1822, John Gemmill Family Papers. SRO, TD293/1.
35 John Stedman to James Stedman, 7 August 1833, no. 18, *Voices*, 36.
36 William Phillips to Mrs Newall, 5 August 1832, no. 13, *Voices*, 30,
37 Simeon Titmouse to — Jackson, 11 September 1832, no. 23, *Voices*, 48.
38 John Luff to Aunt Foster, 29 July 1832, no. 11, *Voices*, 25–6.
39 References to this appear in almost all letters or journals. See, for example, letter of Richard Neal to William and Abigail Neal, 18 November 1832, no. 46, *Voices*, 79, which stated, "I have sent you a letter in July; but I have not had any answer yet: but Hope you will send me one soon." See also Edward and Hannah Bristow letter to brother, 20 July 1833, no. 82, *Voices*, 138.
40 See chapters 1 and 4 above and Elizabeth Jane Errington, *Wives and Mothers, School Mistresses and Scullery Maids* (Kingston & Montreal: McGill Queen's University Press, 1995), chap. 3, for discussion of desertion within the colony.
41 Gemmill Family Papers, John Gemmill to Andrew Gemmill, 21 June 1823, SRO, TD293.
42 Ibid., 6 December 1826. See also a later letter, 2 May 1828, asking Andrew to find the brother of William Miller, who wanted him to write because he was "anxious."
43 John Gemmill to Andrew Gemmill, 6 August 1827.
44 Ibid., 17 September 1828.
45 John Copelain to his brother, 28 August 1832, no. 21, *Voices*, 45. William Pannell wrote to his mother and father, William and Jane, that William Baker asked to be remembered to his father and mother and to tell William Baker's brother that he should come out (14 October 1832, no. 35, *Voices*, 65).
46 See Thomas Adsett to his father, 25 June 1833, no. 71, *Voices*, 123, which ended: "Wrote by James Rapson: his wife and family are all well." Also Elizabeth Wackford to Mrs Sarah Green, 25 June 1833, no. 71, *Voices*, 124–5. See discussion in *Voices*, xix. The problems of literacy went both ways. For example, Charles Johnston wrote to his former employer, Thomas Tryon, Esq., announcing his arrival and asking him to pass on news to family members; he also asked Tryon to let him know how his wife's parents were, since they could not write; and he sent on a message to his brother that if he intended to emigrate, he should write and Johnston would "remain here till he comes" (Tryon of Bulwick Collection, Northamptonshire Record Office [NRO], TB869).

47 For example, his August 1836 letter concluded, "John Heather from Petworth wishes you to call at Botting's, to know how his sister is at Redhill: he is well" (James Rapson letter, 30 August 1836, no. 115, *Voices*, 214). See also Rapson letters nos. 2, 12, 38, 76, in *Voices*, and letters of his in-laws, the Tribes, Henry and Charlotte Tribe (12 February 1833, no. 54, *Voices*, 102). The annotations in the published letters of the Sussex emigrants suggest that sometimes letters were communal undertakings, with two or three people writing individual notes to different recipients, well aware that all would read their news (*Letters from Sussex Emigrants* [Chichester, 1837], 37–41).

48 *Chronicle and Gazette*, 11 July 1835. A reward was also offered for information about James Honey, a tailor – either his current place of residence or a certificate attesting to his death (ibid., 19 August 1835).

49 *Chronicle and Gazette*, 17 June 1835. See also notice of John McGill, who was looking for his brother-in-law, James Lapper. The two had parted in Montreal in 1827, and John had had news of him in 1830. But his father was anxious to hear from him and letters would be forwarded (ibid., 26 April 1834). A brother-in-law was looking for John Kenny, who had arrived five years before and was last heard of three years ago; the brother-in-law wanted "to relieve the anxiety of his wife and three children" (*Bytown Gazette*, 7 October 1841). Also, parents looking for their son who had left home three years before; letters addressed to AC would be forwarded (*Kingston Chronicle*, 13 September 1822).

50 *Farmer's Journal*, 13 May 1829. See also *Kingston Gazette*, 25 August 1818, looking for Alexander Langton, who had last been heard of in 1799 or 1800; *Kingston Chronicle*, 13 August 1819, looking for John Spence; *Kingston Chronicle*, 13 April 1821, looking for Donald Campbell, originally of Argyleshire, by agent in York.

51 *Kingston Chronicle*, 13 June 1829. See also *Cobourg Star*, 30 August 1843, Thomas Eyre of Cobourg and Richard Dingley, Esq., of Launceston, England, were looking for Edmund Turner Colwell, from Devon, who would learn something to his advantage.

52 See, for example, *Kingston Chronicle*, 4 July 1823, looking for William Holliday, native of Yorkshire; *Christian Guardian*, 19 April 1837, looking for "Edward, the son of Anthony and Sarah Brown" of London, who was entitled to £2,000 from the estate of his maternal uncle: the solicitors were looking for him. Also *Cobourg Star*, 2 October 1844, Messrs Trehern & White, solicitors, in London were looking for John Blomfield, who had left home nine years before.

53 See discussion in *Voices*, xxxiii-xxxv.

54 See Harrison, *Until Next Year*, 125–7. David Gerber notes in *Authors of Their Lives* (New York: New York University Press, 2006) that sending letters over-

seas could be expensive and required planning and some knowledge of the postal system. For an intriguing discussion of "Using the Postal Service," see ibid., chap. 4.

55 John Scott to Andrew Redford, 29 August 1835, SRO, GD1/813/1. See also letter of Mary McNicol to brother James McNicol, 2 August 1831, NLS, ACC7020. See also James Gemmill and Agnes Smith to John Gemmill, 25 March 1824, who noted the problems of getting letters and included news back as far as 1821 (John Gemmill Family Papers, AO, MU7424). The correspondence seems to have been intermittent until 1832.

56 John Scott to George Redford, 18 September 1840, SRO, GD1/813/4. See also letters of Matthew Waite (Isaac Wilson's nephew) to Jonathan Wilson, in Isaac Wilson Diaries, AO, MS 199, where on 14 January 1841 Waite explained that he could now send letters to any part of Britain for 14 pence, by the Halifax steamer.

57 John Gemmill to "Dear Wife and Family," 2 March 1822, with annotations that it was received on 23 November 1822, SRO, TD293.

58 Ibid., John to Andrew, 19 September 1823.

59 Henry and Charlotte Tribe to Noah Hill, 12 February 1833, no. 54, *Voices*, 102. Cameron notes in *Voices* that suspicions that their mail was "stopped" or tampered with and altered were not unusual amongst the Petworth emigrants.

60 Isaac Wilson, Dear brother, 24 June 1821, Isaac Wilson Diaries.

61 Harriet Pengelly Diary, 5 September 1835, Pengelly Family Papers. In this particular sequence, Harriet became increasingly anxious, because she continued to check the mails (10 September, 12 September, 22 September, 1 October), but the long-awaited letters did not arrive until 3 October 1835. She noted similar delays and frustrations in later months.

62 Mary O'Brien Journals, 1 January 1836, AO.

63 See, for example, letters to Andrew of 1 June and 17 September 1823, SRO, TD293/1.

64 John Worfold, to father and mother, 15 December 1832, no. 48, *Voices*, 85. Mary O'Brien, 25 October 1830, recorded sending letters home with Catermole, who was going over for the Canada Company.

65 John Gemmill to Andrew, 21 June 1823.

66 Dear Brother, 24 June 1821, Isaac Wilson Diaries.

67 Ibid., Dear Brother, 2 August 1828. See also, the arrival of William Brawn, a new immigrant who brought Isaac a package and a letter from his brother, 26 July 1830.

68 Ibid., Dear Brother, 26 April 1832. Some new arrivals brought not just news but also a recommendation from a mutual acquaintance. On 30 January 1832, Wilson told his brother that he was "annoyed" with the acquaintance who had

"strongly recommended" a Joseph Taylor, as he had turned out to be "a good beggar." Patrick Shireff, *A Tour through North America* (Edinburgh, 1835), 164, had letters from friends in Scotland to be delivered to a relation near Galt. "I was anxious to deliver the letters personally," he wrote, and Mr T., the recipient who had arrived in the colony a year earlier, was very pleased to see him.

69 Wilson noted in a letter to his brother, 13 December 1834, Isaac Wilson Diaries, that he intended to send deeds home by private conveyance for exactly this reason.
70 Journals of George Pashley, February 1834, 16.
71 Mrs Murray to son James, 9 November 1834, Murray Letters, NLS, MS162.95.
72 See Wilson letter to his brother, 26 April 1832, Isaac Wilson Diaries.
73 John Gemmill to Andrew, 21 May 1823, John Gemmill Family Papers, SRO. The following year, John wrote, "Respecting your coming to the country we feel most desirous you should" (John to Andrew, 30 April 1824).
74 Ibid.
75 Ibid., 6 December 1826, replying to letters dated 31 August (received 4 November) and 30 March (received 7 July 1826).
76 Ibid., 24 November 1829.
77 Ibid., 21 June 1823. See also letter of 24 November 1829, in which John commented on news in the British papers.
78 Ibid., 8 November 1824.
79 Ibid., 21 June 1823.
80 Ibid., 21 November 1825.
81 Ibid., 21 May 1823.
82 Ibid., 21 June 1823.
83 Ibid., 8 June 1829.
84 Ibid., 17 September 1823.
85 Ibid., 6 December 1826.
86 In a remarkable passage, John passed on remarks from Jennett: "She has not got the imitation of that Black Man you sent her yet," ibid.
87 Andrew to Mother and Father, 2 October 1824, ibid.
88 Ibid., John to Andrew, 30 April 1824.
89 Ibid. 8 November 1824.
90 Ibid., 21 November 1825. This image of the kettle was also invoked by John and Caroline Dearling to Brothers and Sisters (15 July 1838, no. 134, *Voices*, 276–7).
91 Ibid., John Gemmill to Andrew Gemmill, 25 September 1832.
92 Ibid., 8 November 1824.
93 Ibid., 24 November 1829. Five years earlier, John had replied to what appears to have been a thoughtful letter from Andrew: "I take you kind advice ... and

I hope you will daily and hourly take to yourself the uncertainty of time and the precarious nature of all its enjoyments ought never to be forgot and our preparation for our eternal state ought to be our daily or hourly our constant study and employ as the basis of our Eternal felicity" (4 October 1824).
94 Ibid., 24 November 1829.
95 Ibid., 6 December 1826.
96 Ibid., 6 August 1827.
97 Ibid., 25 September 1832.
98 See Errington, *Wives and Mothers*, chap. 1, for an account of Mary making her decision.
99 Mary O'Brien Journals, AO, 13 February 1832.
100 Ibid., 24 April and 8 August 1829.
101 Ibid., 17 May 1831.
102 Ibid., 15 April 1830, 14 February 1832, 13 July 1836.
103 Ibid., 25 July 1836.
104 The Miller Letters, TUA, B-70-1001, 24 March 1845.
105 See, among others, John Gemmill to Andrew, letters of 11 May and 21 June 1823, John Gemmill Family Papers, SRO.
106 Ibid., 4 October 1824.
107 Ibid., 6 August 1827.
108 Ibid., 8 June 1829.
109 Isaac Wilson Diaries. Isaac and his father had arrived in the colony in mid–1811. His father apparently returned home and John stayed. See 21 June and 19 November 1811.
110 Ibid., mentioned in letter of 24 May 1815.
111 Ibid., 30 August 1815. The letters/journal included considerable detail about the War of 1812, Wilson's sympathy with the Reformers in the 1830s, and a host of other political, social, and economic events in the colony.
112 See Isaac Wilson Diaries, 24 June 1817, 7 September 1819, and 15 November 1830.
113 See ibid., 24 June 1817 and 13 July 1822.
114 Ibid., 9 September 1820.
115 Ibid., 24 June 1817.
116 Ibid., 24 April 1824.
117 See reference in letter of 7 September 1819, ibid., and also note that his brother had been given power of attorney to settle affairs in Britain (31 March 1827).
118 Mentioned in a letter 26 July 1830, ibid.
119 Ibid., 13 December 1834.
120 This begins in a letter of Matthew to Jonathan, 30 April 1838. Mary O'Brien's mother also continued to have financial interests "at home" after

she decided to settle in the colony with some of her children. See letters to Anthony, 25 August 1830 and 17 August 1831, Mary O'Brien Journals, AO.
121 Isaac Wilson Diaries, 20 August 1815.
122 Ibid., 27 April 1824.
123 Ibid., 31 March 1827.
124 See, for example, letter of William Upton to his mother, 16 September 1832, no. 27, *Voices*, 53. See also Ann Thomas to Father, 15 October 1832, no. 37, *Voices*, 68–9; Thomas Adsett to Rev. Robert Bidsall, 21 December 1832, no. 49, *Voices*, 87–8. Charles Moore, on the other hand, in a letter to his father (c June 1833, no. 69, 110–11), told his father not to come: "It is not fit for old people."
125 George and Mary Boxall and William Tilly to family, 16 September 1832, no. 25, *Voices*, 50. See also George and Anna Hills to Father, Mother, Brother, and Sister, 8 March 1833, no. 63, *Voices*, 108–9, who "hoped" that family members would "ever be kind" to mother and father now living with them. John and Caroline Dearling to brother and sister, 15 July 1838, no. 134, ibid., 276–7,
126 Redford Papers, John Scott to Andrew Redford, 29 September 1835.
127 Mary O'Brien Journal, 20 June 1830 and 24 September 1835.
128 *Hutton of Hastings*, ed. Boyce, 2 July 1837, 57.
129 Ibid., 61.
130 Isaac Wilson Diaries, 28 October 1828. Newspapers were sent on 26 July 1830. In the early 1820s there were apparently problems having newspapers forwarded from Montreal (9 September 1820).
131 Ibid., 13 July 1822. See also 24 June 1821 and package that arrived with emigrant William Brown, 26 July 1830.
132 See, for example, Redford Papers, letter of Isabel Scott to her aunt Mrs Redford, 16 April 1840.
133 Ibid., John Scott to George Redford, 18 September 1840.
134 Ibid., undated letter, Archibald to his cousin.
135 Ibid.
136 Ibid., John Scott to cousin, October 1844.
137 Ibid., John Scott to Uncle Andrew Redford, 12 November 1845.
138 Ibid., Isabell Scott to Mrs Redford, 15 May 1840.
139 Ibid., William Knox to "dear cousin," 24 April 1843. See also letter to cousin, 14 February 1842; letter to uncle, 26 December 1845.
140 Ibid., John Scott to cousin, George Redford, 18 September 1840.
141 Ibid., William Knox to cousin, John Redford, 24 April 1843.
142 Ibid., John Scott to uncle Andrew Redford, 12 November 1845.
143 Isaac Wilson Diaries, Isaac to brother, 24 June 1817.

CONCLUSION

1 Pengelly Family Papers, Harriet Pengelly Diary, 27 February 1836, Trent University Archives, 70-001/1/4. See also 1, 5, 12 March and 2 April 1836.
2 Ibid., 8 March 1836.
3 Ibid., 5 April 1836.
4 Ibid., diary fragment dated 29 November 1835.
5 Ibid., Robert Pengelly Diary, 11 August 1836.
6 C. Bennett, *The Lanark Society Settlers* (Renfrew, Ont.: Juniper Books, 1991), 121.
7 George Forbes to Father and Mother, 15 July 1848, Forbes Family Papers, Scottish Record Office (SRO), RH4/80.
8 Ibid., George to Uncle, 1 September 1849.
9 Ibid., Dear Father, 19 October 1858, SRO, TD73/124/1/14.
10 John Gemmill Family Papers, John Gemmill to Andrew, 21 November 1825, SRO, TD293/1.
11 Isaac Wilson Diaries, Matthew Waite to Jonathan Wilson, 30 April 1838, Archives of Ontario, MS199.
12 Ibid., 1 September 1838.
13 Redford Papers, John Scott to Andrew Redford, 12 November 1845, SRO, GD815.

A NOTE ON SOURCES

1 Franca Iacovetta, ed., *A Nation of Immigrants* (Toronto: University of Toronto Press, 1995), x.
2 See, for example, the discussion in "Mapping the British World," in *British World: Diaspora, Culture and Identity*, ed. Carl Bridge and Kent Fedorowich (London: Frank Cass, 2003), and introduction to Phillip Buckner and R. Douglas Francis, eds., *Canada and the British World: Culture, Migration, and Identity* (Vancouver: University of British Columbia Press, 2006).
3 Charlotte Erickson, *Leaving England: Essays on British Emigration in the Nineteenth Century* (Ithaca & London: Cornell University Press, 1994), 5.
4 Ibid.
5 Jane Ohlmeyer, "AHR Forum: Seventeenth Century Ireland and the New British and Atlantic Histories," *American Historical Review* (April 1999): 446–62, 449.
6 Donald Harman Akenson, *If the Irish Ran the World* (Montreal & Kingston: McGill-Queen's University Press, 1997), 173. See also Akenson, *Small Differences: Irish Catholics and Irish Protestants, 1815–1922* (Montreal &

Kingston, McGill-Queen's University Press 1988), and *The Irish Diaspora: A Primer* (Belfast: Dublin Editions, 1996).
7 Bruce Elliott, *Irish Migrants in the Canadas* (Montreal & Kingston: McGill-Queen's University Press, 1988), 6.
8 Marjory Harper, "Crossing the Atlantic: Snapshots from the Migration Album," in *Canadian Migration Patterns: From Britain and North America*, ed., Barbara Messamore (Ottawa: University of Ottawa Press, 2004), 18.
9 In *Canadian Migration Patterns*, ed. Messamore.
10 Hoerder, *Cultures in Contact* (Durham: Duke University Press), ix.
11 Ruth-Ann Harris and Donald M. Jacobs, eds., *The Search for Missing Friends: Irish Immigrant Advertisements Placed in the Boston Pilot* (Boston: New England Historic Genealogical Society, 1989), xv.
12 *Invisible Immigrant: The Adaption of English and Scottish Immigrants in the Nineteenth Century* (Ithaca and London: Cornell University Press, 1972), 1.

Index

Advantages of Emigration (William Catermole), 17; advice about accommodation on ship, 98; advice on preparation and provisioning for the voyage, 54–5. *See also* Catermole, William; emigrant guides
America, image of, 5–6, 17, 28, 138, 182n10
artisans. *See* labourers; steerage passengers
assisted emigration, 16, 29, 48, 181n9; organizing passage, 52–3, 55, 57–8, 200n34, 201nn36 and 38. *See also* Dorking emigrants; Glasgow Committee on Emigration; parish emigration; Petworth Committee of Emigration
Atlantic crossing. *See* voyage

Bell, William (*Hints to Emigrants*), 146; accommodation on ship, 209n27; account of birth of child, 92, 146; advice concerning the journey, 199n17, 203n65, 204n75, 205n79; departure, 207n10; disputes on board, 212n104
Brunswick (Edward Talbot's ship), 77; accommodation on board, 208n24
Buchanan, A.C. (emigrant agent in Montreal), 202n52, 204n66

cabin passengers, 75, 81–2, 83–4, 165; attitudes towards other passengers, 83–5, 86, 99; departure, 77; relations with captain, 208n17; routines on the voyage, 82–4, 87; women, 81, 83. *See also* Hutton; Langton; Moodie; O'Brien; Pengelly; ships and shipping; Stewart; Traill
Canada (Land) Company, 24, 54; sending remittances, 191n84
captains of emigrant ships, 62, 75, 77, 83; relations with passengers, 79–80, 87, 95–6, 97–8, 105, 108–10, 208n17, 210n58, 213n112, 216n171; responsibilities of, 66, 70, 80, 83, 85, 91–2; and steerage committees,

87, 88–9; taking advantage of emigrants, 61–2

Carlton (John Hart's ship), 57, 77, 78, 95, 97, 102, 104–5, 106; accommodation, 84; steerage committee, 87–8. *See also* Hart

Catermole, William *(Advantages of Emigration)*, 44, 59, 65–6; agent of Canada Company, 54. *See also* emigrant guides

Chamber's Information, 12, 17; advice on provisioning, 66; availability of shipping, 59; instructions for packing, 53; recommendations about routes, 64. *See also* emigrant guides

children and emigration, 3, 7, 13, 75, 82, 84–5, 90–2, 105–6, 114–15, 128, 211n77

cholera, 91, 104, 116–17; impact on trip upriver, 124–6; quarantine station, 106–7, 124–5, 140

Colborne, Lt-Gov Sir John, 32

Colonial Office, 16, 29, 138, 201n37

Counsel for Emigrants, 17; choice of routes, 64. *See also* emigrant guides

Curler (John Steele's ship), 87, 89, 103–4, 106, 108. *See also* ships and shipping; Steele

Dorking emigrants, 26; baggage allowance, 198n10; problems on board ship, 212n104, 214n120; relations with parents, 46. *See also* Petworth Committee of Emigration

Egremont, Earl of, 29

emigrant agents, 19, 24, 134; advice on the passage, 61–2, 203n56; assistance to reunite families, 122, 124, 126, 132; Lt Lowe, 62. *See also* Buchanan, A.C.; emigrant aid on arrival; Parliament

emigrant aid on arrival, 113, 119–20; state sponsored, 113, 122, 126–8, 221nn49 and 55. *See also* emigrant agents

emigrant aid societies on arrival, 111–12, 113, 126–7, 220n47. *See also* Kingston Emigration Committee; Montreal Emigrant Society; Pashley; Wilson, Joseph

emigrant correspondence: advice on provisioning, 66; difficulties of, 36, 138, 142, 143, 144–7; importance of, 8–9, 13–14, 19–20, 24–7, 28, 138–9, 143, 151–2, 157–8, 161, 187n45; postal service, 144–5, 225n24; private conveyance of letters, 146–7. *See also* Gemmill; Hutton; Knox; O'Brien; Pengelly; Scott; Wilson, Isaac

emigrant guides, 12, 15, 17, 23, 24, 25, 161, 183n14; advice arranging passage, 56, 63; advice on provisioning, 66, 205n83; advice on seasickness, 99; instructions for packing, 53–4; warning about swindlers, 60. *See also Advantages of Emigration; Chamber's Information; Counsel for Emigrants; Sequel to Counsel for Emigrants*

emigrants: diversity of, 5, 6, 10, 15, 63, 164–5, 179n15; numbers of, 5, 13, 16, 178n9; problems for older people, 46, 195n117

emigrant season, 11, 55–6, 122

Index 237

emigrant sheds, 119, 126, 127, 128
emigration meetings, 23, 24
English emigrants, 4, 6, 48, 66, 135, 161, 164, 179n14, 184n21; arrival in British America, 216n161; leaving home, 201n43

families, 15, 27–8, 35; absconding husbands, 9, 36, 37, 47, 128, 142; continuing obligations, 9, 43, 45–7, 134, 153–5; difficulties of emigration, 24–5, 31; escaping family responsibilities, 44, 47, 134, 138; reunions, 36, 112, 113, 128–30, 134, 191n81; wives reluctant to emigrate, 34–5, 38, 190n78, 191n80; wives supporting the project, 31, 190n78
farmers and emigration, 19–21, 23, 25, 54, 179n15, 184n21, 189n68
Forbes, George, 8, 27, 42; decision to emigrate, 40, 48; preparing to leave home, 52; settled in Upper Canada, 160, 162; trip to Upper Canada and reunion with cousin, 129. *See also* labourers, artisans, and emigration; steerage passengers
Friends (Peters' ship), 76–7, 80, 89, 92, 99, 104

Gemmill, Andrew (John Gemmill's son), 8; carrying out father's instructions, 142; decides not to emigrate, 30–2, 150, 162, 189n63; visit to Upper Canada, 160–1

Gemmill, Ann: preparing to leave home, 37, 51, 55, 67, 68; reunion, 112, 128
Gemmill, John, 7, 24, 164; advice to James Hendry on emigration, 24–5; and Andrew's visit, 160–1; continuing family business through Andrew, 152; difficulties with mail, 32, 51, 145, 148; importance of faith, 97, 149, 150, 164; instructions to Ann for her voyage, 5, 29–30, 51, 67; maintaining contact, 141–2; opportunities for son and daughters, 42; prospecting the land, 7, 39, 69; voyage of, 57, 100. *See also* assisted emigration; Glasgow Committee on Emigration
Gemmill family, 7–8, 10, 25; children becoming Canadian, 162; decision to emigrate, 29–31, 35; importance of family, 147–51; private conveyance of letters, 146; reunion, 36; second generation, 162
gender and emigration, 34–5, 76, 82–3, 93, 138, 165, 190n78
gentlemen and women emigrants, 23, 33, 138, 165; advantages on arrival, 115–17, 138, 166; difficulties of emigration, 38, 160, 193n97; motivation for emigrating, 8, 23, 38, 44–5; preparations for leaving home, 50, 54–5, 63–4, 68. *See also* cabin passengers; Hutton; Langton; O'Brien; Pengelly; Stewart; Traill
George (Stewarts' ship), 49, 71, 77, 80

Glasgow Committee on Emigration, 31, 188n56, 200n34. *See also* Gemmill, John
Grosse-Île: arrival at, 106–7, 124–5

Hart, Jean: experience of voyage, 67, 90, 100; and storms, 102; work on the *Carlton*, 91
Hart, John: arrival at Quebec, 106–8; birth of child, 92; children ill (measles), 91, 105, 125; departure, 77–8; first sight of land, 104; games and diversions on ship, 95, 97; head of shipboard committee, 78, 87–8, 106; organizing passage, 57; preparing for arrival, 105–6; at quarantine station, Grosse-Île, 108; routines on board, 94; view of the New World, 105–6
Hart family: conditions on *Carlton*, 84; cooking and provisioning, 90; diversions, 96; and storms, 102. *See also* Scottish emigrants; steerage passengers; voyage
Hendry, James: asking advice about emigration, 24–5. *See also* Gemmill, John
Horton, Wilmot, 16
Hutton, Fanny, 23, 35, 160; arrival at New York, 106–8; delayed at New York, 114; experiences on voyage, 114; neighbours returning home, 33, 48; preparing to leave home, 52, 54–5; reluctance to emigrate, 23, 32–4, 52, 114; reunion with William, 112
Hutton, William, 35; decision to emigrate, 19–24; gentleman, 23, 160; instructions to Fanny, 52, 54–5; settling expedition, 32–3
Hutton family: arrival in New York, 108, 114; receiving packages and continuing financial support, 154–5; return home for visit, 160; reunion, 36, 114; settled, 134. *See also* gentlemen and women emigrants; Irish emigrants

"information wanted" notices, 3–7, 122–3, 128, 134, 164–5, 177n7, 179n14; brothers and sisters looking for siblings and others, 3–4, 43–4, 131, 132–3; colonists looking for emigrants, 130; families divided on journey upriver, 122–5, 127, 130–1; parents looking for children, 3, 4, 7, 46–7; those at home looking for beneficiaries, 143–4; wives looking for husbands, 3, 36–8, 123–4, 127–9, 131, 133–4
Irish emigrants, 3–4, 6, 9, 23, 29, 134, 161, 164, 179n14, 184n20, 191n84; attitudes to, 59, 98, 120, 164; famine migrations, 9, 184n17; fear of voyage, 206n96; leaving home, 60, 63, 201n43

journey from New York to Upper Canada, 108, 114–16. *See also* Hutton; Langton; O'Brien
journey from Quebec to Upper Canada, 108, 111–12, 114, 116–18, 122–4, 140, 218n28; difficulties, 122, 124–5, 128; imposition on emigrants, 119. *See*

also Pashley; Peters; Stewart; Traill; Wilson, Joseph

Kingston Emigration Committee, 132
Knox, William (John Scott's cousin): advice on passage, 62; arranging passage, 64–5; conditions aboard ship, 84–5, 214n132; first letter home, 140; missing home, 160; opportunities in Upper Canada, 28; relations with the captain, 80; requesting newspapers and packages, 156, 157

labourers, artisans, and emigration, 6, 19, 48; difficulties finding work, 111–12, 113, 120, 131–2; gathering letters of recommendation, 68; preparing to leave home, 50, 52–3, 63; reasons to emigrate, 6, 21, 25, 43–4, 193n97. *See also* Gemmill; Forbes; Hart; Knox; Pashley; steerage passengers; Wilson, Joseph
Langton, Anne, 8, 140; amusements on voyage, 83; decision to emigrate, 45; receiving packages from home, 115; routine on voyage, 83; visit home, 160
Langton, Ellen (Anne and John's mother): arrival at John's, 116; departure, 78
Langton, John, 8; advice on emigration, 45–6; decision to emigrate, 48; gentleman emigrant, 45–6; helping migrants to go home, 196n126

Langton, Thomas (Anne and John's father): decision to emigrate, 45–6; departure, 78
Langton family: arrival in New York, 106, 108; New York to Upper Canada, 112, 116. *See also* cabin passengers; gentlemen and women emigrants
life in port (British America), 108, 122, 129–30; taking advantage of emigrants, 122. *See also* Montreal; Quebec
life in port (Great Britain), 59–61, 63, 67, 201n43; taking advantages of emigrants, 60–1

MacGregor, John (*Observations on Emigration* and *British America*), 53, 54; advice on route 64; conditions in British ports, 60, 203n56
Manahan, A. (emigrant agent, Kingston), 126, 127
men: preparing to leave home, 49, 67–8; and voyage, 87, 93, 165
Montreal (Pengellys' ship), 68, 72, 77
Montreal (port of): arrival of emigrants, 111–12, 165
Montreal Emigration Society, 127. *See also* emigrant agents; emigrant aid
Montreal Special Sanitary Committee (1834), 60
Moodie, Susanna and Dunbar, 151; arrival at Grosse-Île, 106; decision to emigrate, 38; last visits before leaving, 68
Murray, William (Willy): difficulties with mail, 147; family's decision

to send him to America, 40, 42–3; passage, 60; preparing to leave home, 40, 52. *See also* Scottish emigrants

Napoleon (Patrick Shirreff's ship), 82
Napoleonic Wars, 5, 9, 11, 15
newspapers. *See* press
New World, images of, 17, 19, 26, 32–3, 45. *See also* America; Upper Canada

O'Brien, Mary: accommodation on ship, 81, 215n149; advice to prospective emigrants, 186n34; arrival New York and trip to Upper Canada, 115–16, 216n161; encourages sister to emigrate, 187n47, 190n79; importance of correspondence, 151–2, 154, 155; maintaining financial interests at home, 230n120; problems with mail, 145; seasickness, 214n133. *See also* cabin passengers; gentlemen and women emigrants
opposition to emigration, 9, 16, 17–19, 48, 184n18

parish emigration: preparing to leave, 52–3, 188n55, 198n10, 201n37. *See also* assisted emigration; Petworth Committee of Emigration
Parliament: attitude to emigration, 16, 181n9; instituting regulations for the trade, 61
Pashley, George: advice on obtaining best passage, 61–2; arrival at Montreal, 111; arrival at Quebec, 108–9, 111; attitude to other emigrants, 59, 64, 120–1, 164; conditions on *Reward*, 84, 86; death of daughter, 78, 91, 98; departure, 72, 76, 78; difficulties with mail, 147; first sight of land, 104; importance of faith, 98, 109, 111, 114, 121–2, 164; journey Quebec to Upper Canada, 114, 120–1; life in port (Liverpool), 63; organizing the voyage, 58–9, 64, 65, 68; private assistance, 129; receiving aid, 126–7; resettling, 134, 160–1; voyage, 100; writing letters, 138. *See also* labourers, artisans, and emigration; steerage passengers
Passenger Acts, 64, 70, 202n52, 203n56
Pengelly, Harriet, 140, 151; arrival at New York, 136–7; death of, 159; departure, 72, 74; diary writing, 62–3; difficulties with mail 145; Emily (maid) decides not to come, 70–1; importance of letter writing, 136–9, 159; journey New York to Upper Canada, 137; life on *Montreal*, 74, 83; reluctance to emigrate, 38, 68–9, 136, 166
Pengelly, Robert: gentleman, 138; life on *Montreal*, 83, 95; organizing the voyage, 62–3; return home for visit, 159
Pengelly family: access to captain, 80; arrival at New York, 115; decision to emigrate, 38; departure, 72, 77; gentlefolk, 38; journey to Plymouth, 62; life in port,

63; settled, 134; tired of voyage, 102. *See also* cabin passengers; gentlemen and women emigrants

Peter Robinson expeditions, 16, 27, 29, 48. *See also* assisted emigration

Peters, Elizabeth: arrival at Quebec, 108; cooking, 89–90; departure, 72, 76–7; first sight of land, 104; life on *Friends*, 74, 96; life in steerage, 85, looking after children, 90–1, 92–3; preparing for arrival, 105; problems with water, 99; relations with cabin passengers, 98–9; relations with captain, 80; seasickness, 99, 100; seeing other ships, 94; sewing, 92–3; work on board, 76–7

Peters, William: departure, 77–8; first sight of land, 105; journey Quebec to Upper Canada, 165; length of voyage, 104; preaching, 76, 93, 97

Peters family: conditions on *Friends*, 89; departure, 76, 77–8; seasickness, 100–1; settled, 160; Sunday services, 97. *See also* labourers, artisans, and emigration; steerage passengers

Petworth Committee of Emigration, 29, 42, 48; advice for and organizing passage, 53–5, 57–8, 65–6, 188n55, 203n64. *See also* assisted emigration

Petworth emigrants, 29, 46; advice about packing and provisioning, 54, 66–7, 188nn51 and 55; concern about parents left at home, 154; difficulties with mail, 145, 146, 228n59; journey Quebec to Upper Canada, 218n28; maintaining contact, 140, 142, 143; relations with cabin passengers, 214n120; reunion with families, 130. *See also* labourers, artisans, and emigration; steerage passengers

Poor Laws, 58, 188n55

Prescott, Upper Canada: conditions in, 112, 119, 120, 139

press, 13, 24; accounts of life in port, 59–60, 122; accounts of voyage, 28–9, 70, 71, 206n95; advice to emigrants, 46, 55; availability of shipping, 56–7, 59–60; influence on emigration, 14, 17, 19, 183n12, 200n28; publishing emigrant correspondence, 26; reports of emigration, 15–16, 26, 55, 83

Quebec: arrival at, 106–8, 165; cholera epidemic, 116–17; conditions in port, 108, 174, 217n182; linked to Irish and Scottish ports, 60. *See also* journey from Quebec to Upper Canada

Quebec Emigration Society, 121nn54 and 55

Radcliffe, Mrs William: accommodation, 65–6, 82; problems with water, 99; seasickness, 100

Radcliffe, William, 72, 74. *See also* cabin passengers; gentlemen and women emigrants

Rapson, James (Petworth emigrant), 143, 145; writing for others, 227n47. *See also* Petworth emigrants

Redford, Andrew (John Scott's uncle), 12; advice about packing, 53; decision not to emigrate, 13; directions about the mail, 144–5
Reid family, 49, 71, 77
Reilly, John: account of birth of child, 92; cabin accommodation, 80–1; conditions on ship, 79, 81–2; departure, 79; diversions on board, 96–7; problems with water, 99; relations of cabin and steerage passengers, 86, 88; view of steerage, 84, 86. See also cabin passengers; gentlemen and women emigrants; steerage passengers
remittances, 35, 191n84
reverse migration, 33, 48, 161, 166, 190n78, 197nn137 and 138
Reward (George Pashley's ship), 58–9, 63, 76, 84, 98, 111. See also Pashley
routes recommended, 50; via New York, 62, 63–4, 203n64; via Quebec, 55, 63–4; with no preference, 58, 204nn66 and 69

Scott, John: advice on emigration, 12–14, 17, 24, 26, 27; becoming "Canadian," 156; death of father, 163; difficulties with mail, 144–5; land available for young single cousins, 41–2; maintaining contact with home, 163–4; missing home, 155–6, 159; opportunities of emigration, 28, 42, 187n48; support from home, 13, 154
Scott family, 16; decision to emigrate, 35; indifferent correspondents, 156–7; missing home, 156, 160
Scottish emigrants, 3–4, 6, 135, 161, 164, 179n14; leaving home, 57, 60, 66, 71; on voyage, 86, 204n7
Sequel to Counsel for Emigrants, 17
settlers' accounts. See emigrant guides; press
settling expedition, 24, 32, 35, 69, 185n27. See also families; Gemmill, John; Hutton, William
shipboard committees. See steerage committees
shipboard journals, 75–6, 87–8, 103, 159, 207n7; difference in records of men and women, 76, 93–4; importance of, 75–6. See also Hart; Pashley; Pengelly; Peters; Steele; Wilson, Joseph
ships and shipping: Atlantic networks, 43, 60, 200n29; availability, 55–6, 57, 59–60, 200n29; cabin accommodation, 62–3; cost of the crossing, 24, 56–8, 62, 64–6; nature of accommodation, 56–7, 66–7, 79, 80–2, 84, 165, 209n27; steerage accommodation, 62, 64–6, 82, 84, 86. See also voyage
shipwrecks, 28–9, 70, 74, 206n95
Shirreff, Patrick, 82; account of emigrants' reunion, 130, 191n81, 228n68
single or unattached emigrants, 39–46, 48, 193n96
Special Sanitary Committee of Montreal, 210n51
Steele, John: arrival at New York, 106, 108; children playing on

board, 93; coping with shipboard fights, 96, 108; head of shipboard committee, 87; steerage passenger, 87; tired of voyage, 103–5. *See also* steerage passengers

Steele, Mary: work on board, 93

steerage committees, 78, 87–8, 106, 210n54. *See also* captains of emigrant ships; Hart, John; Steele, John

steerage passengers, 58, 75, 82, 83–4, 86; compared with cabin passengers, 83–4, 106–7; conditions of, 84–6, 101, 210n51; cooking, 88–90; and departure, 77; relations with cabin passengers, 86, 97–9, 209n40; women, 84. *See also* Hart; Pashley; Peters; Reilly; Steele; voyage; Wilson, Joseph

Stewart, Frances, 151; cabin accommodation, 81; departure, 68, 71; difficulty of leaving home, 68; journey Quebec to Upper Canada, 117–18; life on *George*, 83; preparing to leave home, 49–51; relations with captain, 79–80, 208n17

Stewart family: access to captain, 80; decision to emigrate, 35, 166; departure, 77

Talbot, Edward: cabin accommodation, 208n24; departure, 77

Traill, Catharine Parr: account of journey upriver, 116–17, 218n18; arrival at Grosse-Île, 106

Traill family, 8, 10, 151; decision to emigrate, 38; departure, 68; encourage others to emigrate, 144; gentlefolk, 38; journey Quebec to Upper Canada, 112, 116–17, 218n18; reunion with family, 129; settled, 134. *See also* cabin passengers; gentlemen and women emigrants

travellers' accounts. *See* emigrant guides

United States: as preferred destination, 6, 27, 192n95, 204n66

Upper Canada: images of, 26–7, 38, 56, 105, 107, 184n18, 186n39, 192n95, 198n5; opportunities of, 28, 32–3, 44–5, 193n97

voyage, 79, 165; apprehension about, 10, 28, 50, 68–9, 70, 72, 166, 215n135; bad water, 66, 99–100; childbirth on board, 92; children, 75, 90–1, 93, 105, 106, 211n77; the departure, 69, 71, 72; diversions and disputes, 93–6, 212n104; end of journey, 104–5, 215n149, 216nn160 and 161; financing, 29, 62; general routines, 75, 78–9, 82, 93, 96, 98, 209n33; like a prison, 79, 94, 102–5; preparing to leave home, 50–1, 53–4, 59; provisioning, 65–7, 82, 88–9, 94, 99, 102, 212n104; relations of cabin and steerage passengers, 79–80, 82–6, 88, 97–9, 209n40, 214n120; seasickness, 62, 80, 89, 90, 99–101, 139, 209n33, 214n133; storms, 85, 87–8, 90, 101–2; Sunday services, 78, 80, 97–8, 213nn111 and 112; women and work on board, 75, 89–91, 92–3, 105. *See also* captains of emigrant ships; ships and shipping; shipwrecks; steerage committees

Welsh emigrants, 5, 6, 179n14

Wilson, Isaac: arrival of emigrants with letters and parcels, 68, 146–7, 155; becoming "Canadian," 157–8; carrying on business through brother, 152–4; circumstances of settlement, 153, 194n105; death, 162; difficulties with mails, 145, 146, 229n69; maintaining contact with home, 162; nephew's correspondence with uncle, 162–3

Wilson, Jenney: work on board, 90–1

Wilson, Joseph: arrival at Quebec, 108; conditions in steerage, 86; departure, 78; difficulties with the cook, 89; at emigrant sheds, 126; finding work, 134; first sight of land, 104; journey Quebec to York, 112, 118–19, 165; preaching, 93, 97; routines and diversions on ship, 93, 95; seasickness, 90, 99–100, 101; settled, 160; storms, 101–2; tired of voyage, 102; view of New World, 105. *See also* emigrant aid; labourers, artisans, and emigration; steerage emigrants

women and emigration: making decisions, 50; opportunities in Upper Canada, 34, 41, 45, 194n107; preparing for voyage, 49–50, 67–8; work during voyage, 75, 89–93, 98–9, 165. *See also* families